SEC OF LIGHT

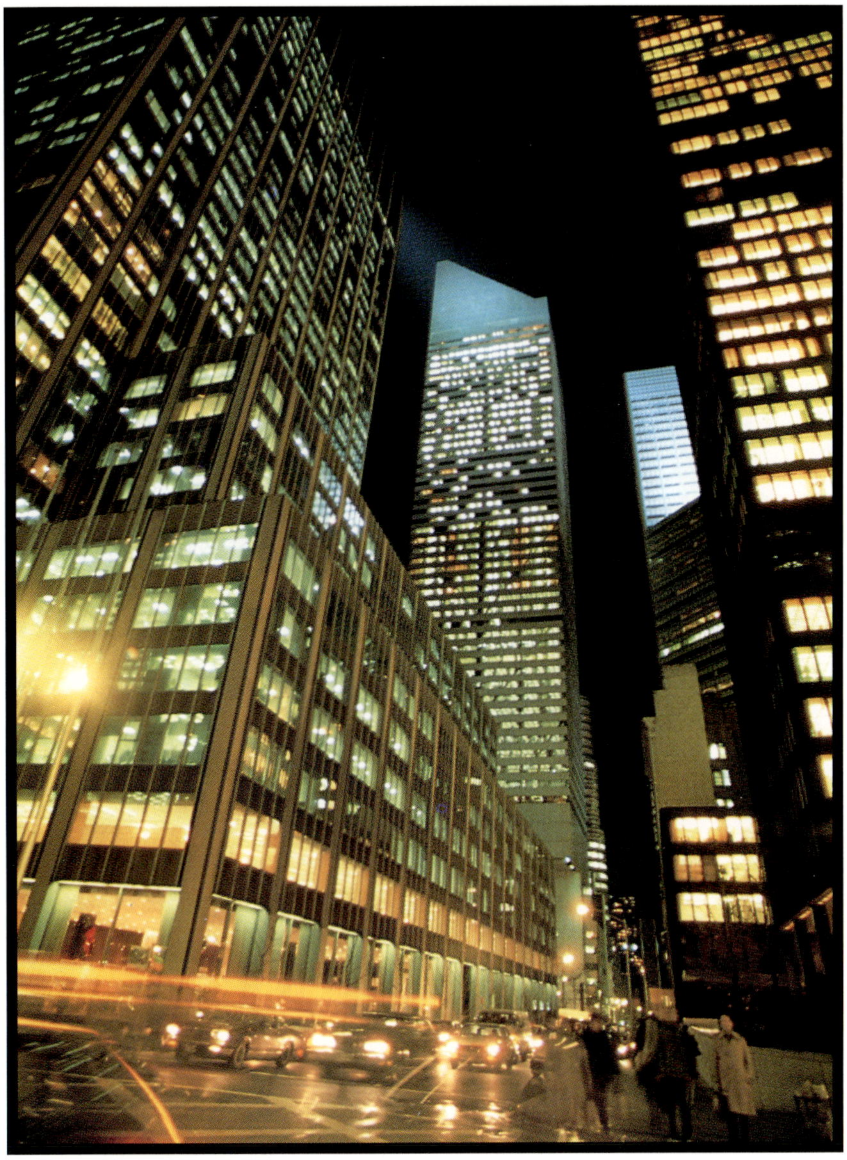

Making the most of light

CASSELL

ACKNOWLEDGEMENTS
Front cover: (main pic) TPL, (bottom left) Adam Eastland, (bottom centre) Mei Lim, (bottom right) TIB, 1 TIB, 2-3 ICL, 4-5 TPL, 5 ICL, 6 TPL, 7 TPL, 8-9 Michael Busselle, 9 Zefa, 10 John Heseltine, 11 Nick Meers, 12 Michael Busselle, 13(t) EP/Shona Wood, 13(b) TPL, 14 EP/Han Lee de Boer, 15 Michael Busselle, 16(t) Adam Eastland, 16(b) Michael Busselle, 17(t) Stuart Windsor, 17(b) Michael Busselle, 18(t) EP/Shona Wood, 18(b) TPL, 19(t) TIB, 19(b) John Heseltine, 20 TSI, 21(l) EP/John Suett, 21(r) Jahreszeiten Verlag, 22 Collections, 23 John Heseltine, 24 Marie Claire Maison, 25 Jahreszeiten Verlag, 26-27 EP/Mike Henton, 28(t) Mei Lim, 28(b) Richard Platt, 29(t) EP/Simon Page-Ritchie, 29(b) ffotograff, 30 Robin Bath, 31 ICL, 32 Jerry Young, 33(t) EP/Simon Page-Ritchie, 33(b) Michael Busselle, 34 Jonathan Vince, 35(t) Swan Photographic, 35(b) Zefa, 36(l) Jonathan Vince, 36(r) Michael Busselle, 37 Zefa, 38 Richard Platt, 39 TIB, 40 Jonathan Vince, 41 RHPL, 42(t) Ed Buziak, 42(c) Roger Howard, 43(t) EP/Trevor Melton, 43(b) TPL, 44(t) EP/Trevor Melton, 44(b) Jonathan Vince, 45(t) Roger Howard, 45(b) EP/Trevor Melton, 46 EP/Trevor Melton, 47 TSI, 48 EP/Michael Busselle, 49(t) TSI, 49(b) EP/Michael Busselle, 50(t) EP/Trevor Melton, 50(c) EP/Michael Busselle, 50(b) Philip Dunn, 51(t) Dev Raj Agarwal, 51(b) ICL, 52(t) TIB, 52(b) Bruce Coleman Photo Library, 53(t) EP/Graeme Harris, 53(bl) Rhoda Nottridge, 54(t) John Heseltine, 54(bl) Patrick Thurston, 54(br) Alastair Scott, 55 ICL, 56 RHPL, 57 TIB, 58(t) Michael Busselle, 58(b) TIB, 59 Roger Howard, 60(t) TPL, 60(b) Zefa, 61 TIB, 62(t) Mike Key, 62(b) Jonathan Vince, 63(t) Jonathan Vince, 63(b) Zefa, 64, 65(t) Zefa, 65(b) TIB, 66 Katz, 67 Roger Howard, 68(t) Robin Bath, 68(b) Zefa, 69(t) TPL, 69(b) RHPL, 70(t) Jonathan Vince, 70(b) Robin Bath, 71(tl) RHPL, 71(bl) Zefa, 71(r) TIB, 72-3 TSI, 73(t) Robin Bath, 73(b) RHPL, 74(t) TSI, 74(b) ICL, 75-78 EP/Michael Busselle, 79 Michael Busselle, 80 TSI, 81 TIB, 82 Robin Bath, 83 TIB, 84(t) Britstock-IFA, 84(b) TIB, 85 Zefa, 86(t) TPL, 86(b) TIB, 87-90 EP/Graeme Harris, 91(t) Ardea, 91(b) TIB, 92 TIB, 93-96 Jim Henderson.

Key: EP - Eaglemoss Publications; RHPL - Robert Harding Picture Library; ICL - Images Colour Library; TIB - The Image Bank; TPL - The Photographers' Library; TSI - Tony Stone Images

Consultant editor: Roger Hicks

First published 1994 by Cassell
Villiers House, 41/47 Strand, London WC2N 5JE

Distributed in Australia
by Capricorn Link (Australia) Pty Ltd
P. O. Box 665, Lane Cove, NSW 2066

British Library Cataloguing-in-Publication Data
A catalogue record for this book is available from the British Library

ISBN 0-304-34492-3

Printed in Spain by Cayfosa Industria Grafica

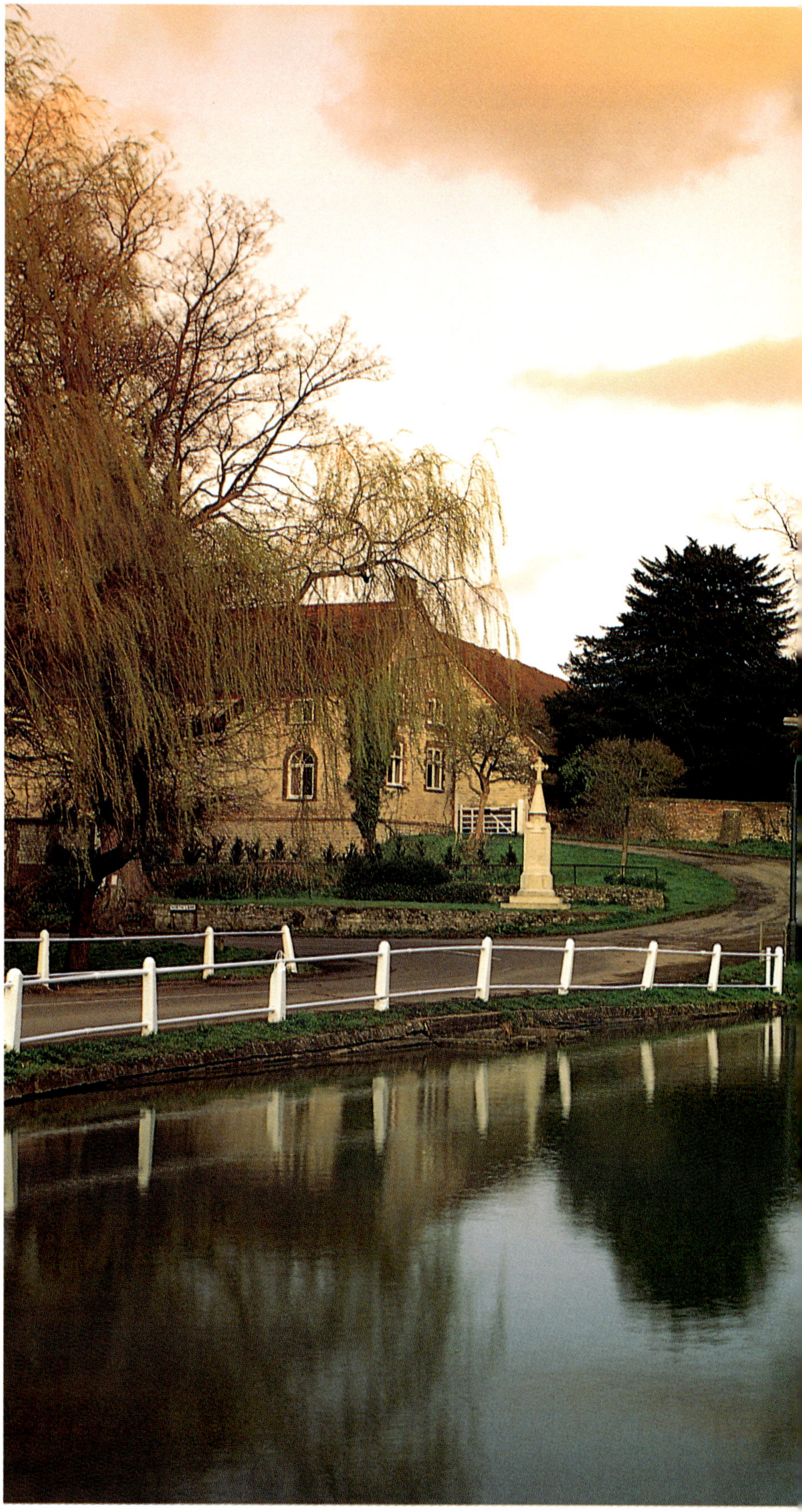

CONTENTS

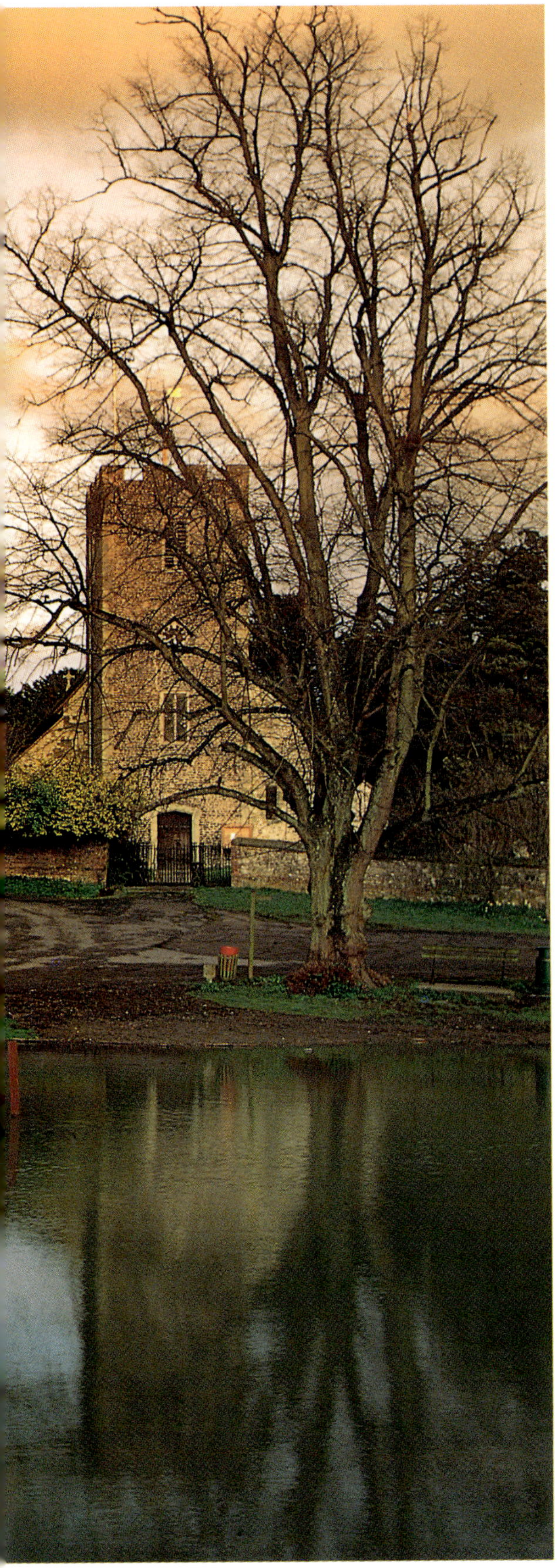

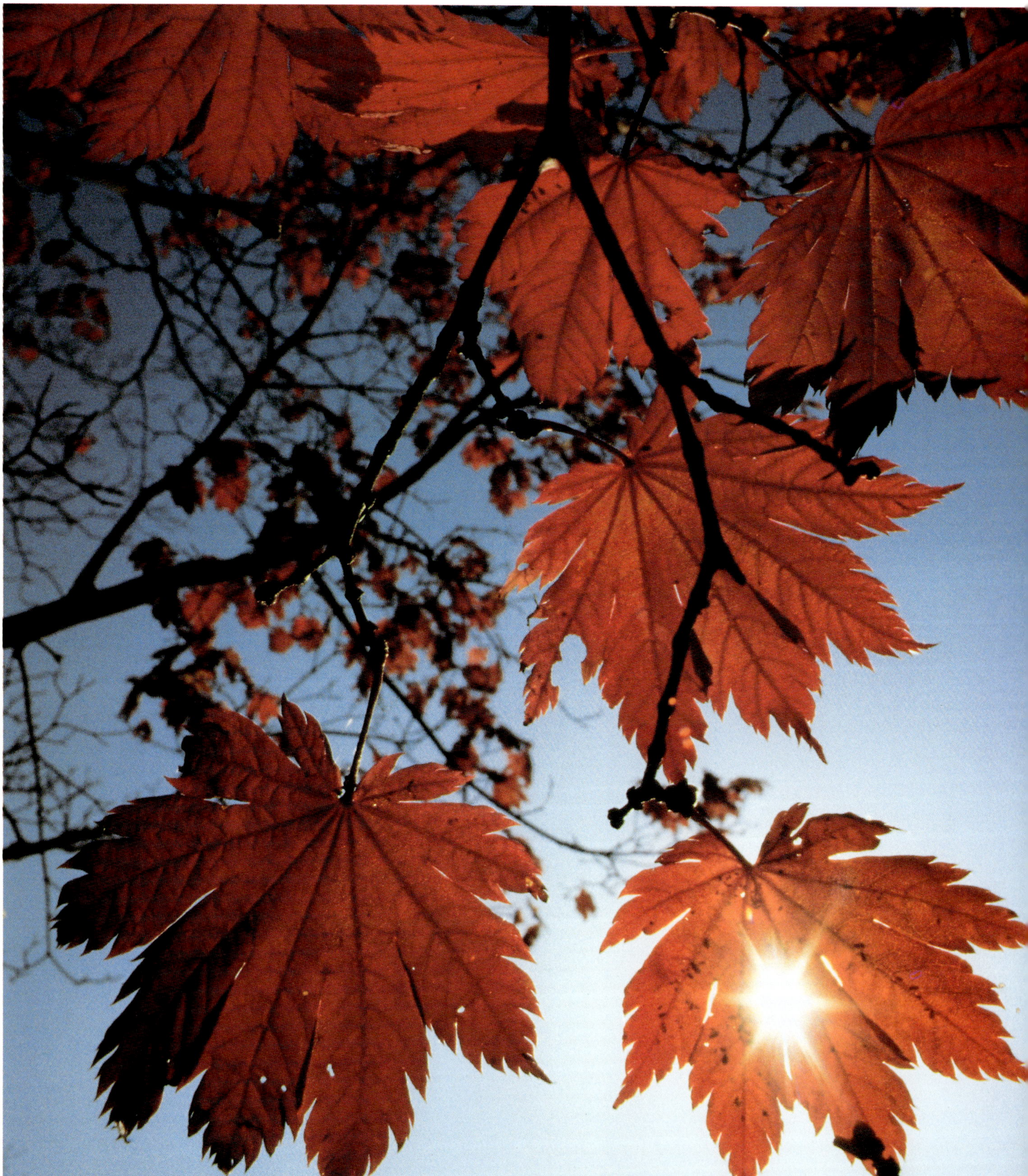

INTRODUCTION

One of the most infuriating phrases in photography refers to the 'quality of light'. Those qualities of light which are scientifically measurable, such as colour, direction and intensity, seem to have little or nothing to do with this term as it is used by photographers (and painters). San Francisco, St Ives in Cornwall and the Greek islands: all have at one time or another been praised for the 'quality' of the light to be found there.

But why does one place appear to have better (or worse) light than another? The answer is easier to recognize than to articulate. The warm light of evening, or the slanting, clear light of dawn often seem to be better than the midday sun, which in turn may have more 'quality' than a cloudy, overcast day. Dramatic storm light, with the sun breaking through lowering clouds, has more 'quality' than flat, featureless light, and dappled sunlight through trees has more 'quality' than blazing sun.

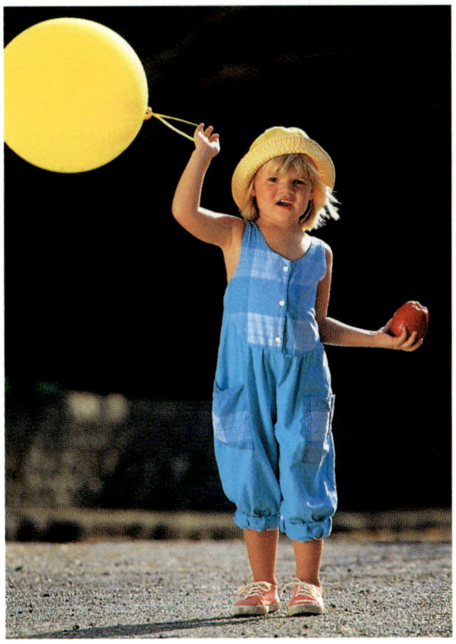

Artistically, 'quality of light' is almost indefinable, and often depends on the photographer's skill in handling the available light. With the right treatment, even 'poor' light can be used to create superb pictures. 'Working with diffused light' on pages 15-18 demonstrates this clearly: all of the pictures on those pages were taken under conditions where most photographers would have simply packed up their cameras and given up.

Equally, bright tropical sunlight can prove too harsh and full of contrast for many subjects, even those which are apparently promising. The advice to 'keep the sun over your shoulder' has served generations of photographers. But although it may be a good rule of thumb, knowing when (and how) to break the rules is an essential part of learning how to take great photographs.

Nor are you obliged to take the light exactly as you find it. Reflectors, diffusers and fill-in flash can all modify daylight, often in a way which is almost imperceptible to the novice: the difference is that the resulting photograph is in some way lifted out of the ordinary.

For that matter, mastery of filters can create many dramatic yet natural-seeming effects. Heavy-handed use of filters will normally make a picture worse, not better; but used with discrimination and understanding, filters can transform your photographs. On pages 29-50, we show you how to filter for extra saturated colours; how to remove reflections; how to change the apparent colour of the light; and how to use graduated filters ('grads') to create memorable pictures.

Shooting into the sun ('contre-jour'); using reflections and shadows; creating silhouettes - all this and more can be found in this book.

Finally, we show you how to apply everything you have learned about the secrets of light to the entire cycle of the day, from the first rays of dawn through the high sun of noon to the warm, hazy light of evening and on into the night. After all, nightfall does not mean that you have to put away your camera: as the colour drains from the sky, you can shoot dramatic night shots, or use the trailing streaks of light from car headlights and tail-lights to distil the essence of the city. And the final few pages in the book explore the most mysterious light of all – the intriguing Northern Lights or Aurora Borealis.

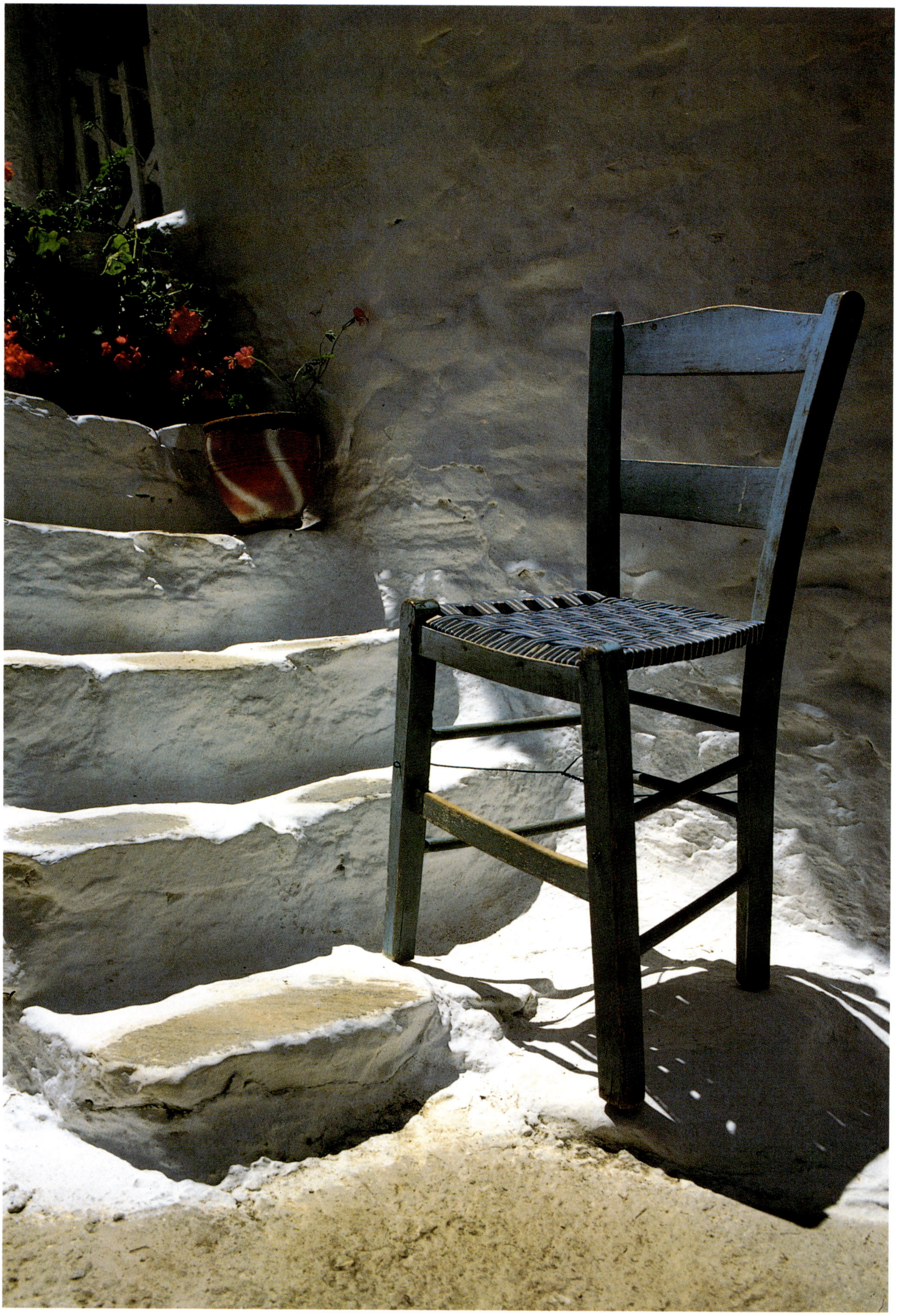

Working with daylight

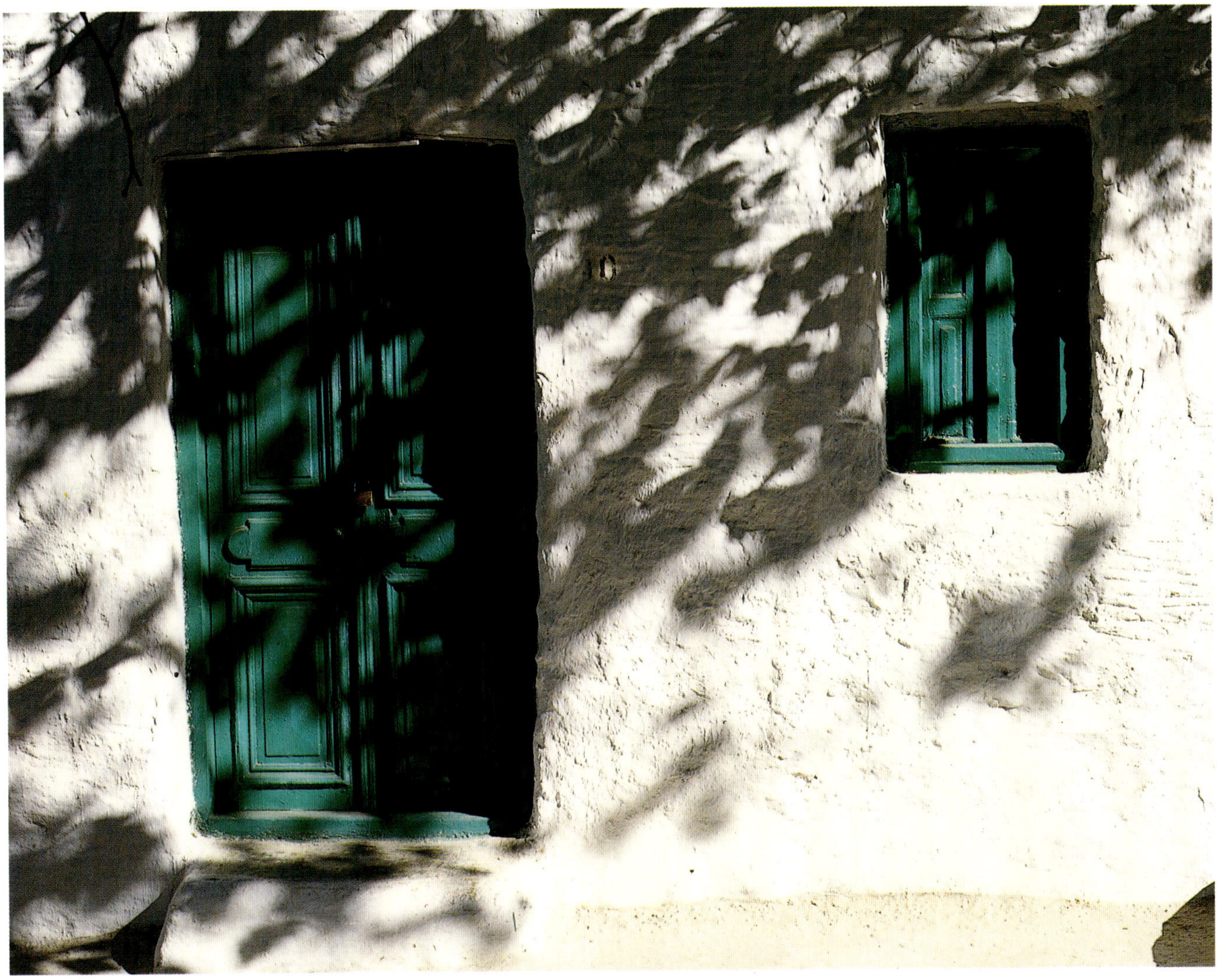

▲ **FOCUS ON SHADOW**
The dappled pattern of leafy shadows on this wall is sharply outlined – a clear indication that the sun is shining brightly. Hard shadows, like these, are produced in conditions of direct daylight.

Daylight continuously changes in both quality and quantity. You can't control it, so you have to adapt to suit it. Understanding how daylight works and how it can affect your pictures is one of the secrets of successful photography.

Whether it's early morning light, a grey, overcast day or a sunset, the sun is the source of all natural daylight. But the character and quality of daylight changes from hour to hour and from season to season, so you need to understand its different forms in photographic terms.

Types of light

Daylight can be divided into four main categories. There is direct, diffused, reflected and indirect window light.

We shall begin by looking at these different types of light, and go on to the different techniques which are required in order to take successful pictures in each one.

Direct light

This is the easiest type of daylight to recognize. It occurs when the sun is shining brightly and the skies are clear. The light falls directly on to the subject. If you imagine the sun as a giant spotlight in the sky, you will be able to picture the bright highlights and strong shadows direct light produces.

A subject such as a sand dune which could otherwise look quite dull is vividly brought to life when patterned or textured by sharp shadows. The contrast between the sunlit areas of the picture and the shadows are extreme. However, direct light is not ideal for portrait photography as it creates unflattering shadows. In any picture, you need to consider whether hard shadows will create a pleasing effect or be a distracting hazard.

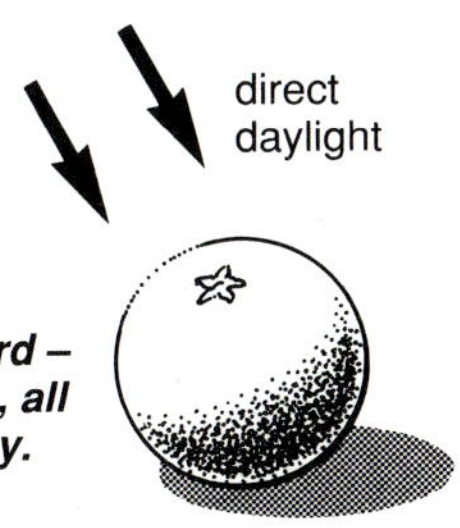

HOW DIRECT LIGHT WORKS
Direct light makes hard – edged, dark shadows, all pointing the same way.

Diffused light

When the sun is obscured by clouds, mist, haze or even a dust storm, the light becomes diffused. Instead of falling brightly from one direction on to a subject, the light is scattered and broken up so that the rays come from many directions. This has the effect of softening the shadow areas and the light itself is less bright.

Many people think that you can't take a good picture on an overcast day. In fact, this is one of the easiest types of daylight for a photographer to work with since it creates virtually no harsh shadows. This makes it ideal for subjects such as portraits.

▼ USING DIFFUSION

Weather conditions affect the kind of light available. Here the light is diffused (scattered) by a combination of cloud and mist. An overcast day is ideal if diffused light is required. Shadows are very soft or almost non-existent.

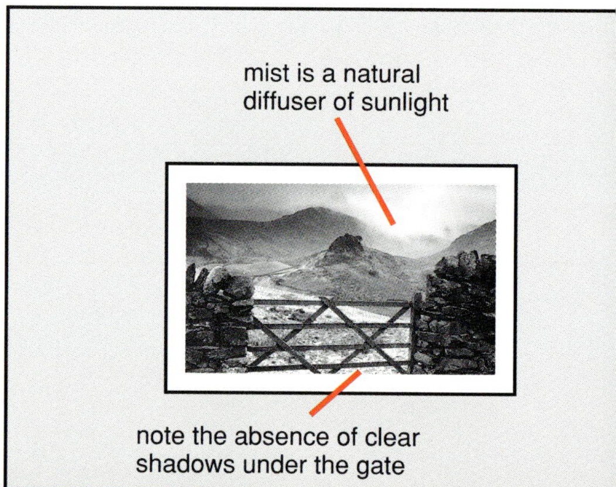

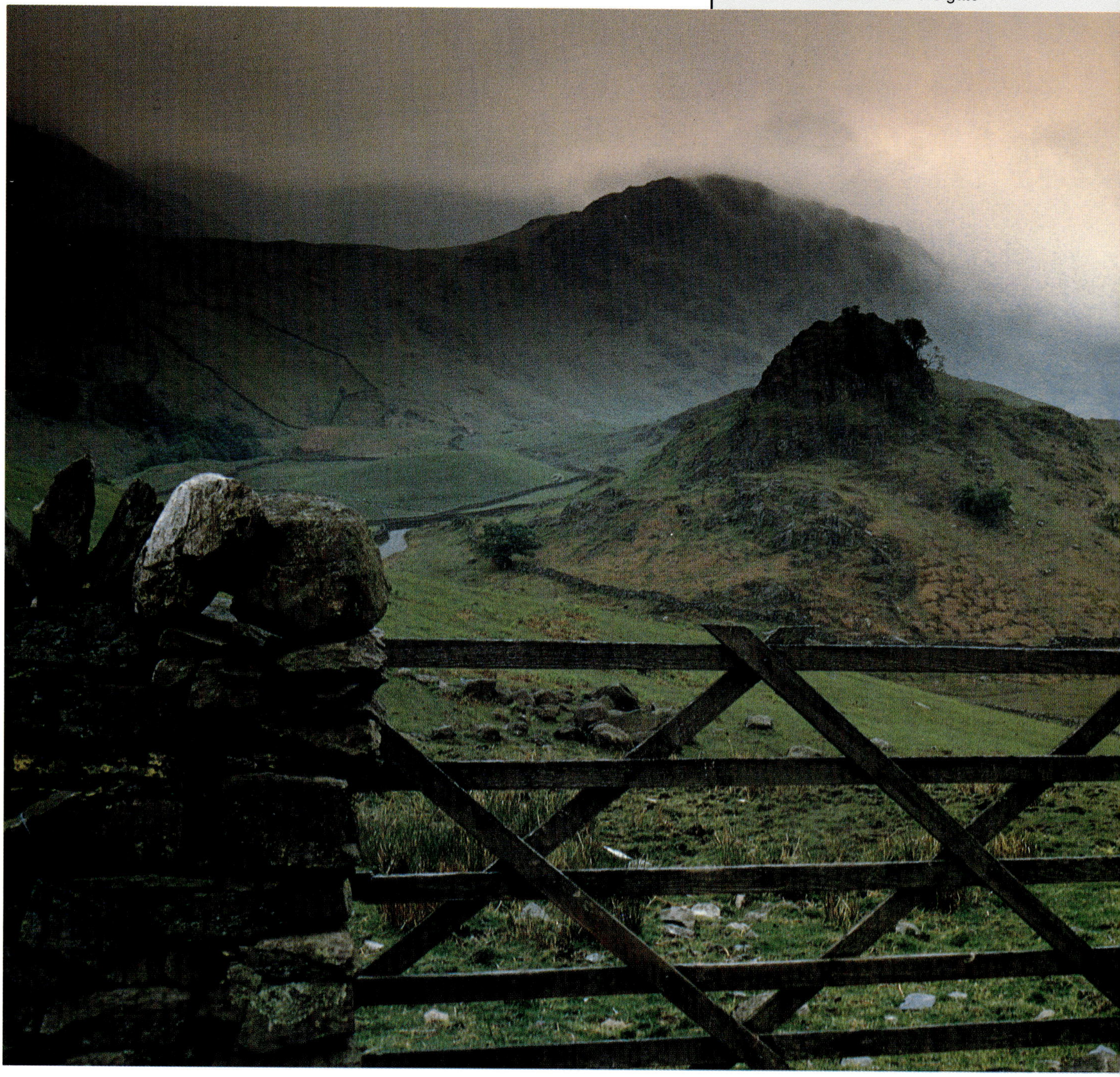

How diffused and reflected light work

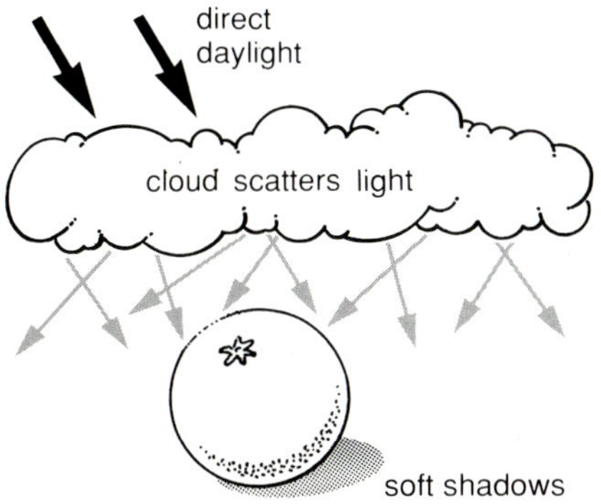

◀ **Diffused light** produces little or no shadow. What shadow there is will be mid toned, with soft edges.

▶ **Reflected light** bounces back into the shadow areas. Again, there is hardly any shadow cast.

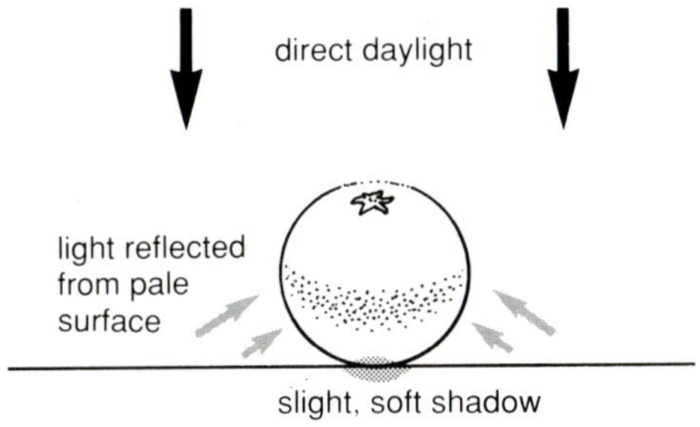

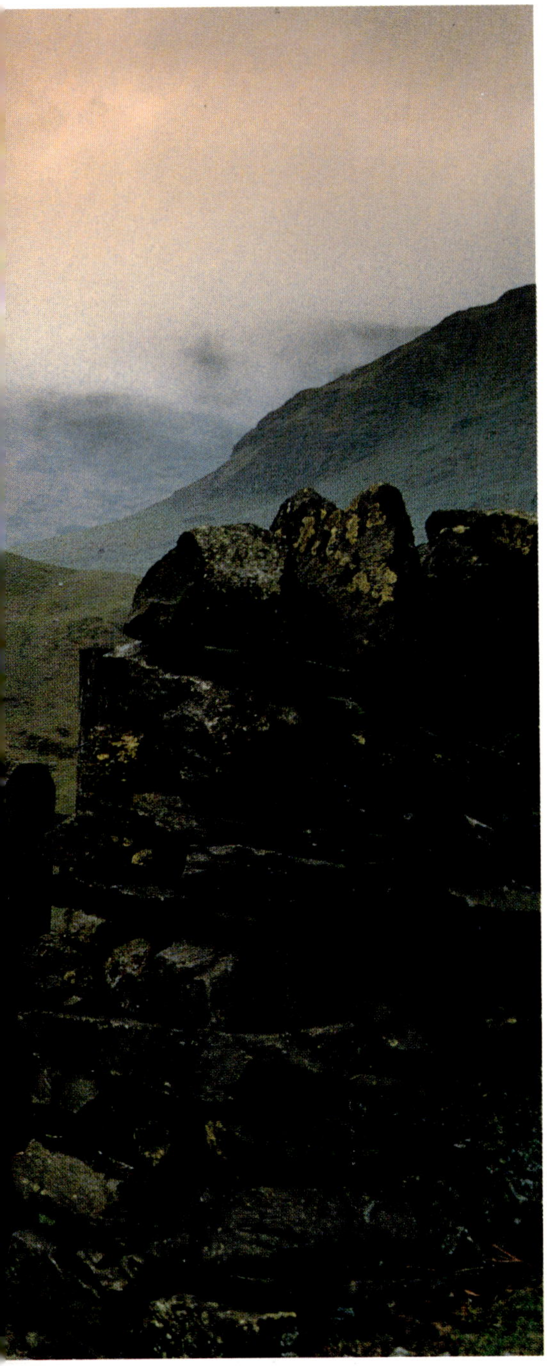

Reflected light

Reflected light is created when direct light bounces off a surface.

Water is a familiar reflector of light. Think how direct sunlight reflects off the surface of a lake or pool. Reflected light bounces back into the face of a swimmer from the surface of the water.

Other surfaces that reflect light naturally may be a whitewashed wall, a gravel path or sand. If you position your subject carefully and move around until you have found the best spot, you can use this reflected light to brighten the dark shadows in a subject flooded by direct sunlight.

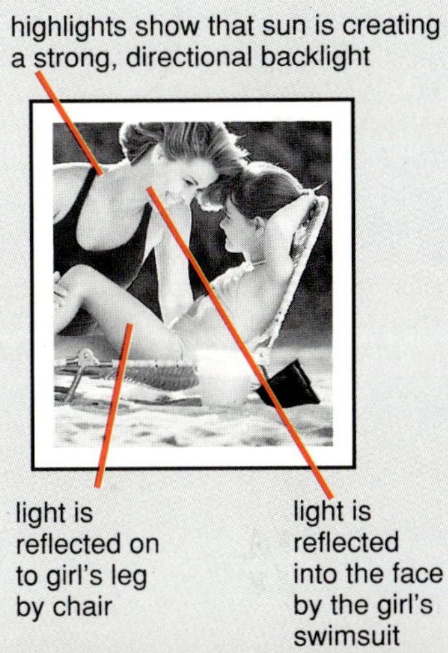

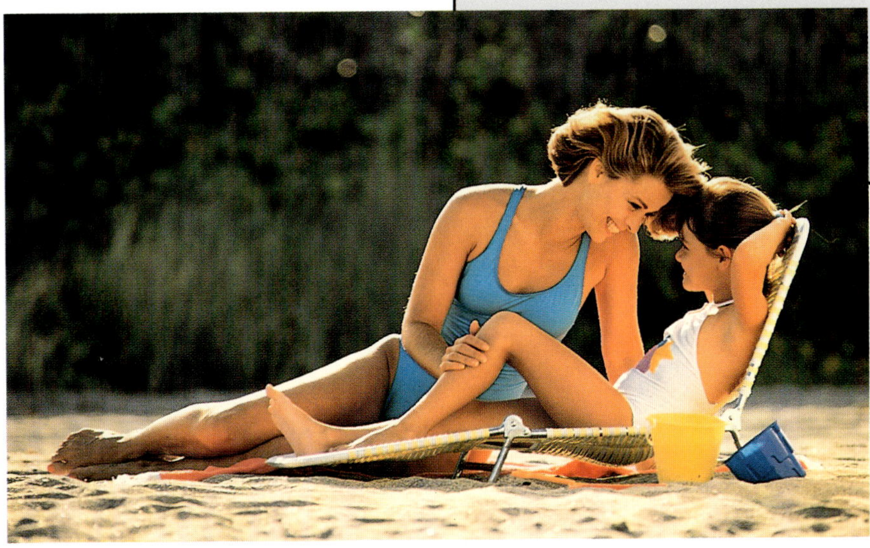

▲ **REFLECTIVE SURFACES**

Imagine this picture with the mother and daughter lying on a dark unreflective rock in bright sunlight. The shadow areas would be very dark, with little detail. But here the light coloured sand, beach chair and swimsuit all act as reflectors and throw light back into the skin tones. This creates soft, modelling shadows rather than harsh, unflattering ones.

Indirect window light

If the sun shines through the window, the effect is the same as with direct outdoor sunlight. It creates bright highlights and dark shadows.

Indirect natural light indoors has qualities of both direct and diffused lighting. When the window faces away from the sun or it is an overcast day, only a certain number of scattered rays can enter the window, giving a very softened version of direct light.

A light wall in the room may also reflect light, creating soft secondary shadows and a gentle additional light which fills in shadows.

▼ USING NATURAL LIGHT INDOORS
The objects in this picture are lit by light coming in through the window. The light outside is diffused by clouds. This gently illuminates the objects, creating very soft shadows with blurred edges. This kind of natural window light is ideal for photographing an indoor still life.

How indirect window light works

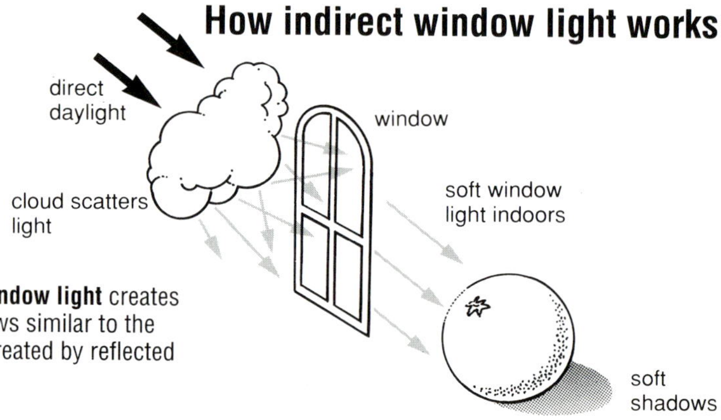

Indirect window light creates soft shadows similar to the shadows created by reflected light.

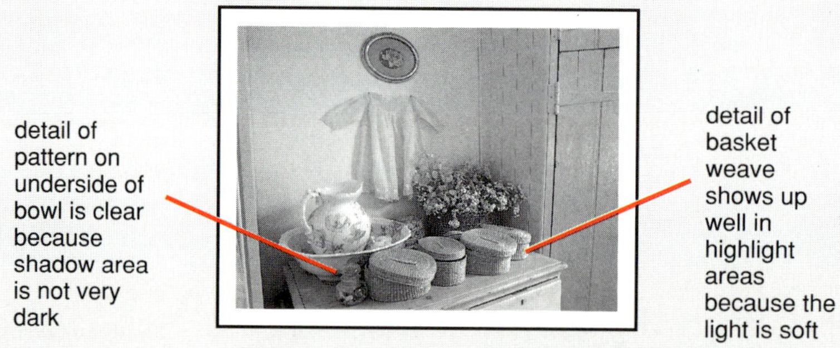

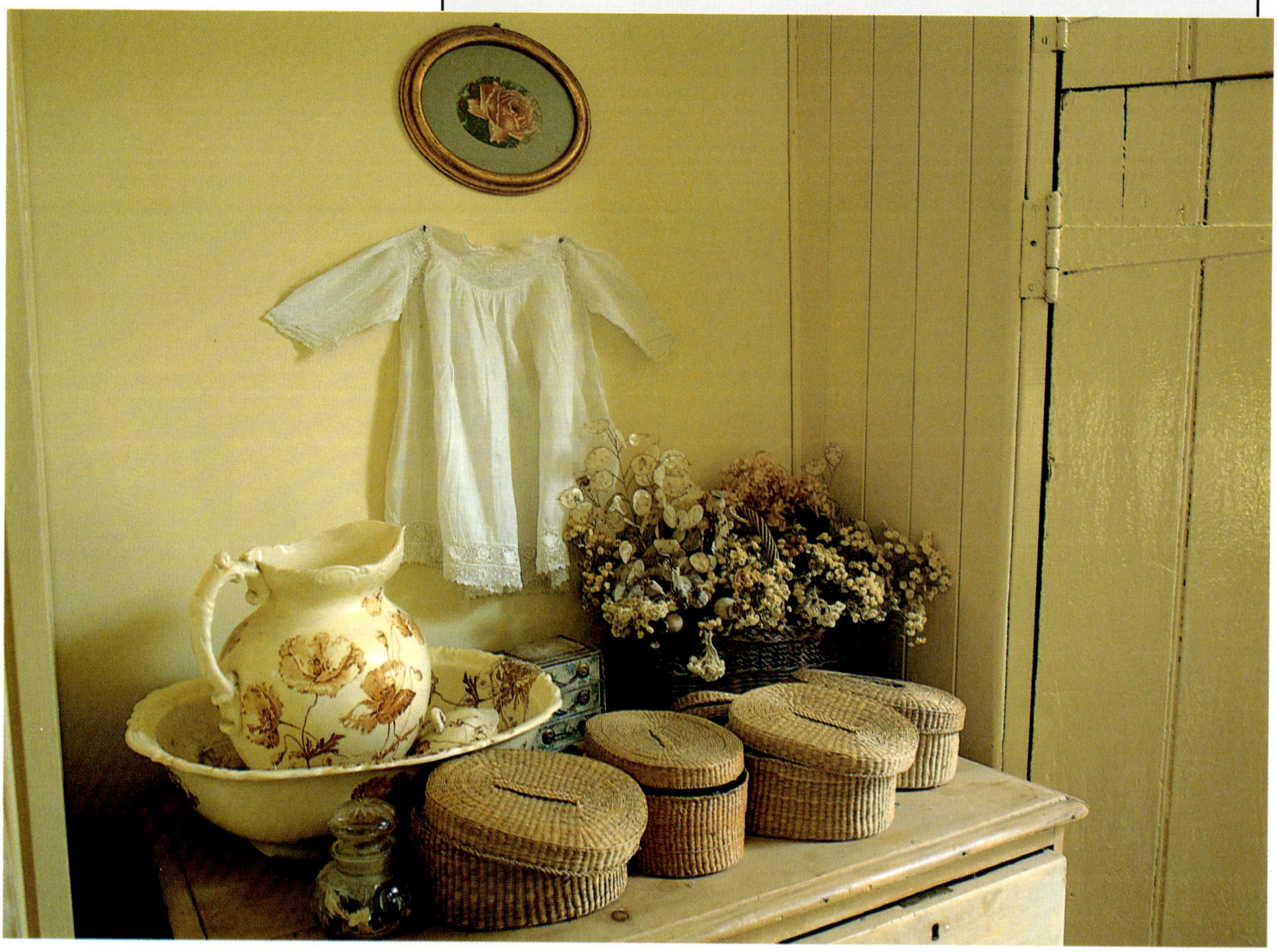

Using direct light

Imagine a sunny, cloudless day. The light shining down on you is the very strongest kind of light available – direct sunlight.

With direct light, there is a huge contrast between areas of light and darkness and you can't create subtle effects. Sunlit parts of a picture have strong, white highlights while cast shadows are dark and sharp-edged. Details that fall inside the shadow area are barely visible.

The graduated shading which emphasizes the roundness of objects is lost in the harsh contrast between light and shadow: something like a football, for example, ends up looking virtually two-dimensional. The advantage of such light, however, is that it picks out textures and emphasizes patterns, thereby adding interest to your photographs.

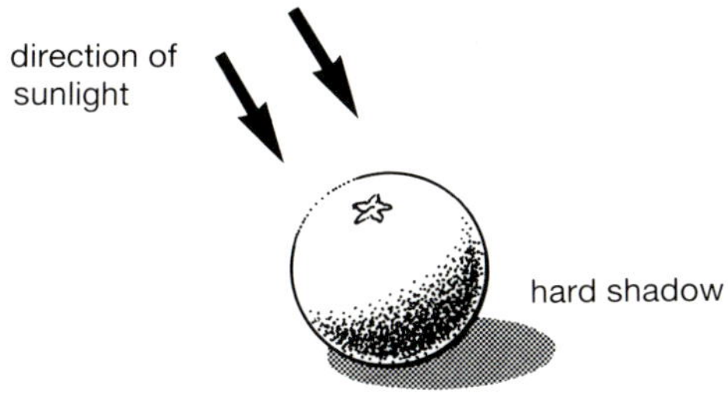

HOW DIRECT LIGHT WORKS
Bright sunlight creates heavy shadows and contrasting white highlights.

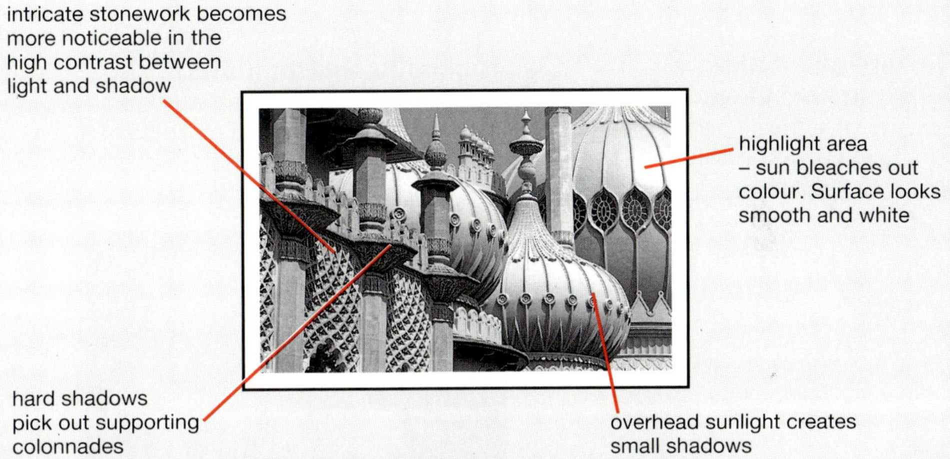

▼ MAKING THE MOST OF ARCHITECTURE
Direct light can sometimes be ideal for photographing buildings. But the point is to catch the time of day when the pattern of light and shade is at its most appealing. Here, the high contrast between lit and shadow areas emphasizes the architectural features. Long, late afternoon shadows might have produced confusing patterns.

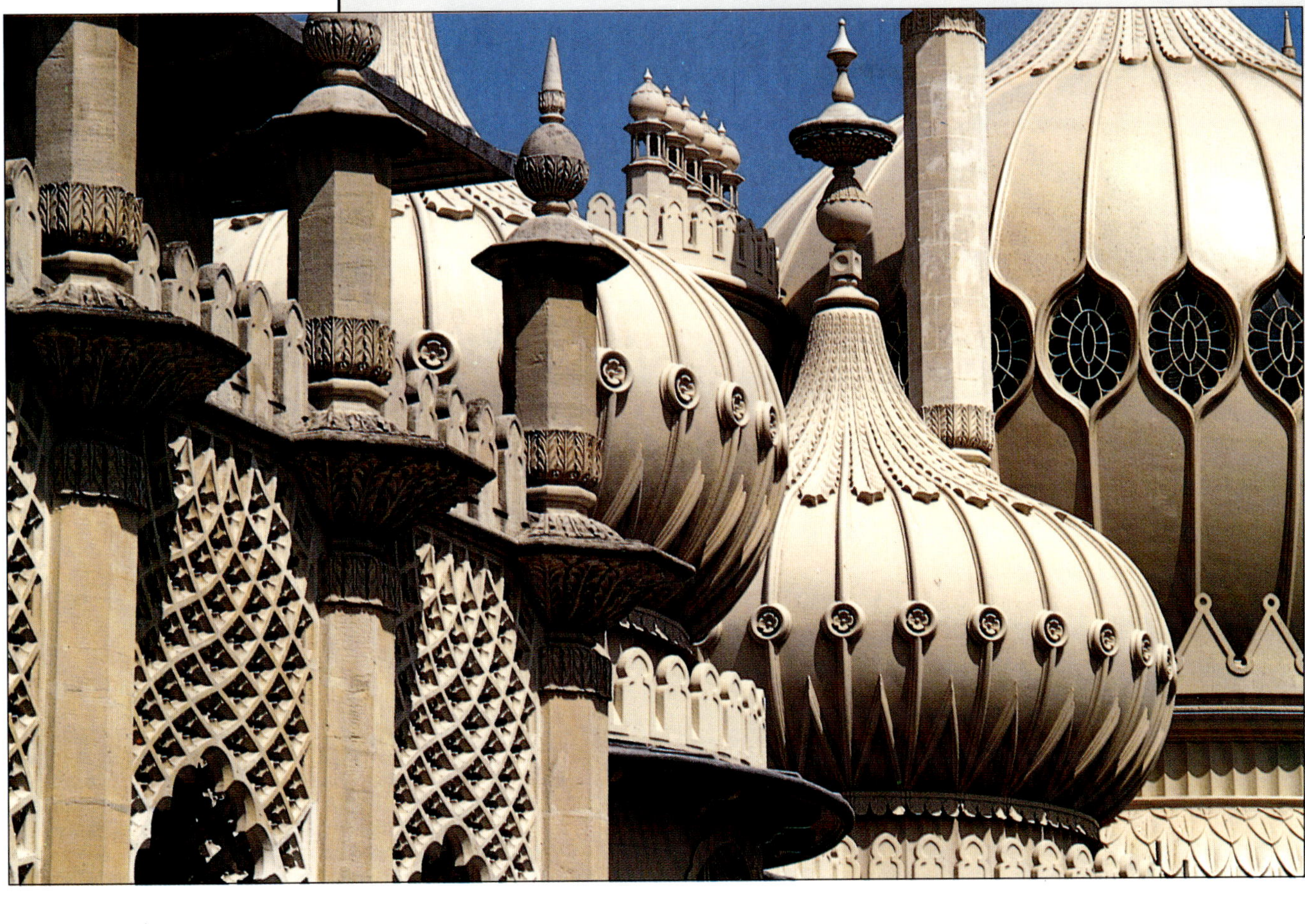

The angle of light

The angle at which the sun is shining can also make all the difference to your shot. In the morning and evening, as the sun rises and sets, the shadows are long. At midday, as the sun is overhead the shadows are at their shortest.

In most parts of the world the time of year affects the length of the shadows. In the winter, the sun shines lower in the sky, so shadows are longer.

Texture and pattern

Direct light tends to bring out the texture of subjects because even the smallest bump or hollow is thrown into extreme contrast with deep shadow.

Texture revealed by direct light can in turn make interesting patterns with contrasting areas of light and shade.

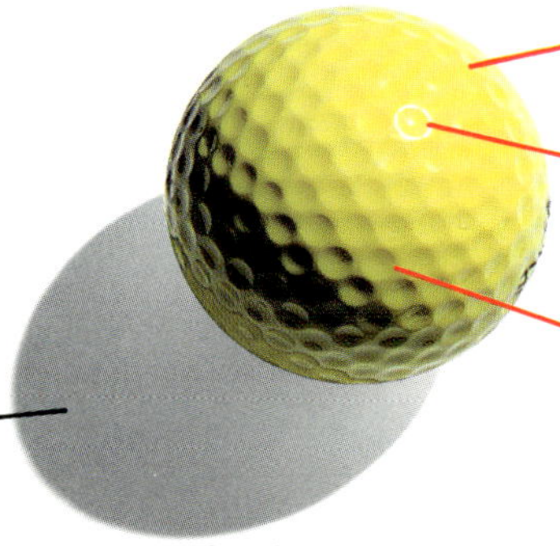

▶ The angle of the sun is high up to the right. One side of the ball is scorched to white and the other is plunged in deep shadow.

Highlights and shadows

In full sun, highlights can be so bright that colours and textures are completely bleached out, while at the other extreme, you cannot see anything in the dark shadow areas.

Before taking a picture in direct sunlight, look carefully at the highlights and shadows and see how you can make best use of the patterns they create. These may well turn a run of the mill picture into an unusual shot.

Tip: Shadow and exposure

The extreme contrast created by direct light can make working out exposure hard. The human eye sees detail in a huge range between light and dark. Film is less sensitive. It can't pick out detail in such a vast brightness range.

You must choose an exposure which is correct for the highlights or for the shadows – you can never get both right. Either the highlight areas will be overexposed and too pale or the shadow area will be so dark that no details show. However, you can deliberately throw shadows into darkness or have bright highlights, for a creative effect.

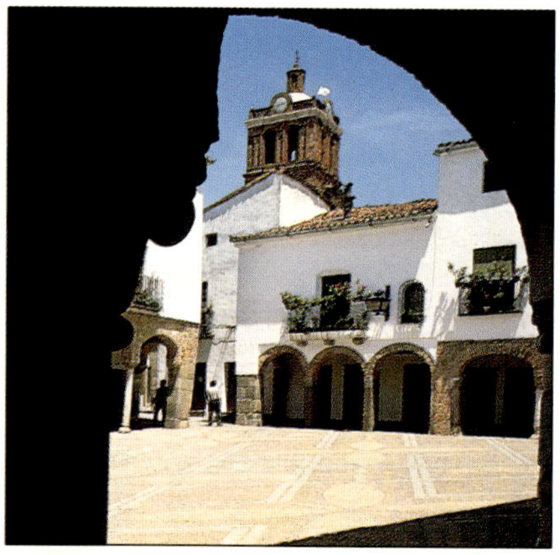

◀ The photographer decided to sacrifice foreground detail so that the central square would be correctly exposed. The contrast between light and shadow means that the archway in the foreground and the man standing under the arches in the background become silhouettes. This extreme contrast helps to evoke the feeling of a place where the sun is hot and the shade cool and dark.

If the photographer had chosen to show the detail of the archway, the rest of the picture would have ended up drastically overexposed.

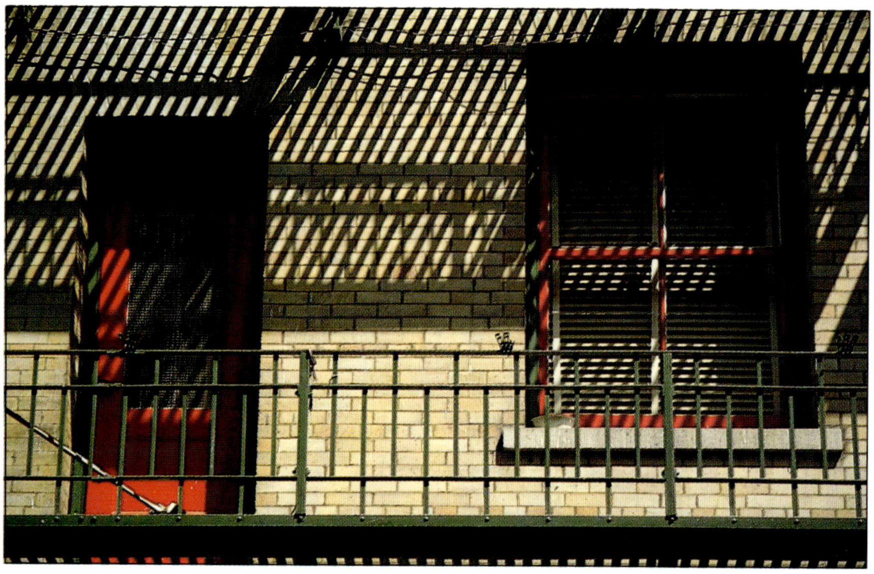

◀ UNUSUAL PATTERNS
The shadows in this photograph were formed by the metal walkway above the apartment. Overhead sun means that the metal casts shadows on to the side of the building, forming an interesting pattern.

▶ EFFECT OF THE ANGLE
For this shot, the sun is quite low in the sky, lighting the dunes sideways. If the photo had been taken at noon, the sun would have been directly overhead. This would have meant there were few shadows and the dunes would have appeared flat and shapeless.

Changing highlights and shadows

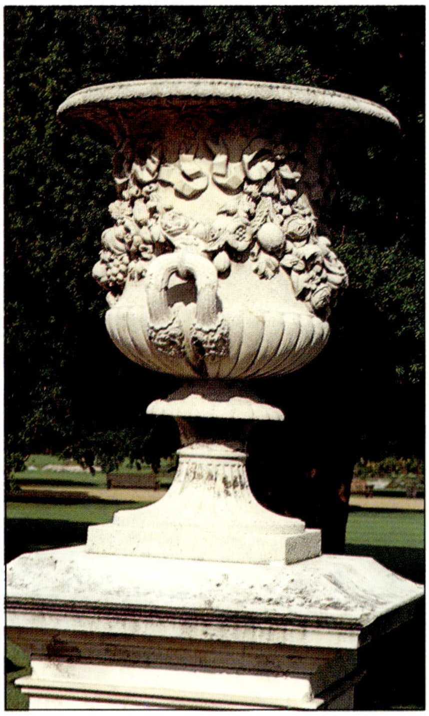

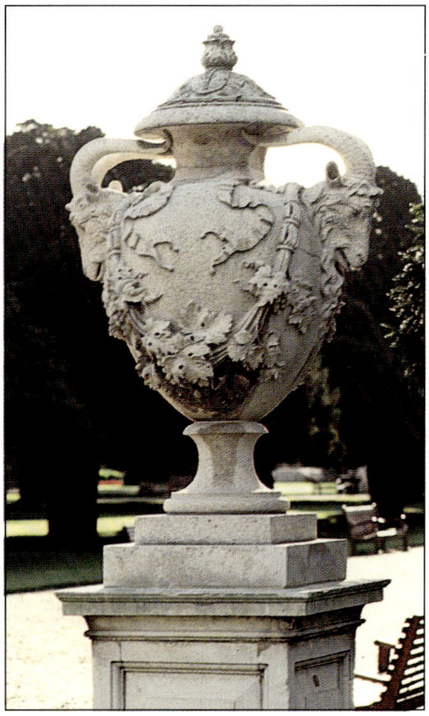

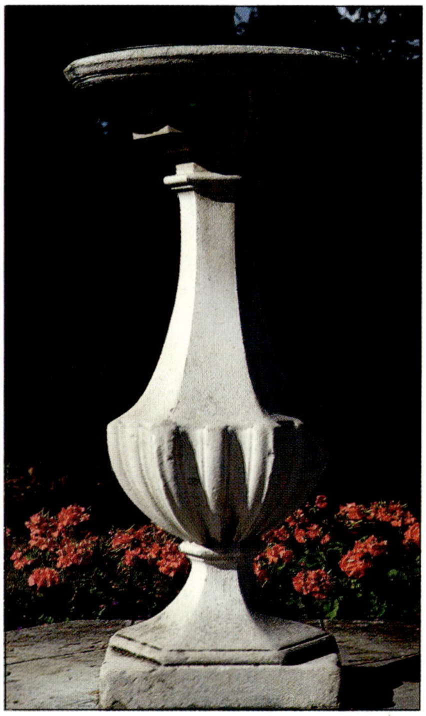

TOPLIGHT
When the sun is overhead, it casts shadows directly downwards. The area under the lip of the vase is thrown into complete darkness. Some details on the relief decoration on the vase show up well because the downward pointing shadows emphasize their pattern.

BACKLIGHT
With the sun behind the urn, everything except the edges of the vase is thrown into shadow. To prevent the subject becoming a silhouette, a correct exposure has to be taken from the shadows. This means the sky in the background is overexposed, making it appear white rather than blue.

SIDELIGHT
When the sun is low in the sky, the shadows are cast sideways. They throw one half of the picture into darkness and emphasize the vertical curves of the stonework and the pattern at the base of the sundial.

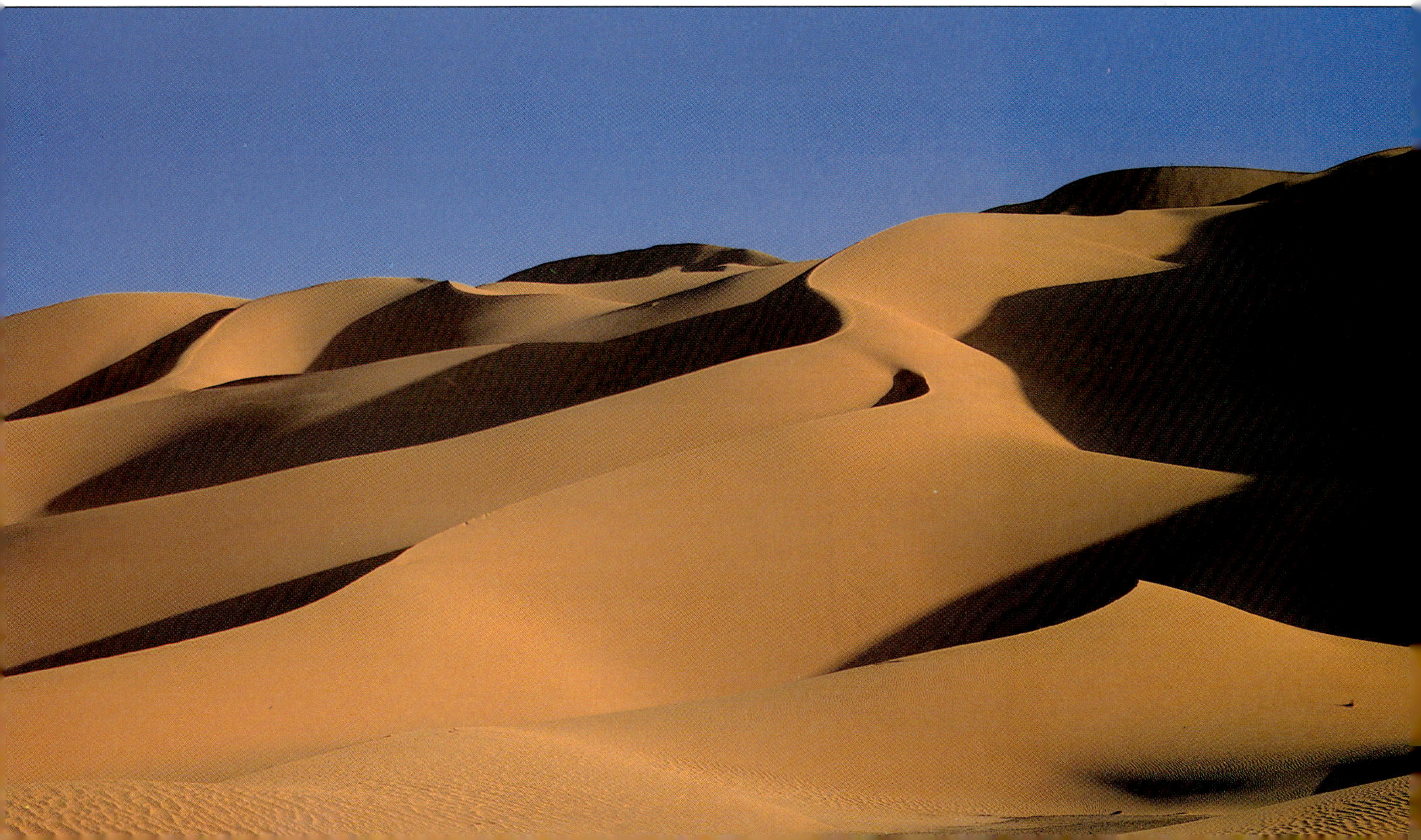

Portrait lighting

Using direct light for portraits can produce some interesting results, not all of which are flattering. Different effects depend upon the direction from which the light is coming.

1 TOPLIGHT
This is uncomplimentary to the human face. It throws the eyes, cheek hollows and jaw into shadow. Here it emphasizes lines under the eyes and diagonal lines down the side of the nose. The forehead, tip of the nose, and top of the head and cheeks are highlighted.

2 BACKLIGHT
This outlines the head and hair with strong highlights. The whole face would normally fall into deep shadow. In this picture, the exposure has been measured from the man's face to prevent him becoming silhouetted. With a correct exposure, backlighting can show facial detail without hard shadows.

3 FRONTLIGHT
The trouble with frontlighting is it makes people screw up their eyes because they are looking into the sun. Pictures shot with frontlighting often look a bit like portraits taken in a photo booth – there are few shadows, the subject looks uncomfortable and the face resembles a mask with slits for eyes and mouth. The only shading appears unattractively under the nose.

CHECK IT!

Remember direct light
- ❑ creates hard-edged shadows and strong highlights.
- ❑ can be used creatively to show up texture and pattern.
- ❑ can complicate pictures with detail.
- ❑ can be used for high contrast.
- ❑ is not ideal if subtle effects are required.

4 SIDELIGHT
This is sometimes unflattering for faces, sometimes not. Half the face is thrown into shadow, which can look quite menacing or, as here, show character in a portrait. With hard shadows details such as the nose and raised eyebrow become more dramatic.

1
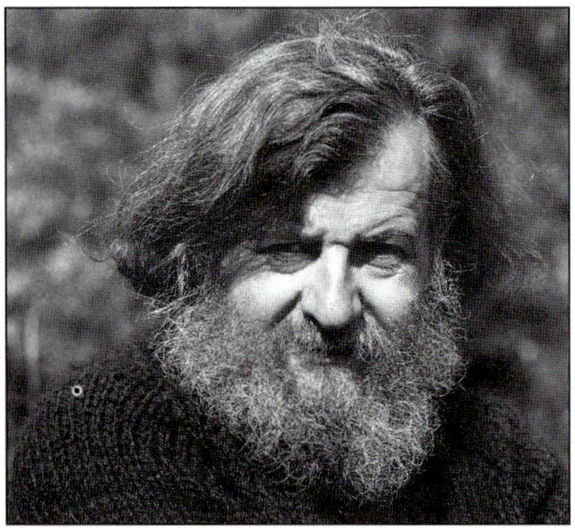

2
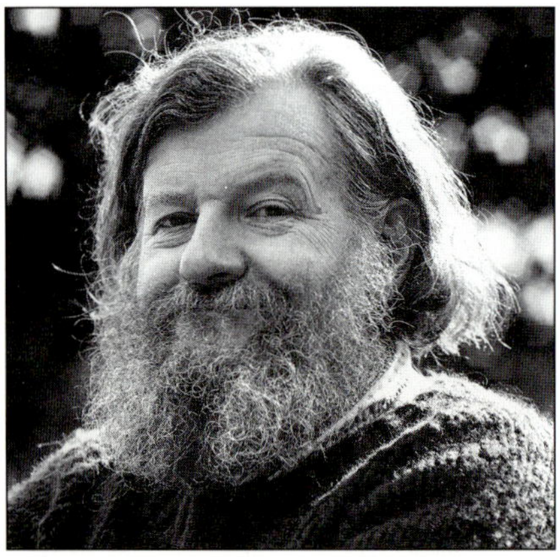

3
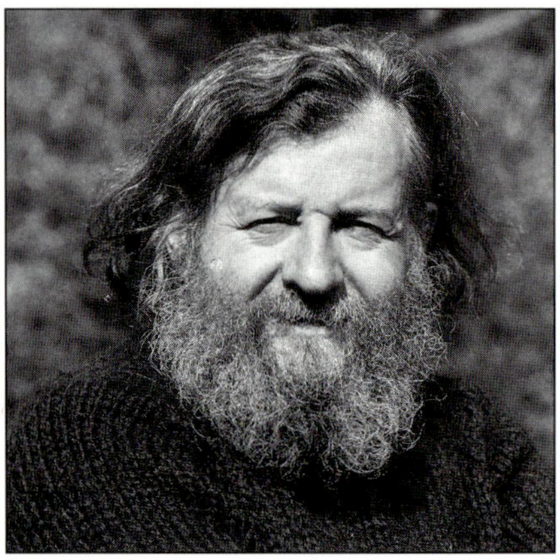

4
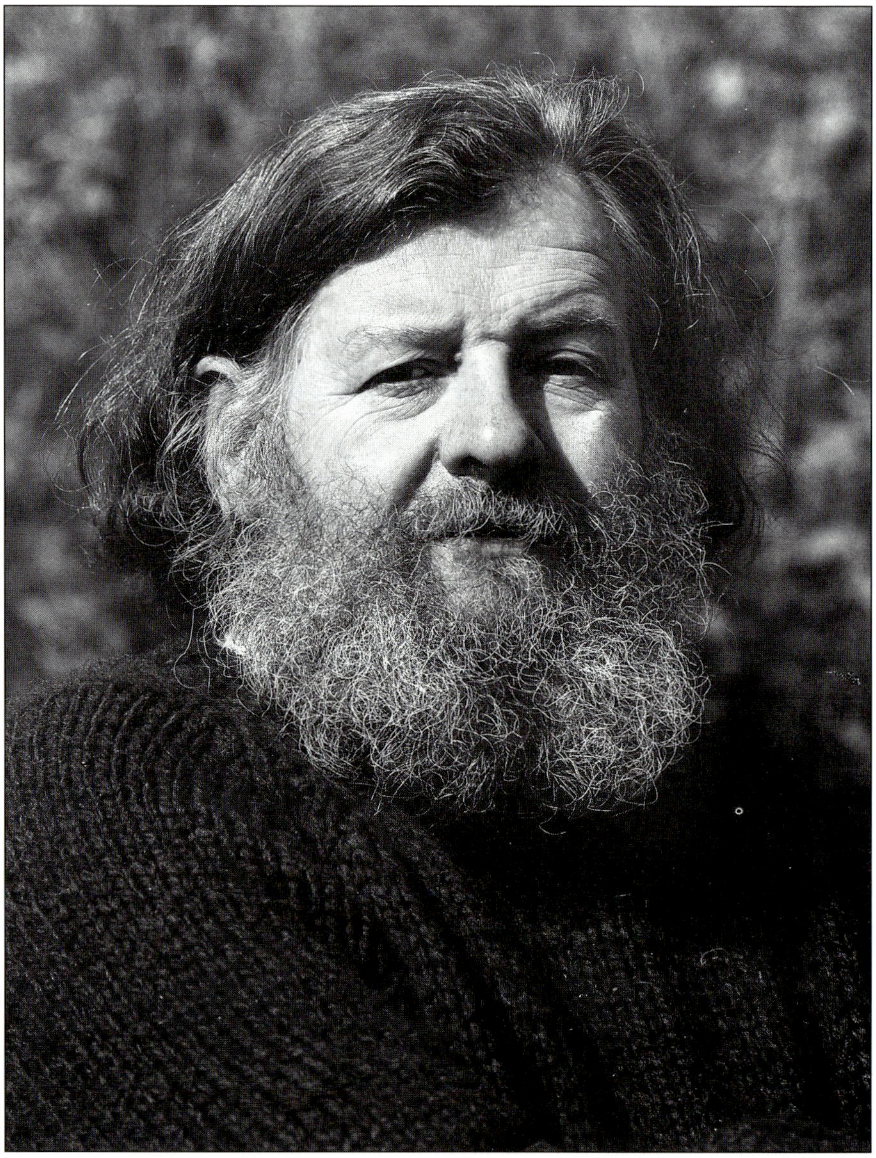

Using diffused light

Many photographers believe that to take a good picture the sun must be shining. But diffused light on an overcast day has its own special qualities and it can free you from some of the particular problems direct light brings.

Diffused light casts few shadows. This makes it easier to use than direct light because shadows sometimes complicate a picture's composition. Diffused light comes gently from all around, so that when you are taking portaits, for instance, you see subtly moulded features instead of rather unattractive shadows – and you don't have to worry about the person squinting into the sun. When you're photographing architecture, diffused light reveals detail and texture that can be lost in direct light.

Another advantage of diffused light is that the colours and details you see through the viewfinder accurately represent what you will get on film, with no extremes to fool the camera.

In direct light, your eyes penetrate shadows and highlights to pick out detail which film can't recreate. And your brain 'tells' you what colours you are seeing even in areas masked by black shadow or white highlight. The camera can't do this, so your pictures may have more contrast than you intended. Diffused light creates no such problem.

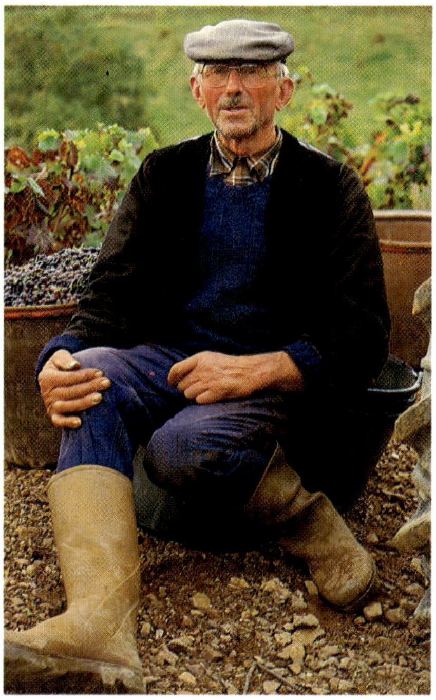

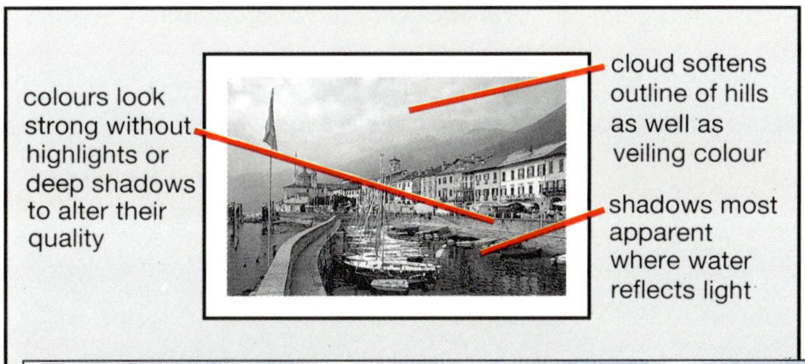

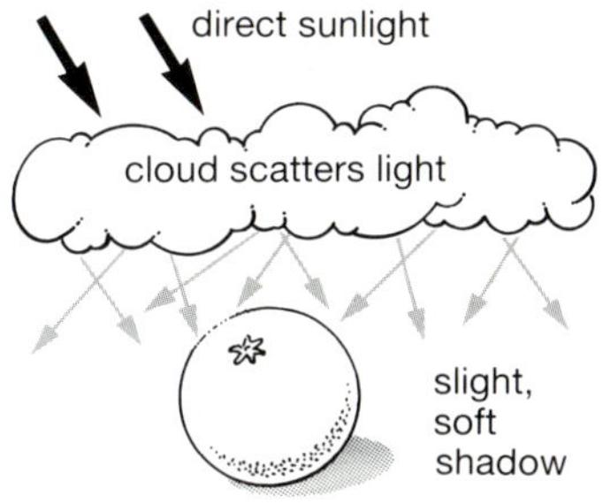

▲ PORTRAITS
For portrait photography diffused light works well. Because there are very few shadows, you can clearly see detail in the features.

▼ SUBTLE SCENES
Overcast days create diffused light – good for reflecting tranquillity.

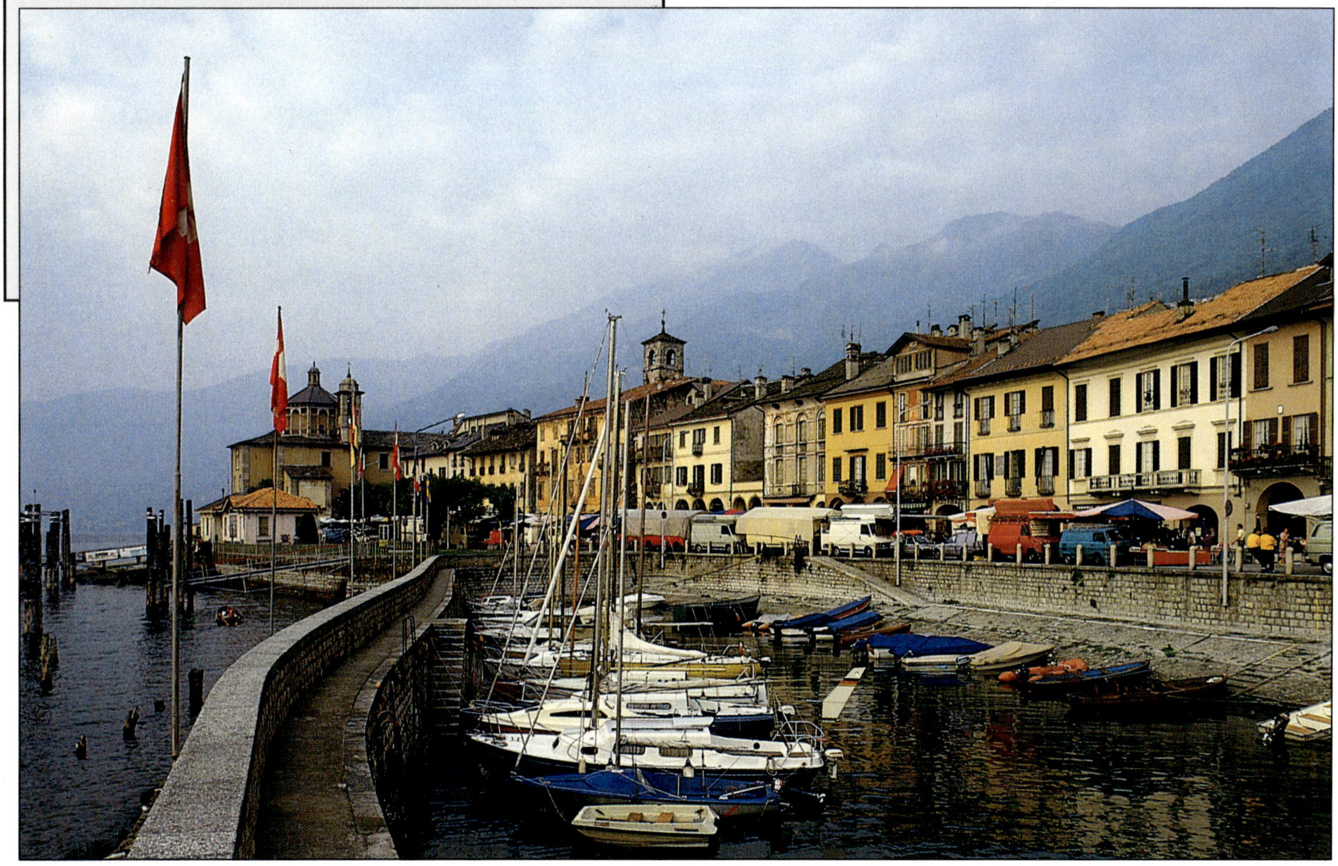

Diffused light and colour

Colours lose some of their brightness in diffused light because highlights and shadows are much more muted. In bright, direct sunlight strong shadows are created, the highlights are intense and white, and colours are bold.

On a cloudy day the highlights are spread out, giving an even appearance to the colours, and distracting shadows are lost. These conditions are ideal for pictures where it's important to emphasize texture or to show off a block of colour.

For example, imagine the bonnet of a red car in bright sunlight. The area where highlights fall appears white and the lit area of the bonnet looks bright red. Under cloud, there are no obvious highlights and the whole of the bonnet appears to be a solid red colour. The difference is quite noticeable.

Because of the cloud, pictures in diffused light look more grey or darker overall than photos taken in direct light. This subdues the colours, but it makes contrast between them stand out all the more.

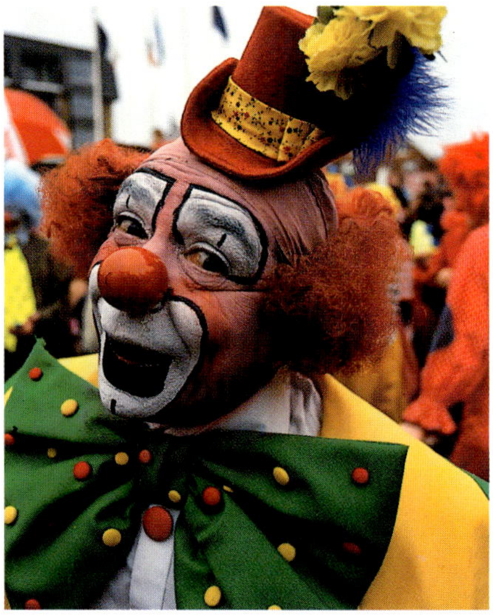

▲ CLEAR COLOURS
Without distracting shadows and highlights, the colours are evenly bright and colour contrast stands out at its strongest. One advantage of diffused light is that you see the colours as they will appear in the photograph.

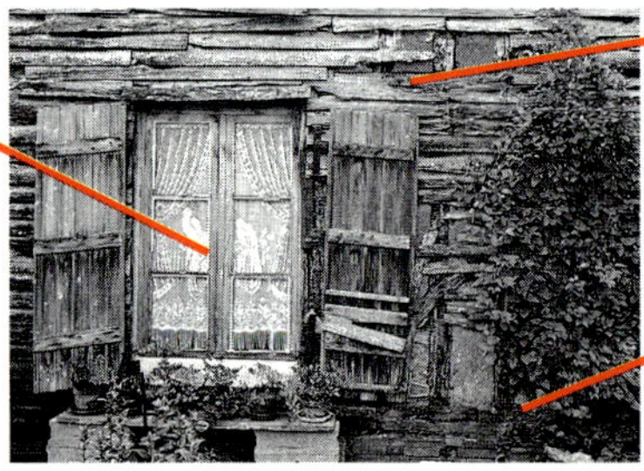

▼ TEXTURE AND DETAIL
Cloudy days are ideal for shooting intricate subjects without confusing shadows. Every tiny detail is captured because of the diffused light.

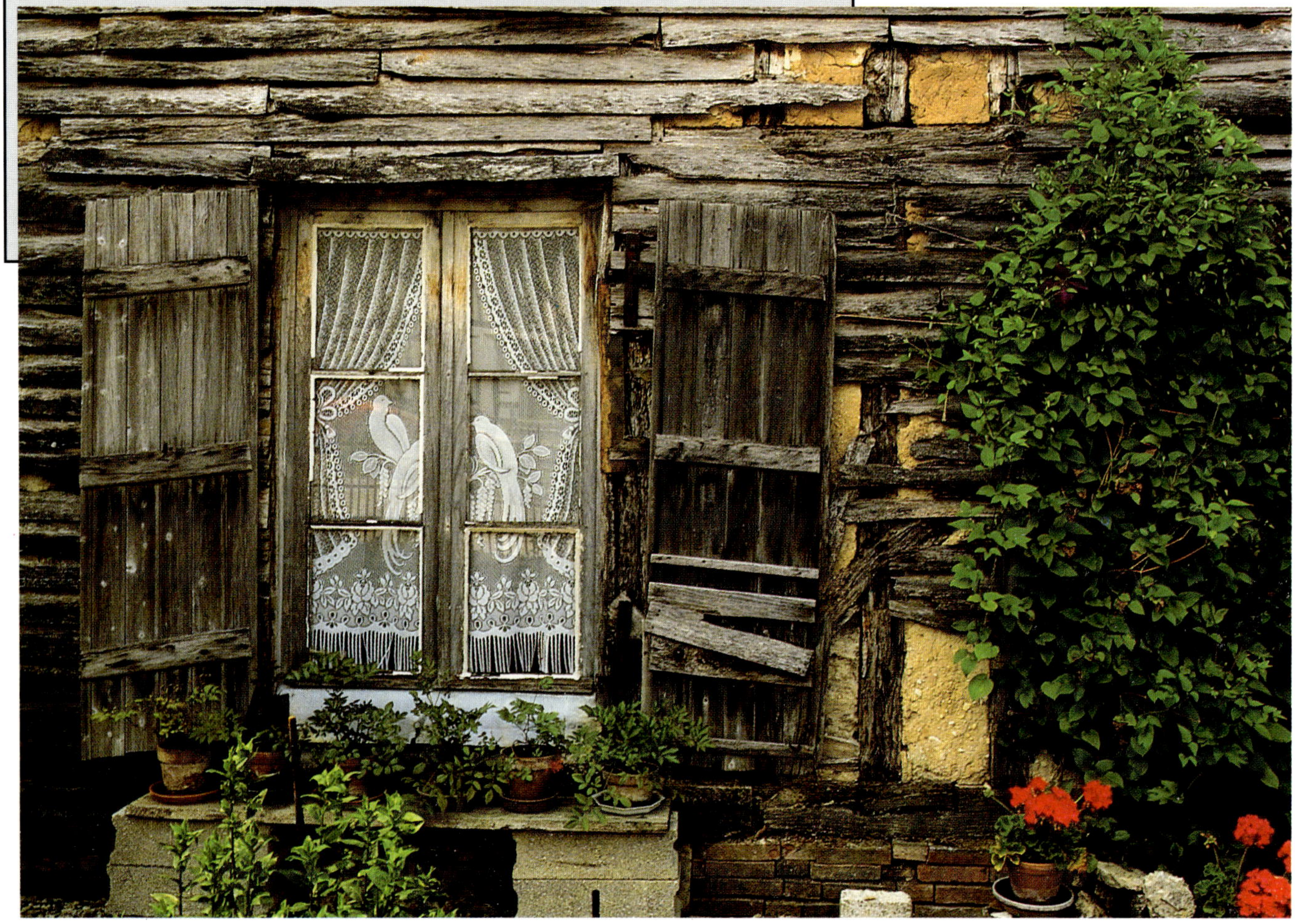

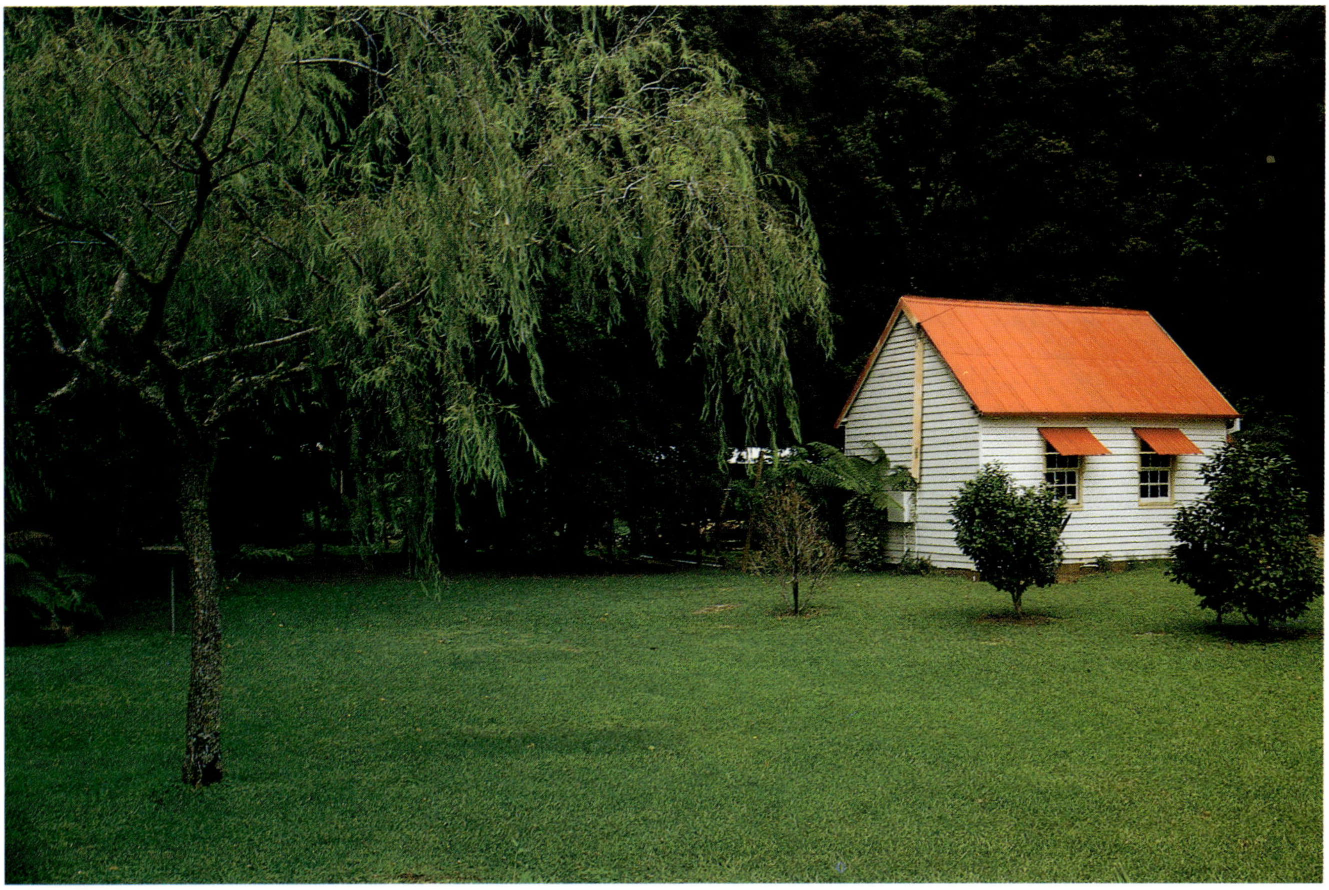

Tip: Extra care with exposure

On an overcast day, the whole sky becomes the light source, as the clouds diffuse the sun's rays.

Take care measuring the exposure when using a built-in light meter. If the picture includes a large area of sky, the meter will read the subject as much lighter than it appears. This is because the light meter is deceived into thinking that the scene is much brighter than it is. It underexposes everything except the sky and the picture comes out far too dark.

The solution is to point the camera down at the ground to cut out most of the sky when taking the light reading.

▲ COLOUR CONTRAST
The vivid contrast between the red and white house and the greenery gives this picture interest. If it had been taken on a sunny day, the contrast between the red and green would be less noticeable – both colours would have had highlights and the whole picture would be very bright. In diffused light, the greenery looks dark and so the contrast between it and the red of the house becomes more striking.

▼ CREATING PATTERN
The impact of the scene stems from the geometric lines of trees, the uniform colour and the details of the leaves. Direct light would have created a conflicting pattern of harsh shadows.

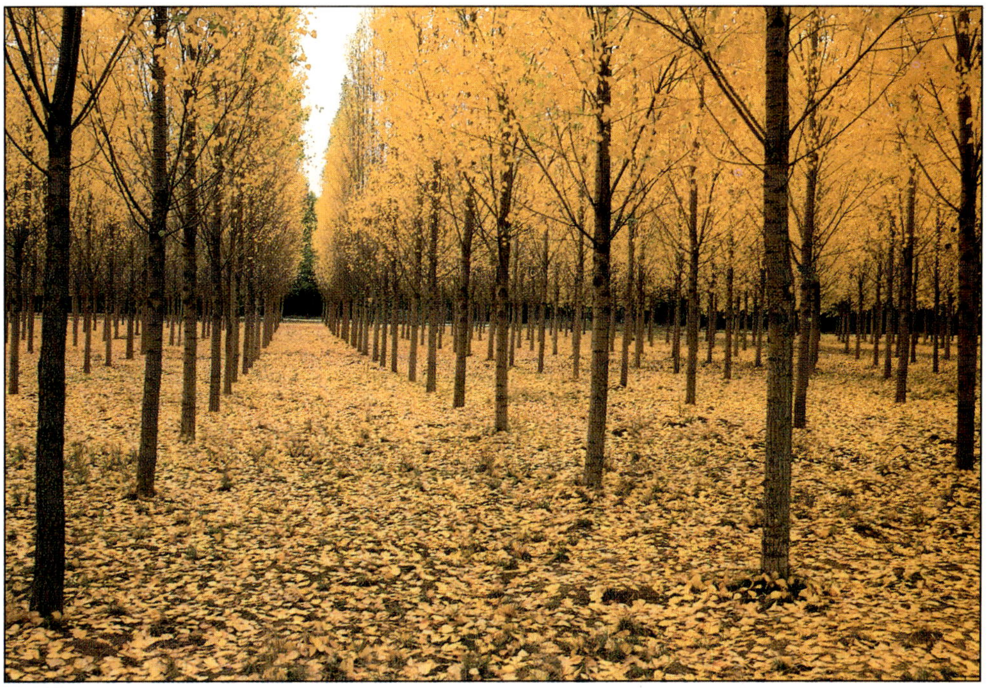

Diffusion and the weather

As light shines through a layer of cloud, minute drops of water in the cloud scatter the rays of light in every direction. The result – diffused light.

Clouds are the most common way in which sunlight is diffused. However, there are many other weather conditions which scatter the sun's rays. Sometimes you get more than one at a time, for instance fog and cloud.

Thick cover – dust, smoke, mist, smog, fog or heavy cloud – casts a murky cloak over a scene. This can help to create moody shots, but the effect may be rather monochromatic, as weak colours tend to blend together. The outlines of objects are also less well defined.

CHECK IT!

Diffused light:

❑ Occurs when the sky is overcast or when other weather conditions prevent direct sunlight.

❑ Is a good modelling light for portraits and can create subtle, moody effects.

❑ Re-creates colours as you see them and brings out colour contrast.

Comparing direct and diffused light

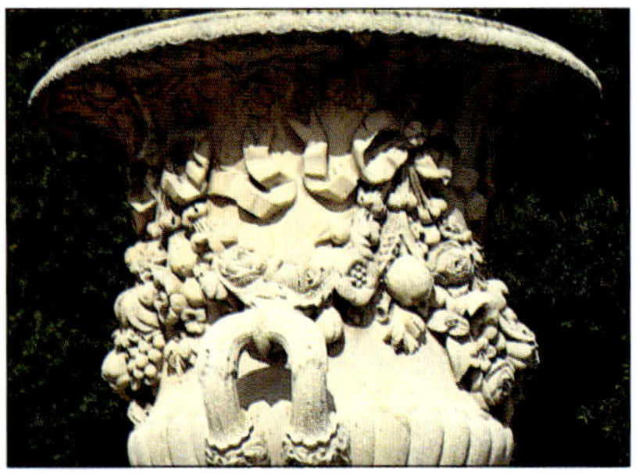

▲ **DIRECT LIGHT**
Hard shadows are cast by direct light. It creates greater tonal contrast between light and dark areas.

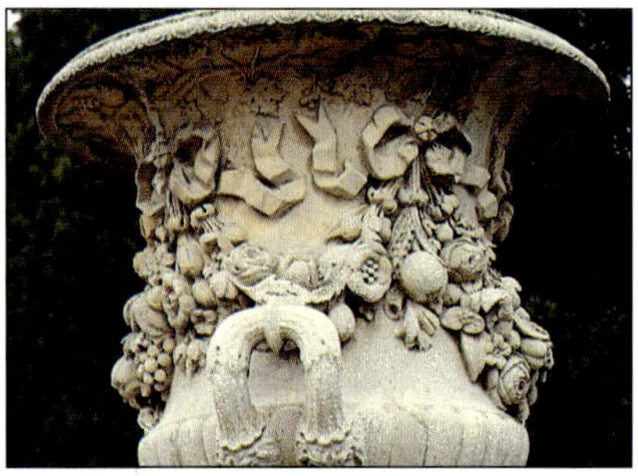

▲ **DIFFUSED LIGHT**
Detail and texture are shown up in diffused light. The background loses detail, making the vase stand out more.

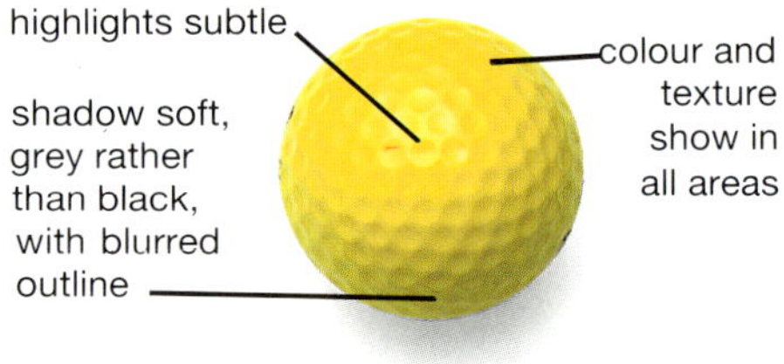

▲ **SPREADING LIGHT**
Diffused light spreads the highlights over a larger area than direct light, making colours weaker. Shadows are soft or barely visible.

▼ **USING HEAVY CLOUD**
You might not normally think of taking a photo on such an overcast day. However, for an uncluttered image, the blanket cloud cover filters the sunlight so successfully that the chair has only a very soft shadow.

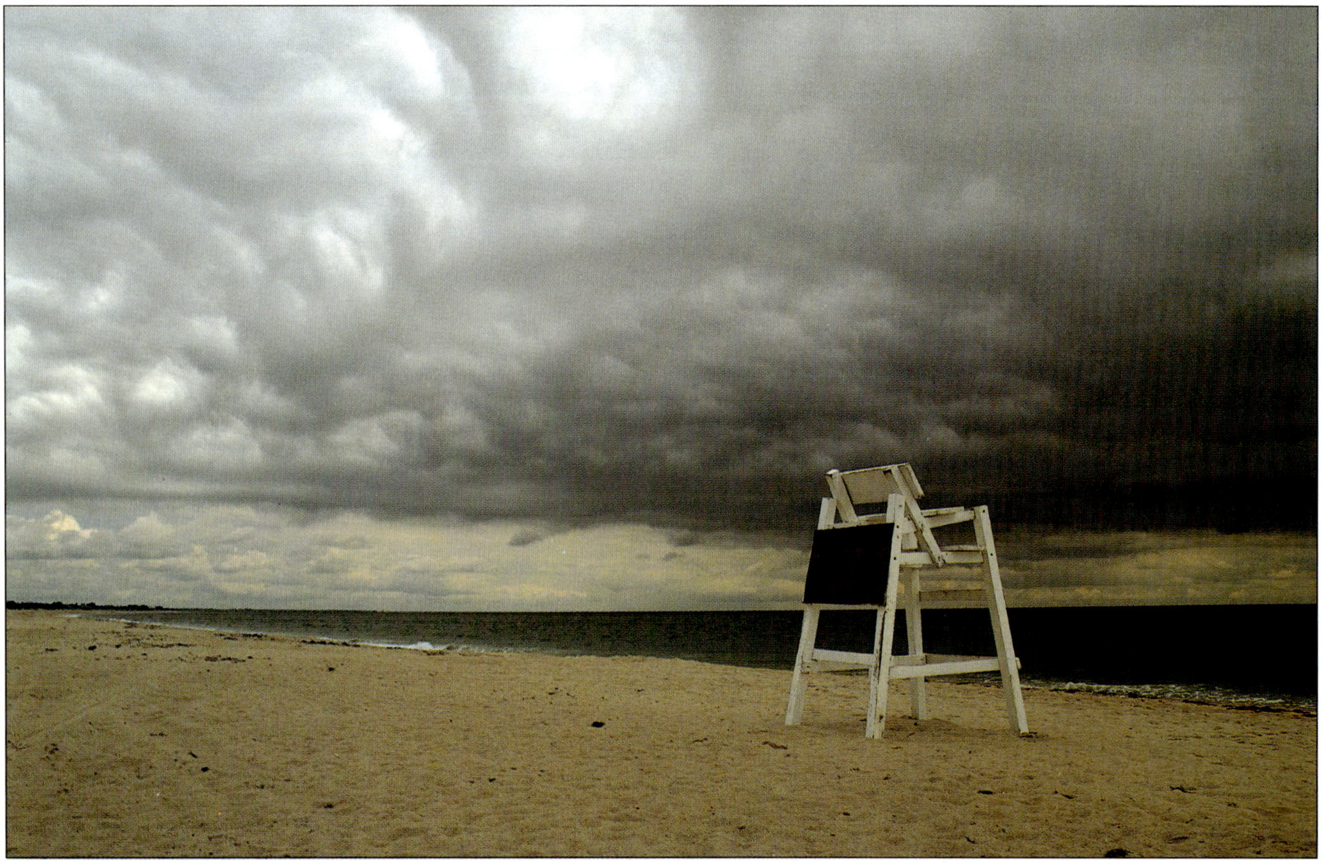

Using reflected daylight

When sunlight bounces off a pale or shiny surface it produces a secondary daylight source called reflected light.

A white wall, sandy beach or pale plastic table top are all good reflectors of light. They bounce light back into the picture. If the surface is a dark colour, the light does not bounce back off it. A black wall absorbs most of the light shining on to it.

Using water

Water is the most familiar, and the most dramatic, light reflector. When sunlight shines on to water, it makes thousands of tiny highlights on the surface. These highlights are so intense that they can be dazzling. The reflections they bounce back shimmer and shift. So instead of an evenly lit area, your subject is dappled by the play of light on the water.

A note of caution when photographing watery subjects – the highlights on water are usually much brighter than the subject, such as a boat. Because of the wide brightness range you have to expose for one or the other: choose whether you want to record the details of the subject or the highlights on the water. It is not possible to keep detail in both.

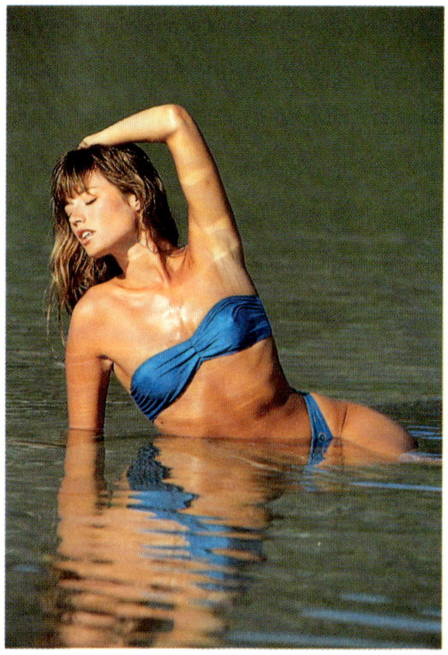

▶ **REFLECTED HIGHLIGHTS**
Note the creative potential of reflected light. The white bands of light on the model's stomach and arms are the effects of sunlight reflected back up from the water.

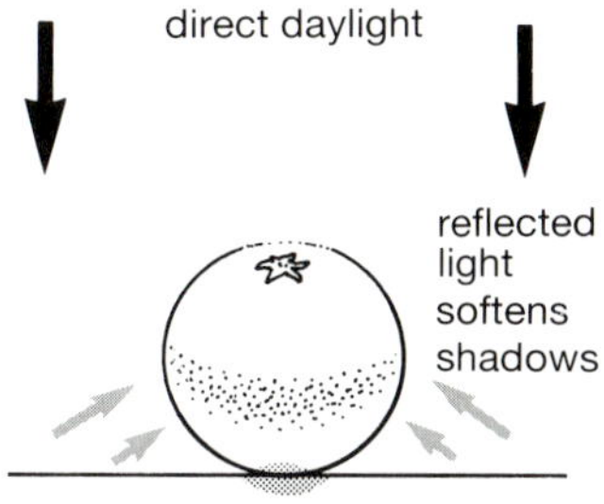

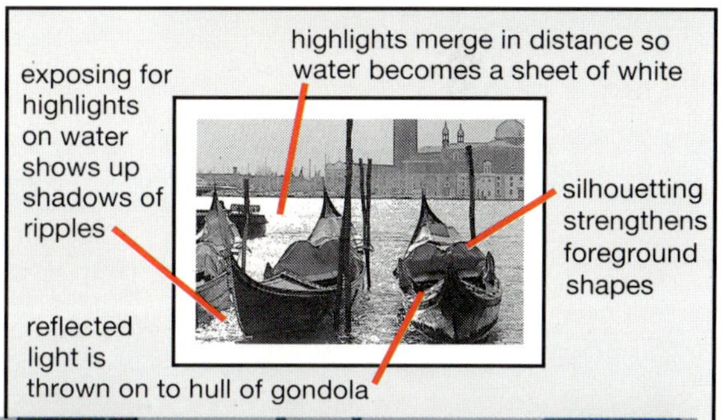

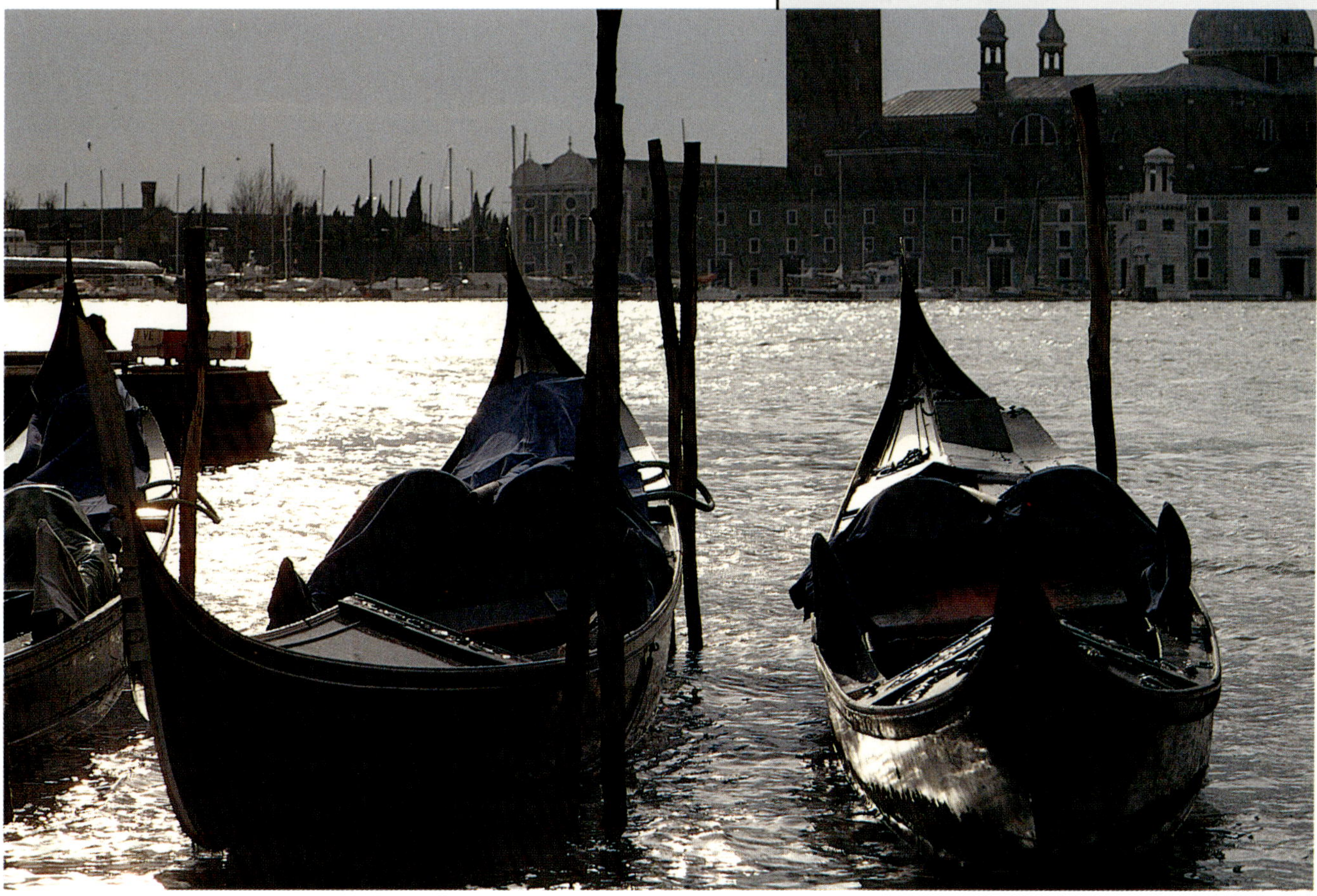

▼ **REFLECTIONS ON WATER**
To achieve a pleasing photograph of the highlights on the water, the photographer has chosen to put the boats in silhouette. Reflected light from the water helps to illuminate the hull of the boat on the right, so it is not in complete shadow.

What reflected light is like

Angle Light can be bounced on to a subject from any angle, so you can get round the problem of harsh shadows in direct sun by making use of naturally reflective surfaces.

For example, imagine someone standing beside a white wall, with the sun shining on one side of their face. Light bounced off the wall illuminates the other half of their face, which would otherwise be in shadow. Bear this in mind when taking pictures in bright sidelight.

You can also stand or sit people *on* a light surface. If a child is lying on a white sandy beach, some of the sun's light shining down will be reflected back upwards from the sand on to the child, softening the shadow areas.

Strength Reflected light is most intense when the sun is shining directly. If the light is diffused, far less is reflected.

Colour The colour of the surface which reflects the light may affect the colour of the reflection. For example, if light is reflecting off a bright yellow beach towel the sunbather lying on it will have a yellow colour cast in your photo.

▼ USING A REFLECTIVE SURFACE
A white sheet acts as a reflector of light. By putting the little girl on a white surface, light is reflected back at her and her teddy.

reflected light from sheets gives child's limbs a gently modelled and rounded appearance

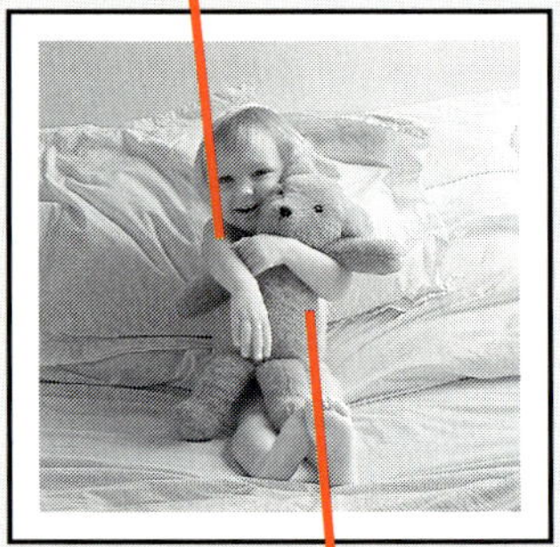

soft quality of the window light helps to retain detail, so that texture of fur is clear

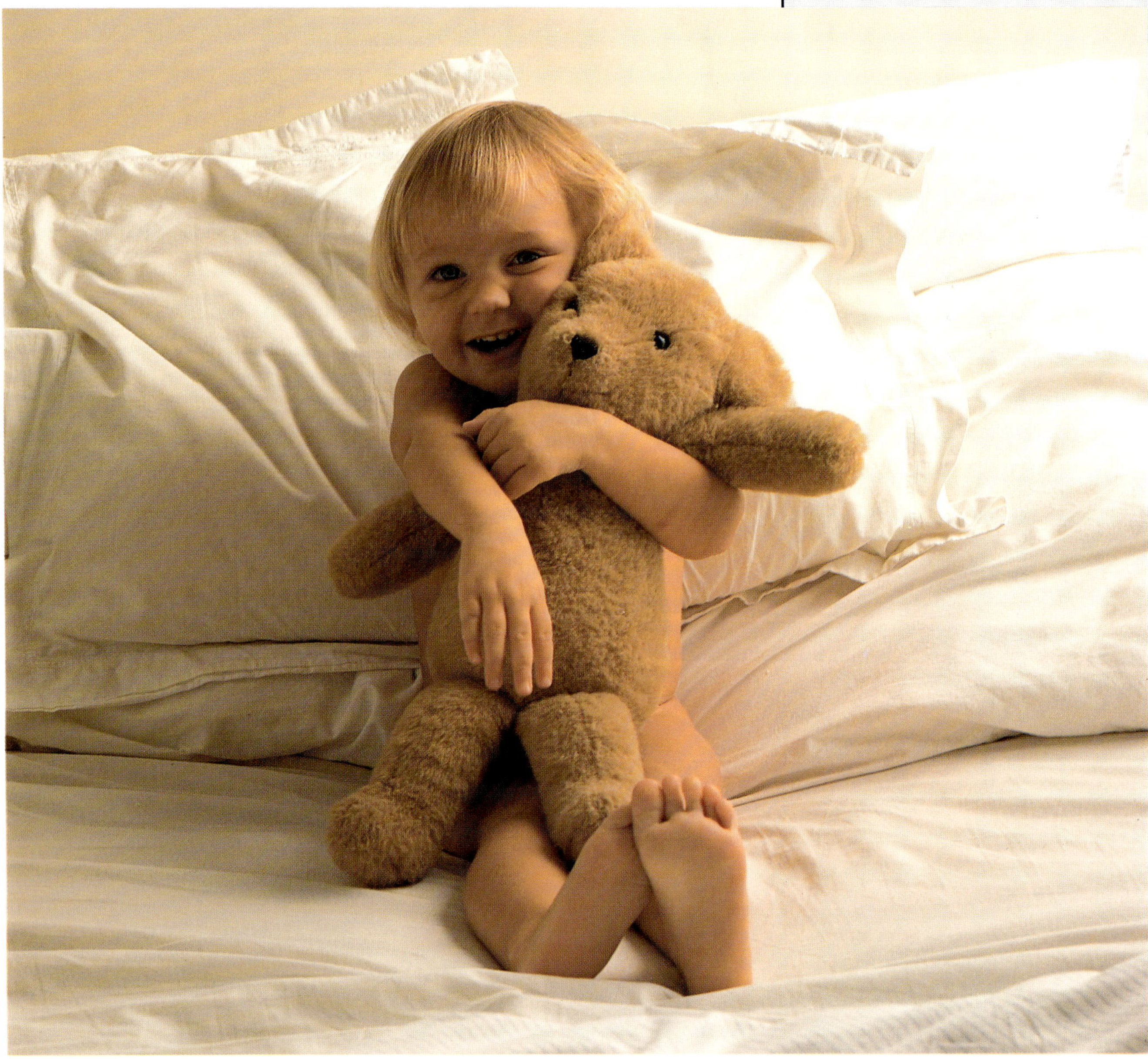

Comparing direct and reflected light

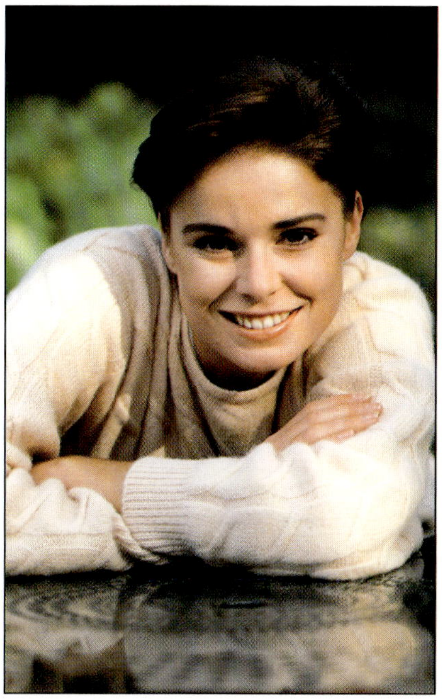

▼▲ ***A white tablecloth shows how much reflected light can affect a picture. Light is thrown up from the tablecloth into the face of the girl, removing unflattering shadows while adding a distinct colour cast.***

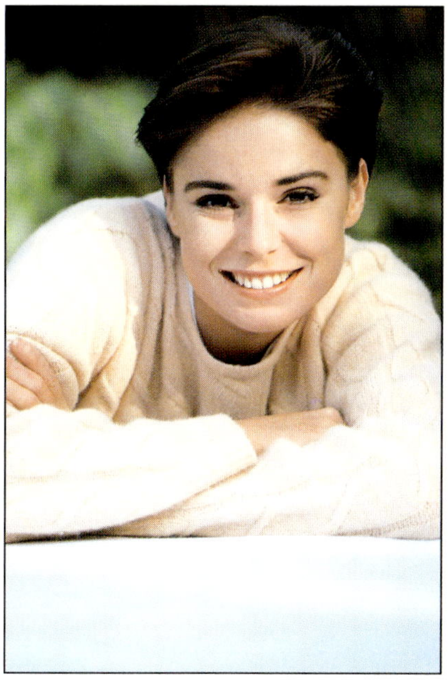

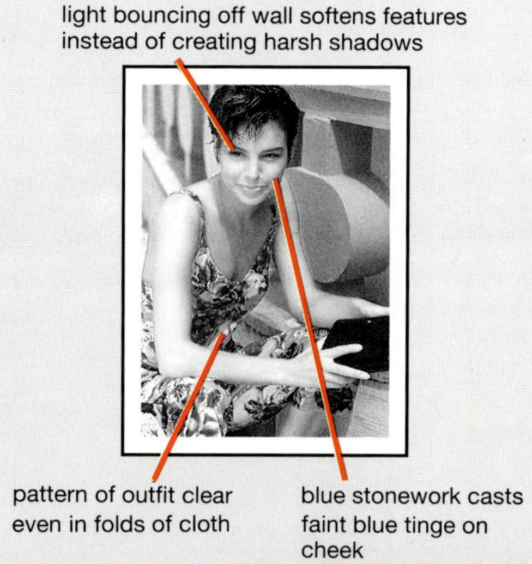

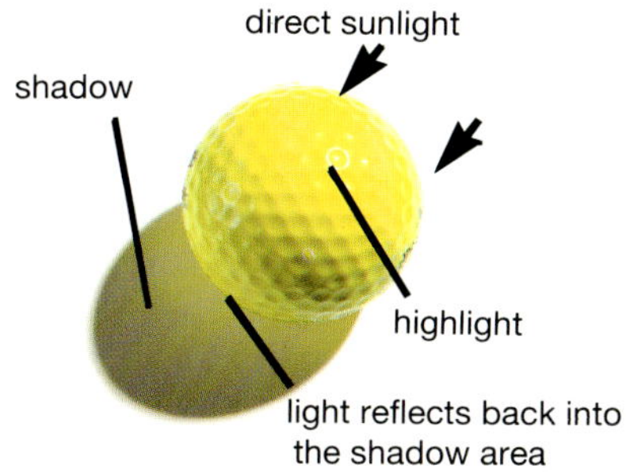

▲ **BRIGHT LIGHT**
Light reflects back into the golf ball from the left side, opposite the sun, putting highlights into the underside. The ball has a reflective surface, which is why the shadow looks a bit yellow.

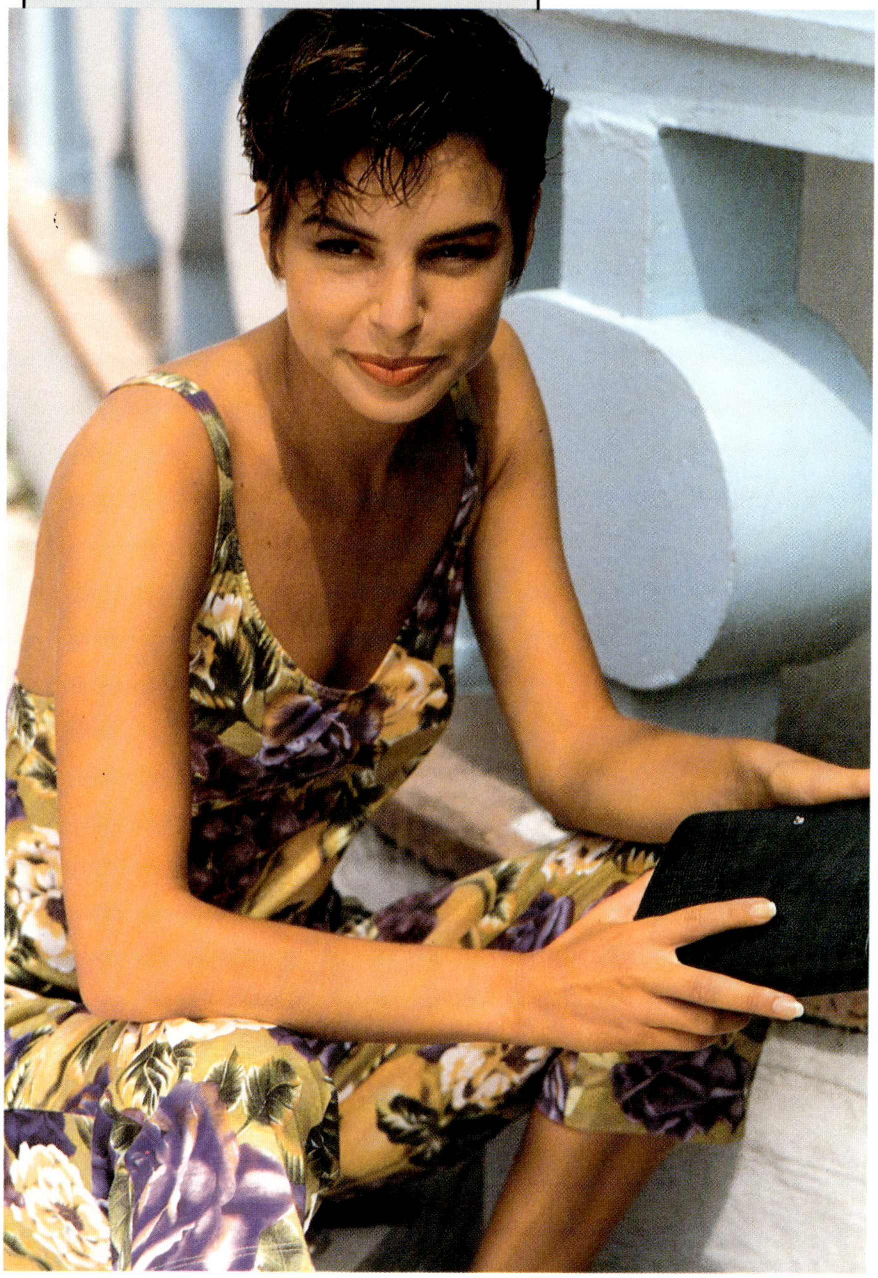

▶ **REFLECTIONS FROM WALLS**
By placing the model next to a light-toned wall, the photographer ensured that reflected light stopped her skin and dress from becoming too dark in the shadow areas.

Window light

Light from a window can work well for photographing all kinds of subjects. It creates soft highlights and shadows which are good for showing off shape and some detail. It is useful for photographing both people and objects.

Direct window light If you are sitting indoors, have a good look at an object which is near to the light coming in through the window. If the sun is shining straight in through the window, there will be hard shadows and strong highlights on the object.

The light behaves in the same way as the direct light you get outside on a sunny day. The shadows cast and the image of the window frame itself can make interesting compositions.

Indirect window light The kind of window light most useful to the photographer is indirect (diffused) light. If the light coming in through the window casts only soft shadows on an object, then it is diffused light. Another way to check this is to look at the weather. If it is a cloudy, overcast day and the sun is obscured then the light is diffused.

One direction

The sun's rays are scattered in all directions when the light is diffused outdoors. However, when diffused light shines through a limited space such as a window or door, the light falls in only one direction. So although it is a diffused type of light, it is different because it has a direction.

The great advantage of this kind of window light is that you don't have to worry about complicated hard shadows or extremes of contrast – which are the hallmarks of direct light.

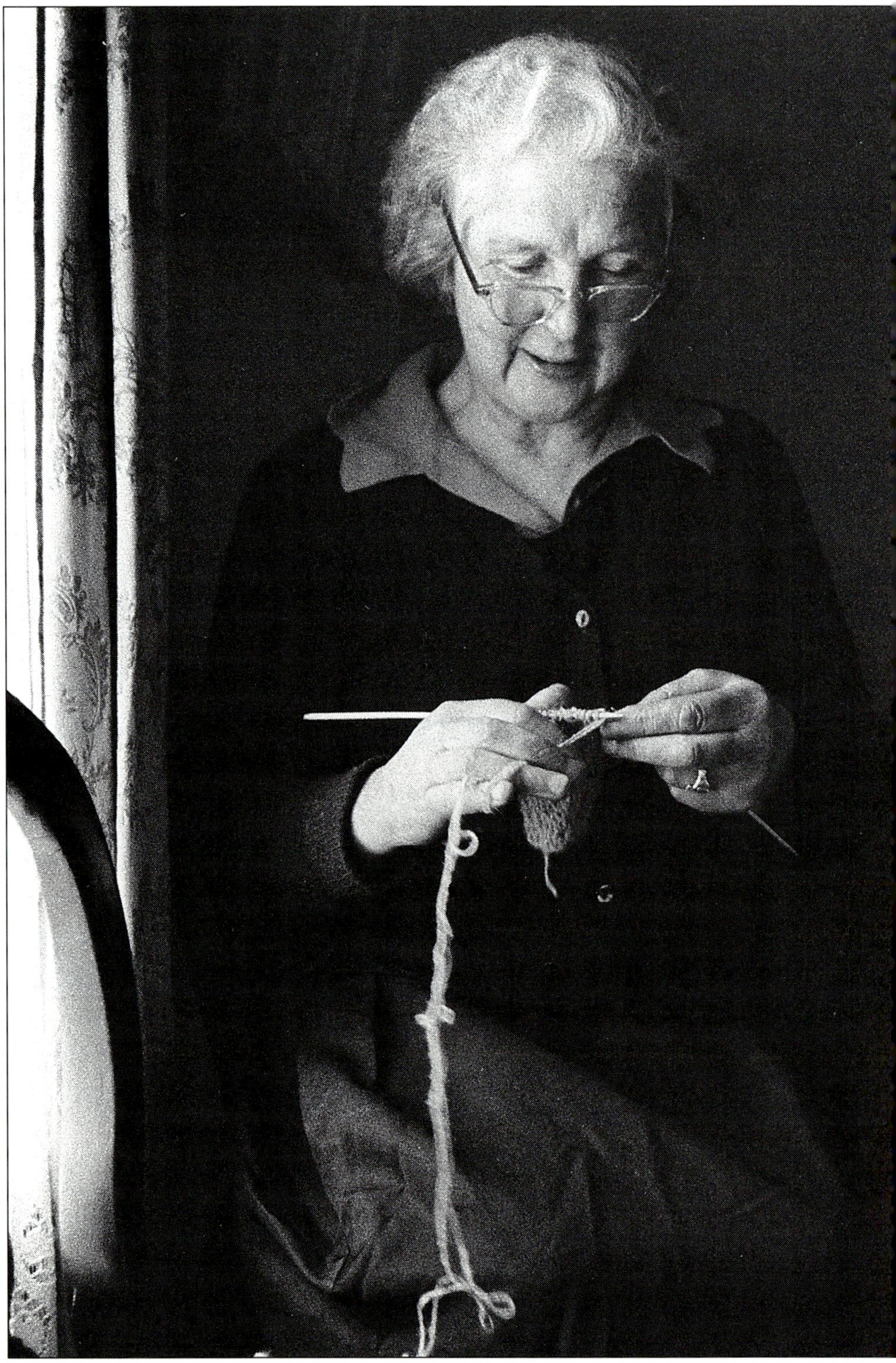

Tip

North-facing portrait light

It may be worth picking a north-facing window if you are using window light to illuminate your subject. The sun never shines in directly from the north (or south in the southern hemisphere) so the shadows are soft and don't move throughout the day. This means that it is a good light for revealing detail without being too harsh.

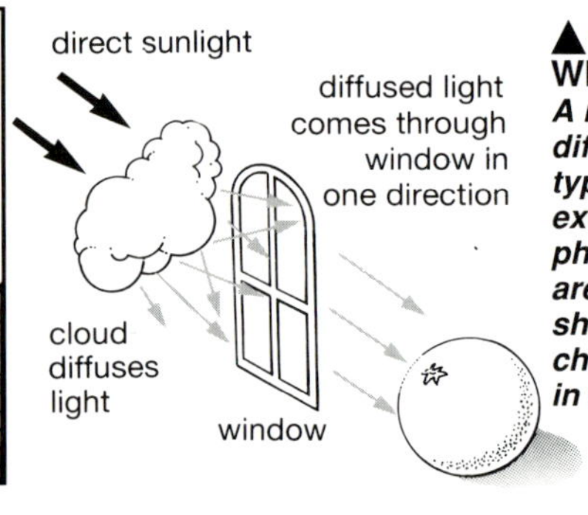

▲ PORTRAITS WITH WINDOW LIGHT
A net curtain at the window diffuses the sunlight. This type of sidelighting is excellent for portrait photography. The features are defined by soft-edged shadows which show character without harshness in this gentle portrait.

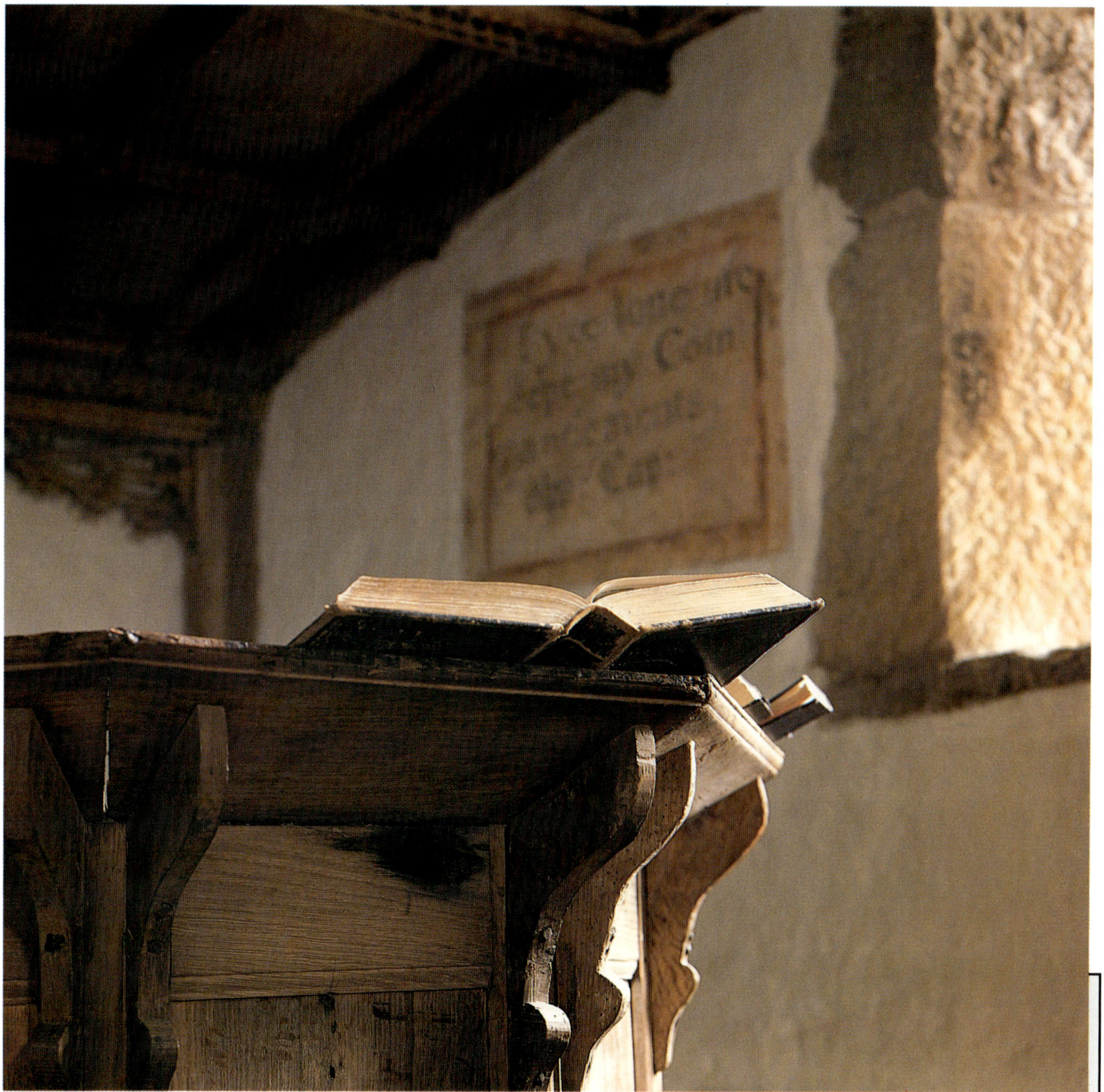

▲ **KEEPING DETAILS**
Window light can be good for picking out detail. Although the area closest to the window is quite bright, the left side of the picture is not thrown into dark shadow because there is plenty of diffused light.

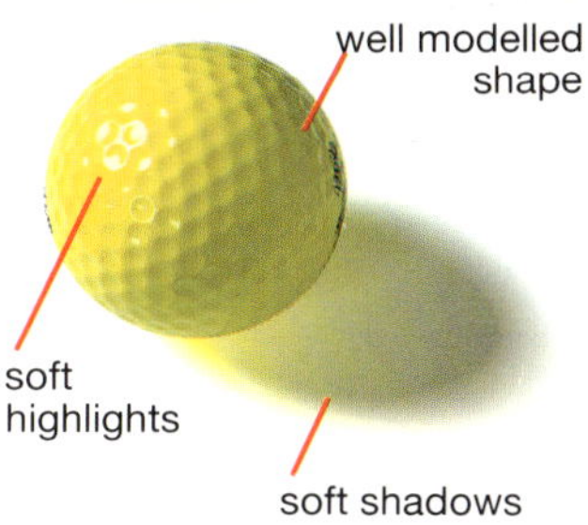

▲ **A SOFT MODELLING LIGHT**
Diffused window light coming from one direction casts soft shadows and soft highlights. Almost all the dimples on the ball are visible – it's a good light for retaining details.

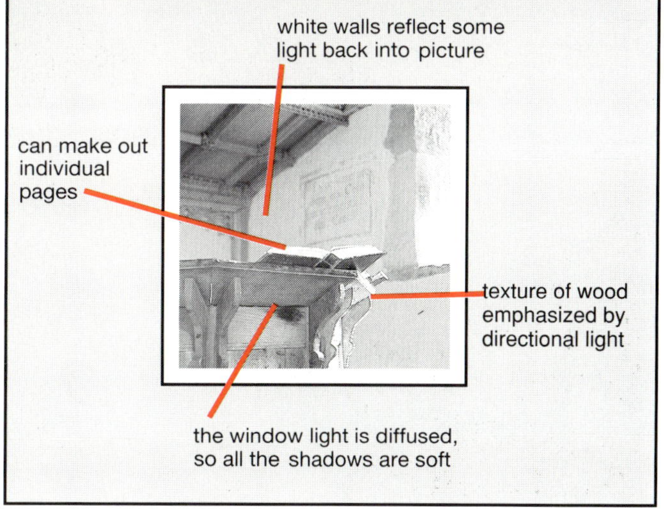

Light from several sources

Often there is more than one window or a door letting light into a room. If the light shines straight in from one direction, it creates dark shadows. If the subject is also lit from a second, different angle then this may help to lighten the shadows.

Take care, though, that one light source dominates the scene. The second light source should simply soften the shadow cast by the first. Double shadows cast by light sources of equal intensity usually look odd or 'wrong'.

Using more than one source of window light can help solve one potential problem. Indirect window light is sometimes so weak that you need to use a very slow shutter speed to get the correct exposure. If you are taking a portrait, it may be difficult for your model to stay still for a long exposure. By placing the subject in a position where they are lit by more than one window, the level of light increases.

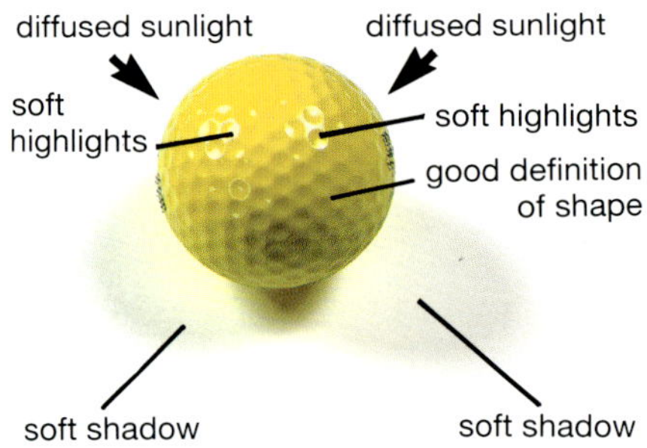

▲ SOFT AND SUBTLE
With diffused daylight hitting an object from two opposite angles, the shadows almost disappear. Two sets of highlights and shadows are created – a double effect that can look odd.

CHECK IT !

To make the most of daylight, remember:

❑ Indirect window light creates soft shadows and soft highlights which are good for modelling.
❑ Reflected light throws light back into the unlit side of a subject.
❑ Only light coloured surfaces reflect light. Dark colours absorb light.

▼ MORE THAN ONE SOURCE
Indirect daylight subtly lights this indoor scene. Using two sources of diffused light opposite each other, the scene is lit very evenly.

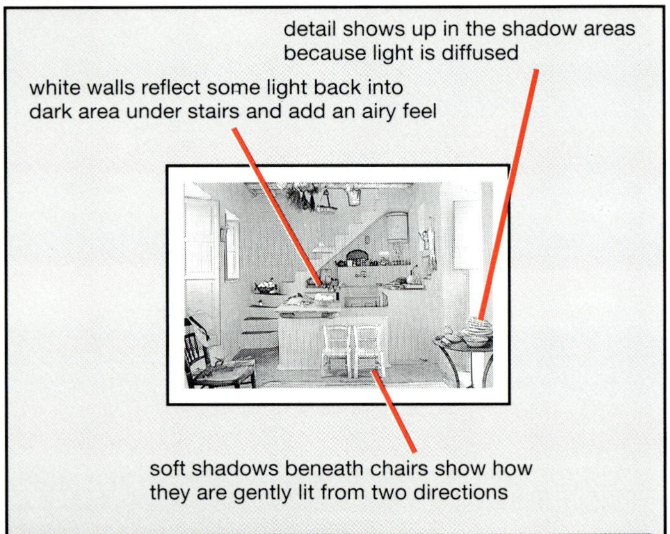

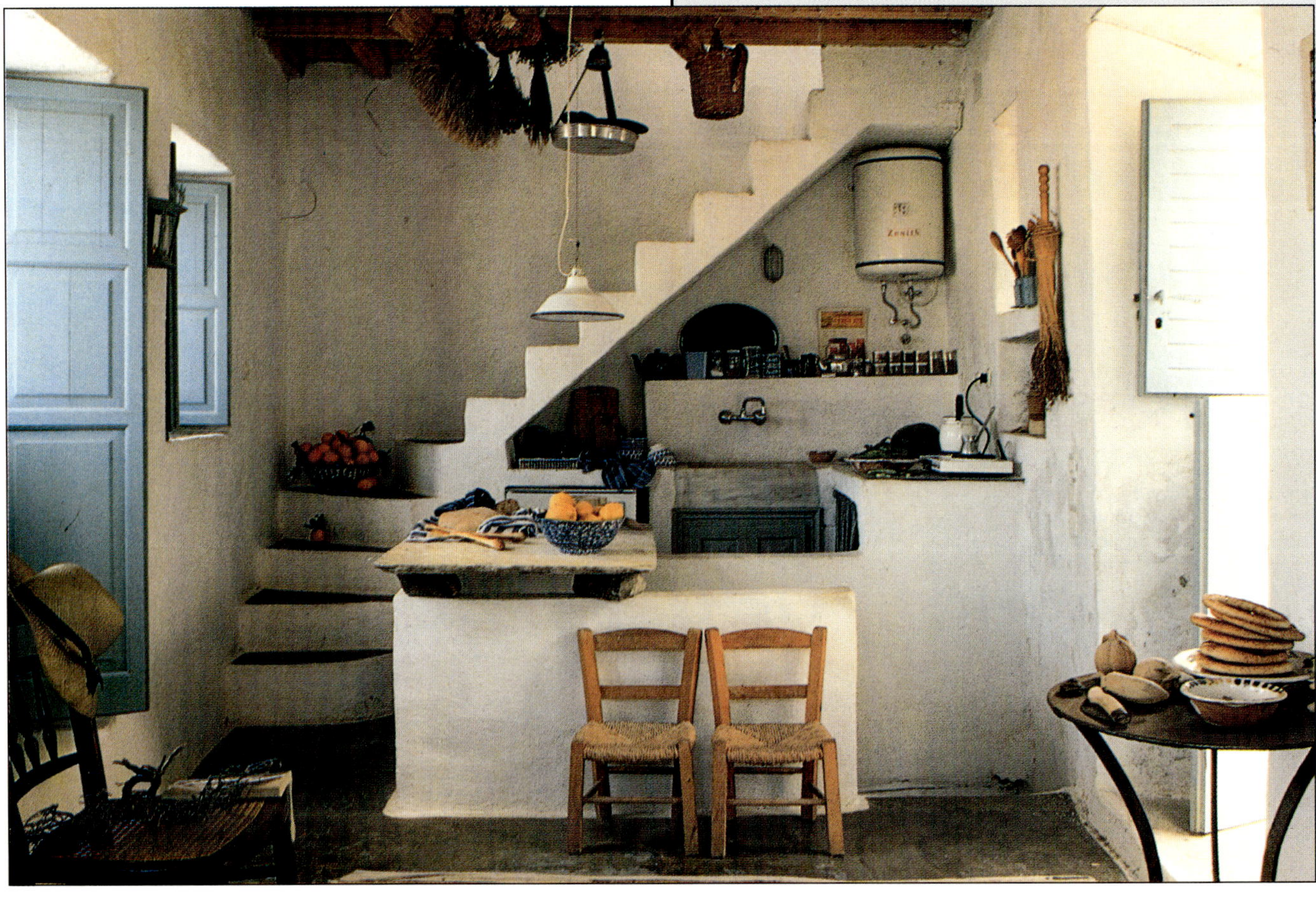

Adapting daylight

There are several ways you can modify sunlight to improve your pictures. But to do it successfully you first need to recognize what type of light is available.

Is the day bright and sunny, creating direct light with dark, hard-edged shadows? Or is it cloudy, diffusing the light so that it is virtually shadowless? If you are using daylight to illuminate an indoor scene, where is the light coming from? Is it coming from more than one direction?

Once you have answered these questions you can see whether you need to adapt the light and if so, how. The four main ways to modify light are by using reflectors, absorbers, diffusers and fill-in flash.

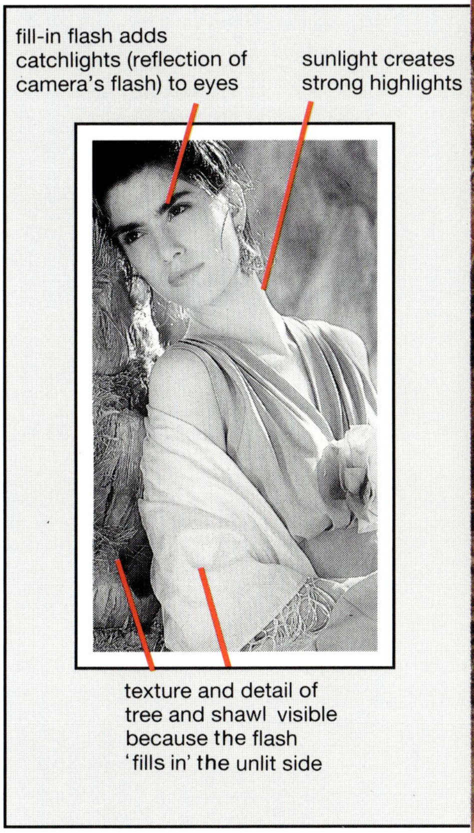

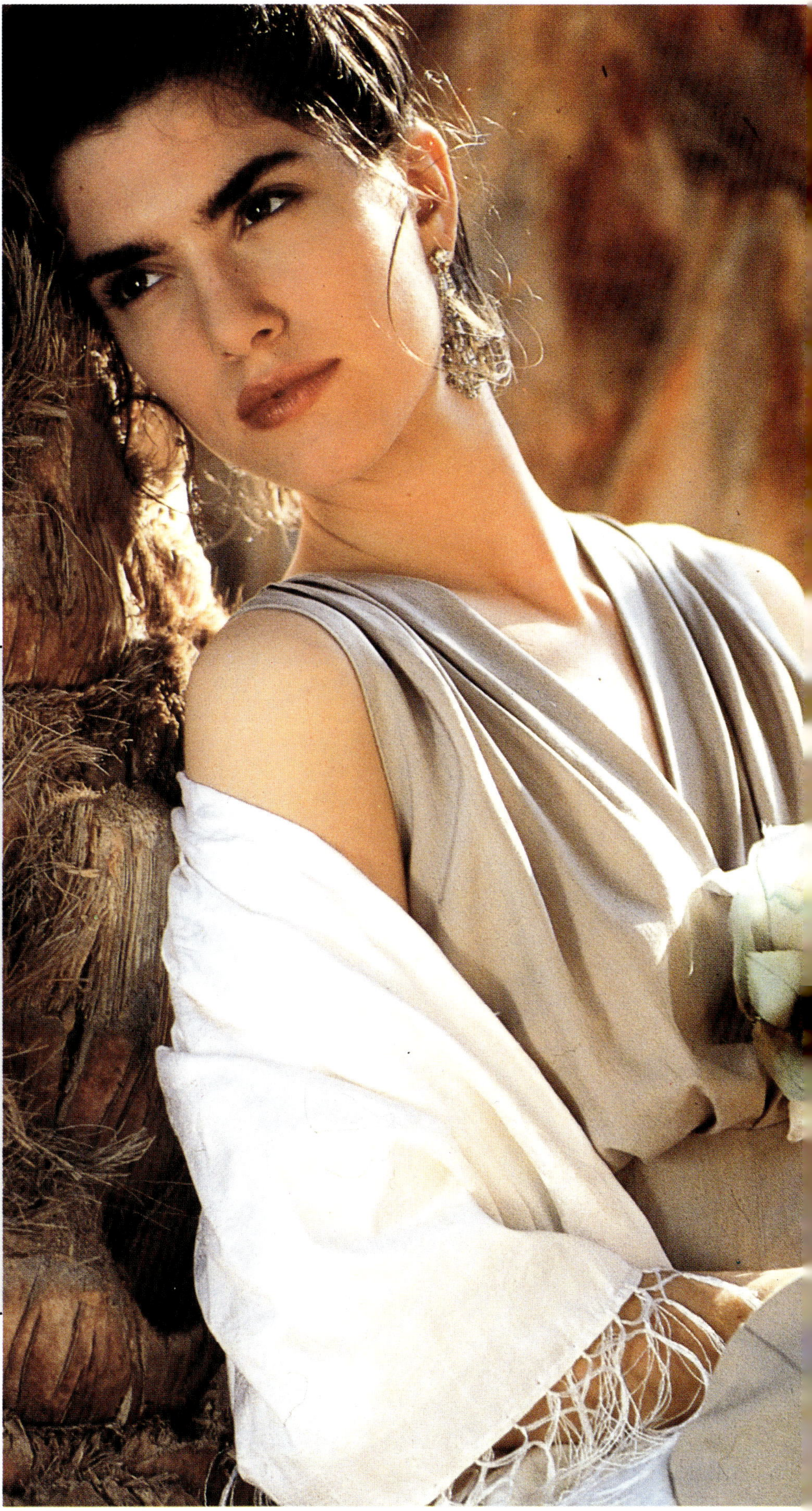

▶ **USING FLASH WITH DAYLIGHT**
Using flash is one way to adapt daylight. If the main subject is in shadow, or diffused light makes the scene a bit dull, flash picks out detail that would otherwise be lost. As a bonus here, it also makes the model's eyes sparkle.

Reflecting light

If you take an indoor portrait lit by window light with the sun shining in directly, the area in the shadows will be extremely dark and you'll lose details of features.

To solve this problem, you need to throw some light back into the picture. The easiest way to do this is to use a light-coloured reflector, so that some of the daylight is thrown back into the dark side of the picture.

Improvising reflectors

There are many simple ways of making a reflector. A piece of white card or an old white sheet or towel all work adequately.

You can improvise reflectors out of all sorts of things. To reflect light up into a face, the whiteness of a newspaper or book held by the subject will throw some light upwards. If the subject is sitting at a table, try adding a white tablecloth to reflect light up.

Silver baking foil also reflects light well. When you are choosing a reflector, bear in mind that if it has a shiny surface, the light it reflects back will create small, hard highlights.

If the reflector has a matt finish or is crumpled, the light that bounces back will be more diffused.

When you are shooting outdoors, it may not be convenient to take along a reflector. In this case, move your subject close to a suitably reflective surface. For example, if you are taking a portrait and there is too much contrast between the highlight and shadow areas, move your subject close to a white wall. Light will be reflected back into the shadow side of the subject, reducing contrast.

If you look around outdoors there are an enormous number of surfaces that reflect light – from the sand on a beach to a white towel hanging up on a washing line.

Tip

Cut the contrast by moving in

When the subject has a long tonal range, you can sometimes control contrast by careful composition. With indoor portraits or still lifes, you can reduce contrast by moving closer to the subject so you cut out surrounding highlight and shadow areas – you don't always need to use a reflector.

Reflecting colours

Although any light-coloured surface acts as a reflector, the colour of the reflector is also thrown back into the picture.

Colour casts are sometimes attractive, sometimes not. A slight orange or reddish light reflected into a portrait can add warmth to natural skin tones, but a green cast usually makes people look ill. Blue is also a cold colour for portraits.

Using reflectors

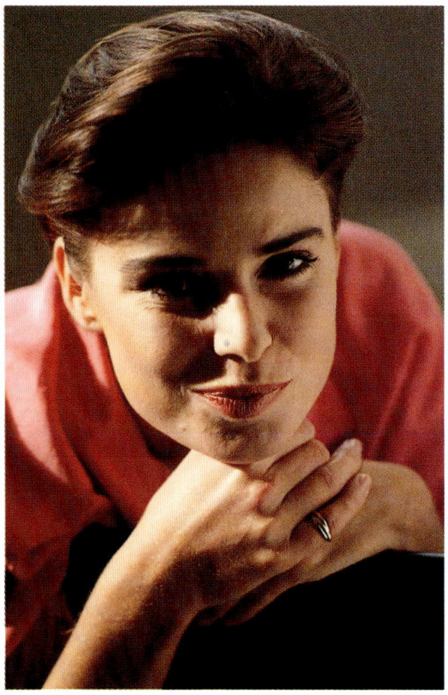

NO REFLECTOR
Without a reflector, the direct sidelight creates hard shadows across the model's face. Because the light is both direct and coming from the side, it picks up the texture of the skin in an unflattering way.

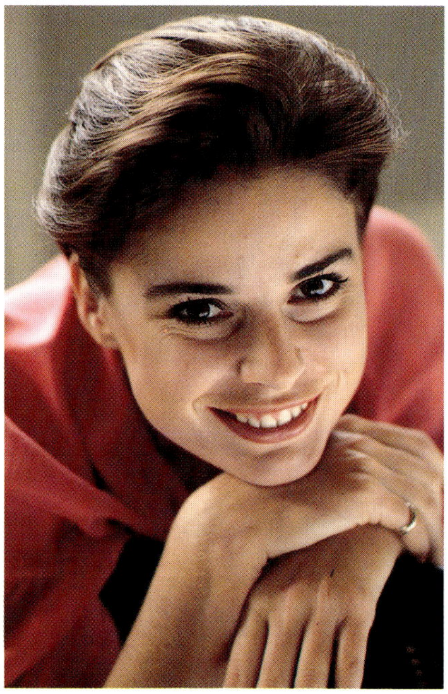

SILVER REFLECTOR
Here the photographer puts a silver-coloured reflective card on the opposite side of the model's face to the light to remove the hard shadows. Because the silver reflector is shiny, the light reflected back throws a slight sheen on to the model's face and is rather a cold colour.

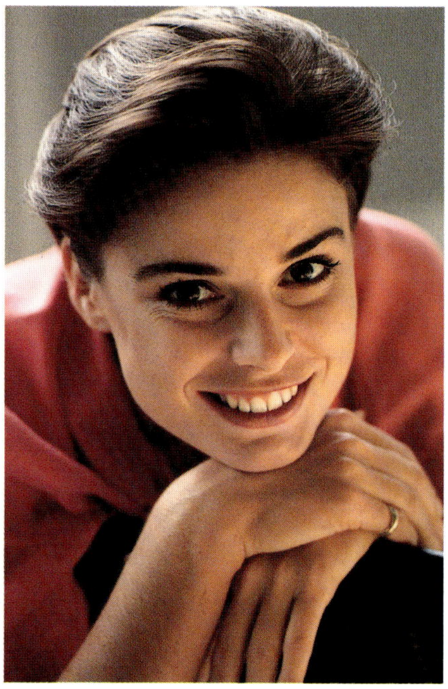

GOLD REFLECTOR
In this picture, a gold reflector card achieves a pleasant, warm effect. As well as filling in the shadow areas it gives a golden glow to the face.

Diffusing light

You can soften the hard shadows and strong highlights of direct light by diffusing it. It's quite simple to diffuse light indoors. If the sun is shining in through a window or door, just hang a net curtain, a white cotton sheet or similar piece of thin material across it. Tracing or greaseproof kitchen paper stuck up against a window will also diffuse direct light well.

It's more difficult to diffuse sunlight outdoors, though with a friend to help you can sometimes rig up a sheet.

▶ DIRECT LIGHT
The light coming straight through the window on to the model casts hard edged shadows, and you can't see much detail in her arms and legs. The mirror also casts an ugly shadow on the wall.

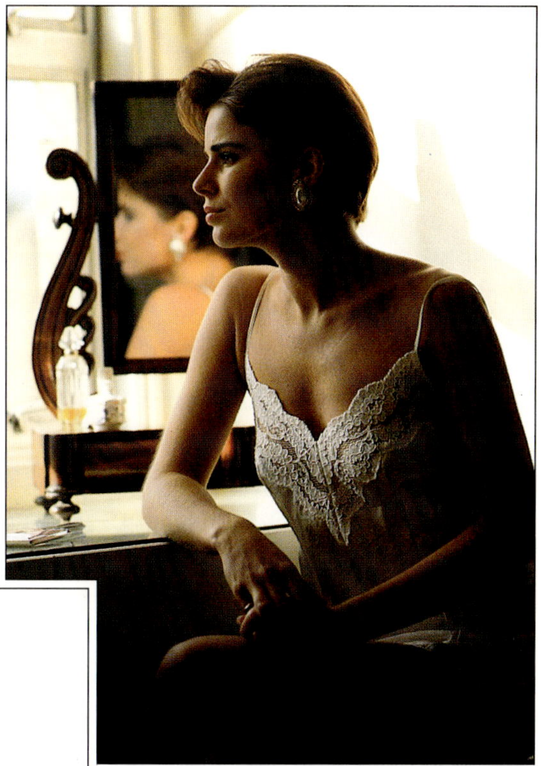

▼ DIFFUSED LIGHT
Here, the photographer has diffused the light by putting a net curtain up against the window. He moved the model out of the shadow so that there is less contrast between the highlights and shadow areas. The result is softer and more flattering modelling.

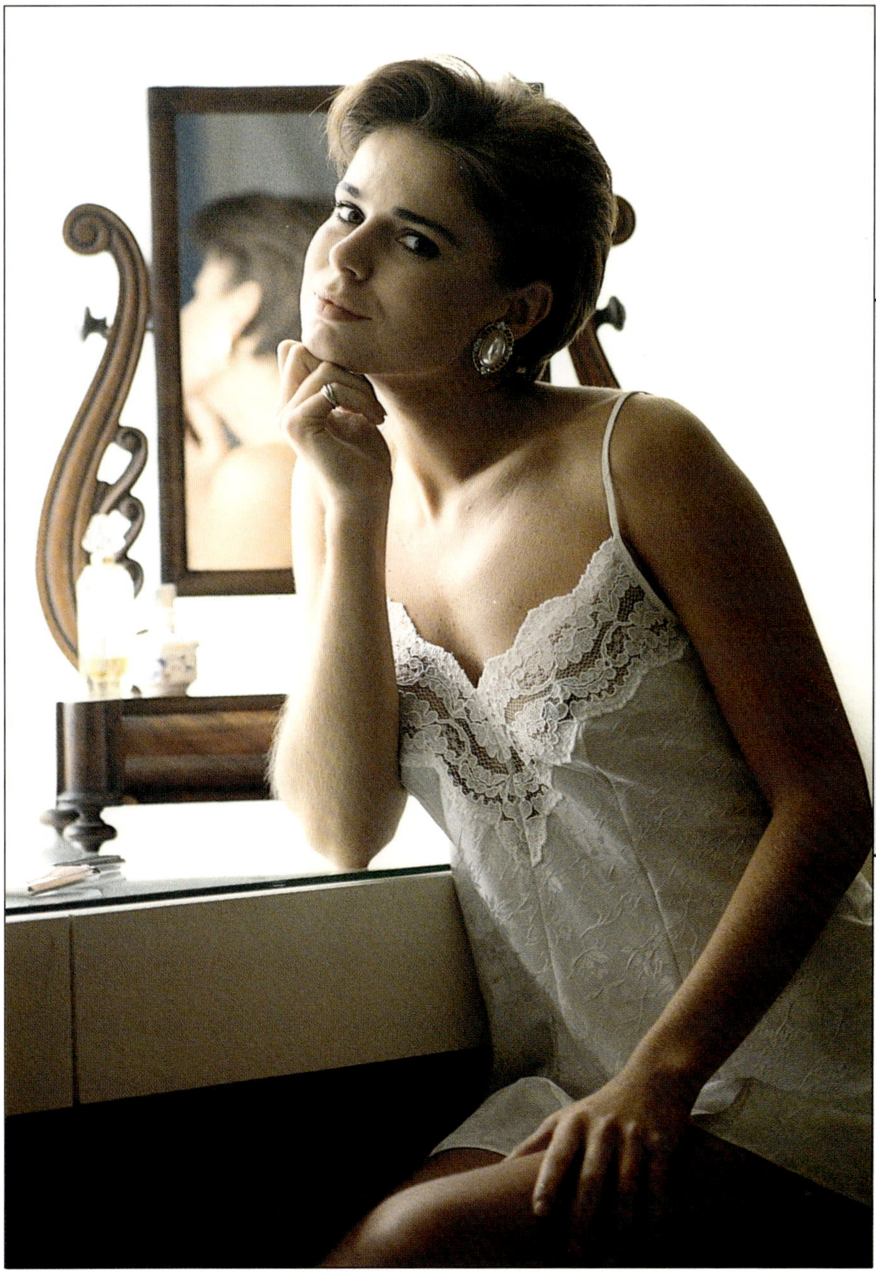

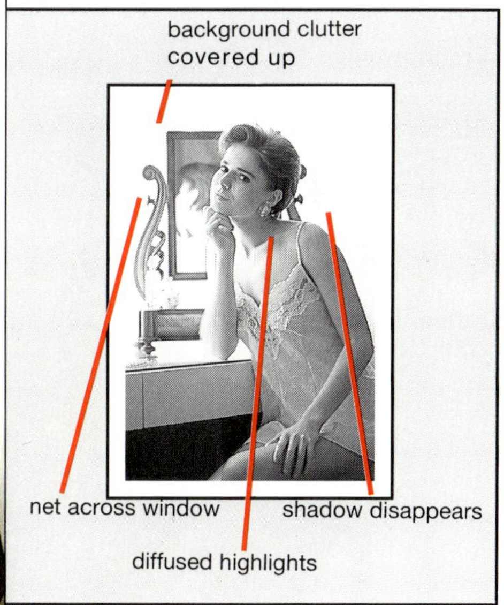

Tip

Absorbing light

Just as a light-coloured or shiny surface reflects light, so a very dark, matt surface like a blackboard absorbs light. This can be useful if the light is diffused and you want to create darker shadows and more contrast.

Using fill-in flash

Fill-in flash is so called because it fills in the shadows. It adds more light to a picture and mixes well with daylight. It works only if the subject which needs to be lit is not too large, and is not too far away from the camera. Exactly how far depends on your flash – check the flash range in the camera spec details.

Detail Fill-in flash is useful for lighting up detail such as the pattern on fabric, or a flower on a dull day.

Outdoor sunlit portraits In direct sunlight, if you take a picture of, for example, a woman wearing a wide-brimmed hat, her face will be thrown into shade. Use fill-in flash to put light back into the shaded area.

Exposure and silhouette A sunset in the background of a portrait will throw the figure into silhouette. This is because there is such a difference in brightness between the sunset and the person. If you want to take a picture of someone against a very bright background, fill-in flash is the ideal way to reduce the contrast between the subject and background.

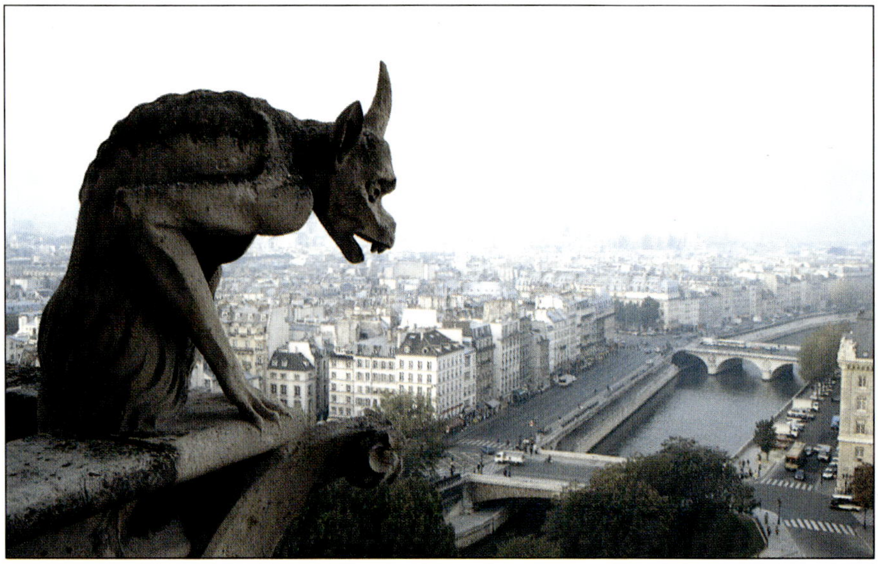

▲ ADDING DETAIL
By using fill-in flash, the details of the gargoyle are clear. Without flash the statue would be much darker.

CHECK IT!

How to alter daylight:

❑ Throw light into shadow side with reflectors or fill-in flash.

❑ Create more contrast and increase modelling with absorber.

❑ Diffuse direct light through tracing paper or net curtains.

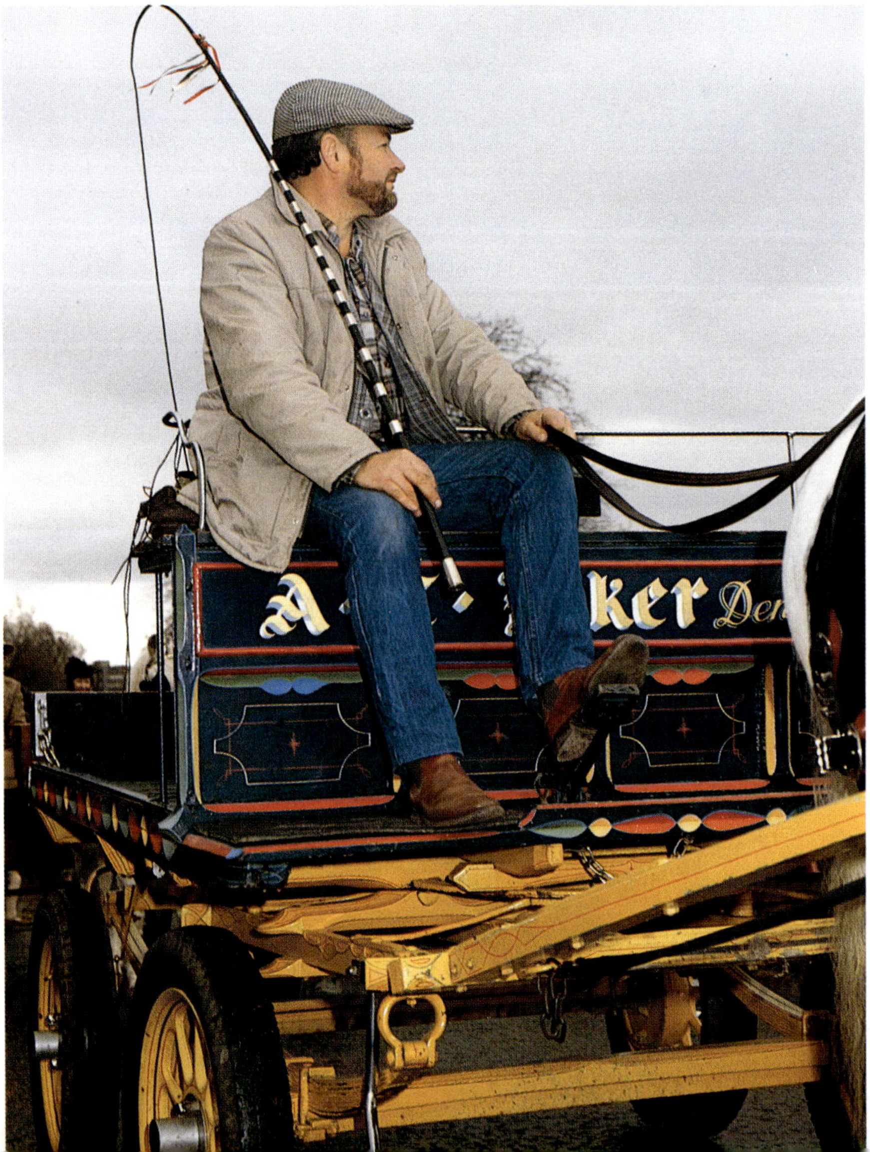

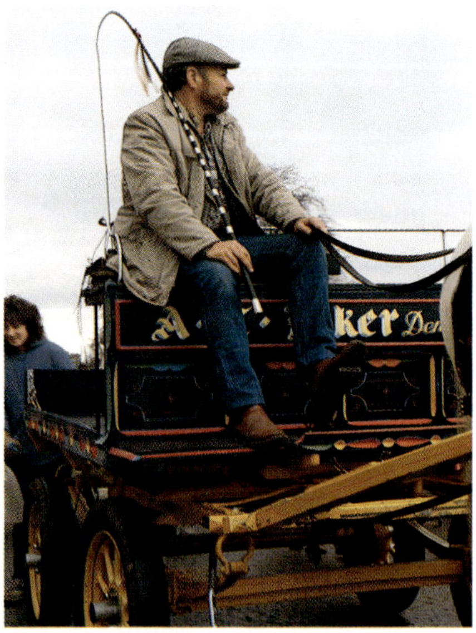

◀ ▲ BRIGHTENING UP
On a dull day, fill-in flash brightens up the colours of the cart. The picture also looks sharper because the hard light of the flash adds small, brilliant highlights.

Polarizing filters

One of the most valuable and versatile filters is also one of the plainest. The humble polarizer looks like a disc of grey glass – only the rotating mount hints that it may be something out of the ordinary.

Have you ever wondered how professional photographers get stunning deep blue skies, while the skies in your own pictures look weak and washed out? The answer is simple – they use a polarizer.

Polarizers are capable of a range of effects, from subtle to spectacular. As well as darkening blue skies, they can also remove unwanted reflections and saturate colours, for punchy photographs that can't fail to catch the eye.

Because polarizers are so versatile, we have devoted several pages to showing the many ways they can be used. For instance, polarizers were originally developed for suppressing reflections and glare, but one of their most important uses in photography is for intensifying the blue of the sky.

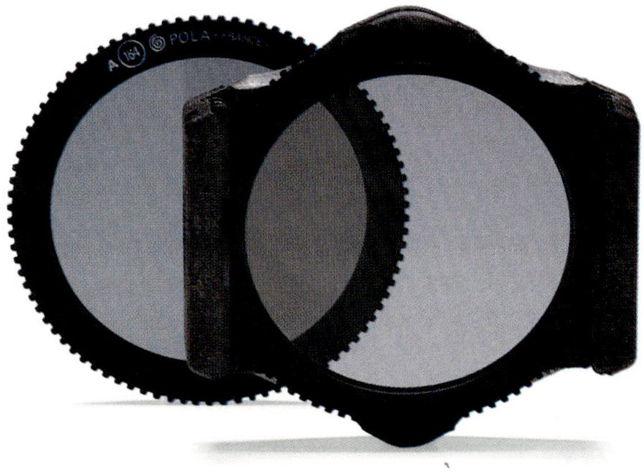

▶ You can buy polarizers to fit system filter holders. These versions are round and have a serrated edge to help you grip and turn them.

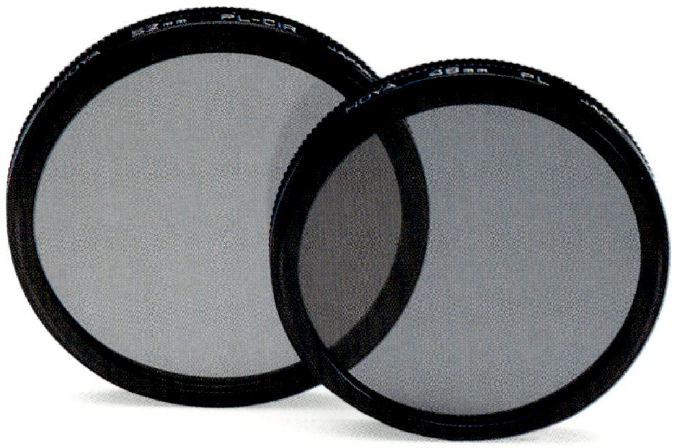

◀ The angle of the polarizer on the lens is crucial, so the glass element of the filter is fixed into a rotating ring that you can twist independently of the filter mount. This means that when the filter is screwed securely on to your lens, you can turn the polarizing element without unscrewing it.

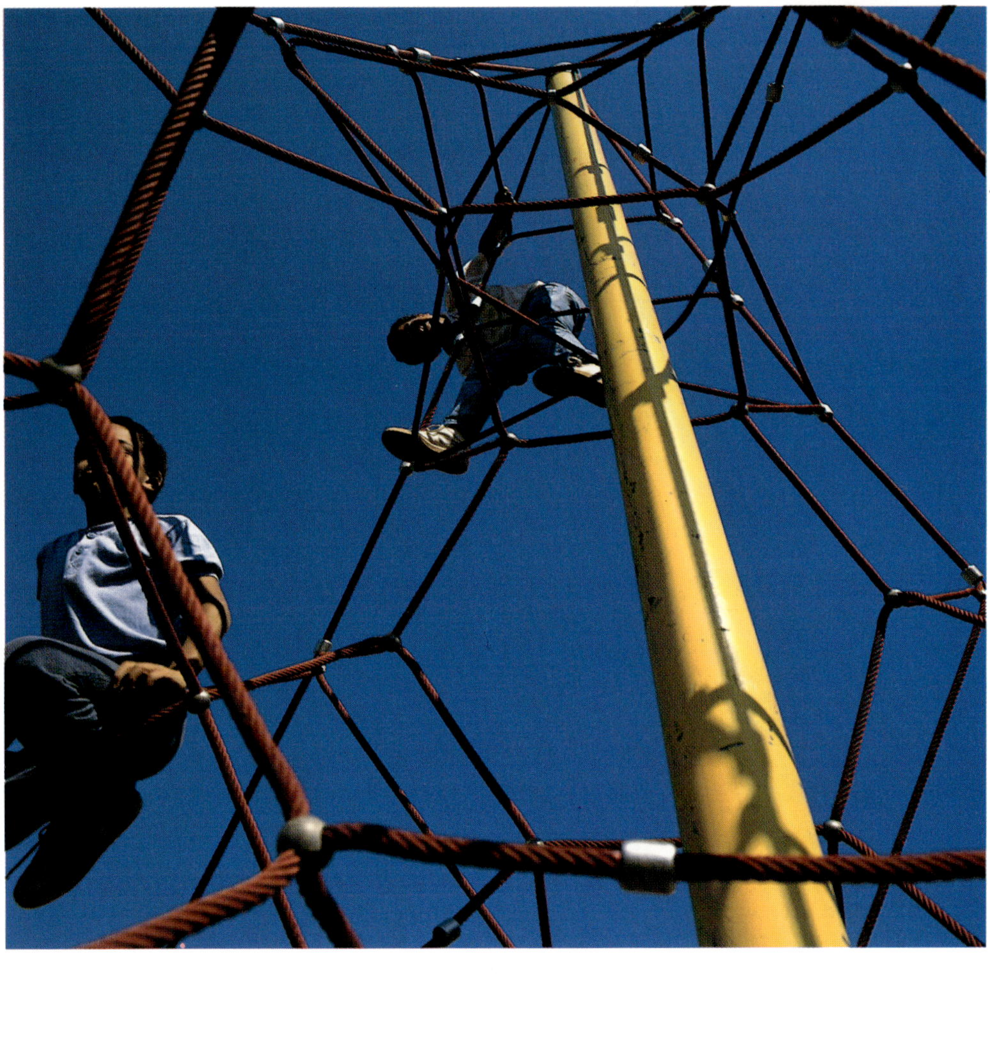

◀ Polarizers are invaluable on sunny days when you want deep blue skies and saturated colours. They're easy to use and the results can be stunning.

Blue skies above

Polarizing filters work by absorbing polarized light, while allowing unpolarized light to pass through to the film (see Back to basics). Blue sky is a rich source of polarized light, so fitting a polarizing filter absorbs light from the sky, darkening it and enriching its colour. A further bonus is that white clouds stand out against the rich blue background.

Take your turn

To use a polarizer with an SLR, simply screw it on to the front of the lens, look through the viewfinder, and turn the filter. You'll see the blue sky darken from its unfiltered shade, through to a much darker shade of blue, then back again. This cycle is repeated twice for each full turn of the polarizing filter.

To what degree the blue sky darkens depends on a number of factors:

❏ How blue it is without filtration.
❏ The focal length of the lens you're using.
❏ What part of the sky you are pointing the camera at.
❏ The time of day.

A polarizing filter will not add colour to a grey sky – it can only enhance the blue that's already there.

How it works

BACK TO BASICS

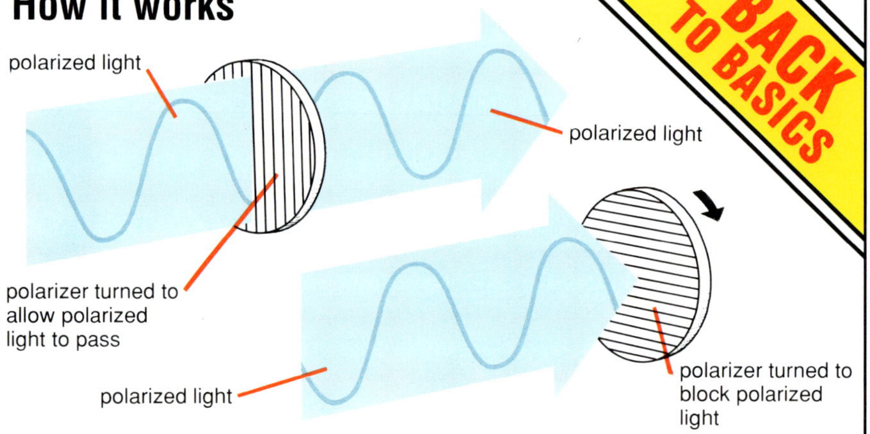

Light rays travel in one direction, but they also vibrate in a wave-like motion at right angles to their direction of travel. Individual rays vibrate in one plane – for example, up and down or side to side or at an angle of 30°.

Normal light is made up of lots of rays of light vibrating in different planes along the light path. Polarized light is made up of light vibrating in one plane only.

Polarizing filters act like bars on a cage. Only the light rays that are vibrating in the same plane as the gaps between the bars can pass through. So when normal light passes through the filter it emerges as polarized light – vibrating in just one plane.

When a beam of polarized light strikes the filter, it passes through only if it is vibrating in the same plane as the gap between the bars on the filter. If the bars are turned to another angle, the filter blocks the polarized beam.

Light from a blue sky is partially polarized. When you turn the filter and the sky darkens, you are moving the bars at an angle that stops the polarized light from the sky passing through to the film. Only unpolarized light that's vibrating in the same plane as the bars on the polarizer gets through.

Generally speaking, the bluer the sky, the more heavily polarized the light is – and the greater the filter's effect. When the light is heavily polarized, the filter can turn the sky virtually black.

Different polarizing filters have different sized gaps between the bars. The size of the gaps affects how well the filter works. Narrow gaps block more light, because the angle of the light rays has to match the angle of the gap precisely. Wider gaps let some light rays that don't exactly match the angle of the bars squeeze through.

Tip: On the dot

With a non-SLR camera, you can't see the polarizer's effect while the filter is on the lens. Instead, hold it to your eye and rotate it until you get the effect you want. Note the position of the white dot on the filter mount, relative to the top of the camera, and then fit the filter to the lens at the same angle.

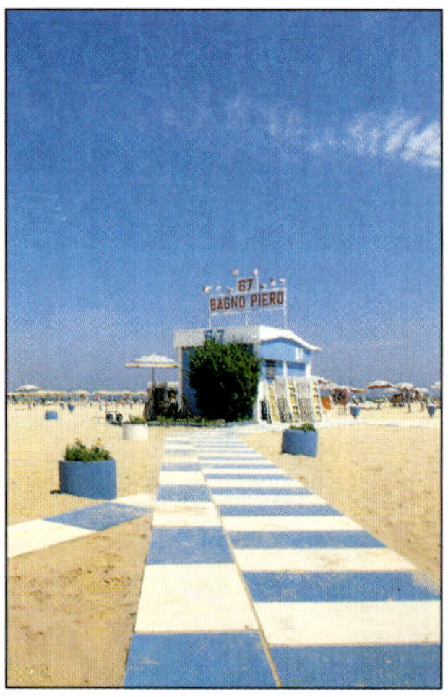

▲ ***Without a polarizer on the lens the sky is recorded as a weak blue – both polarized and unpolarized light reaches the film.***

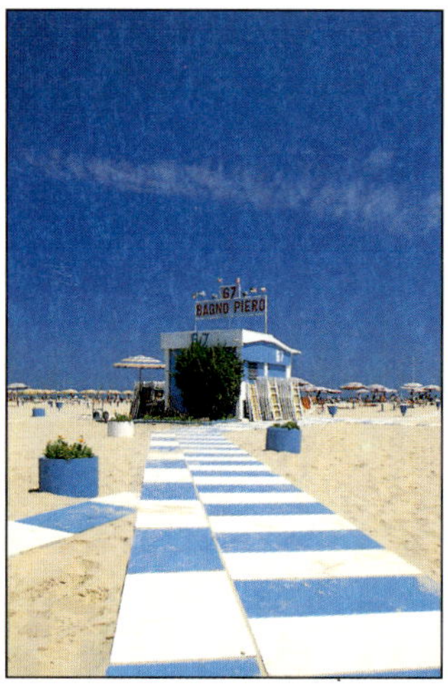

▲ ***Fitting a polarizing filter and turning it slightly darkens the sky – the filter blocks some of the polarized rays of light.***

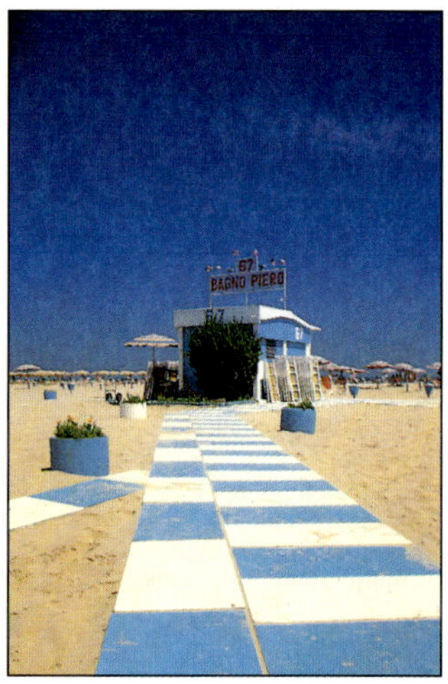

▲ ***Continue turning the polarizer and the sky darkens further – the filter blocks all of the polarized light coming from the sky.***

Chasing the blues

Often you will have decided on your composition before you fit a polarizing filter to the lens. However, if you can move around the subject, you may find that other camera angles increase the polarizer's effectiveness and give deeper blue skies.

The area of greatest polarization – and also the area of the sky that the polarizer affects most noticeably – lies in a band running across the sky at 90° to the sun. Once you've figured out the sun's position and where to point the camera, rotate the polarizer and check how much the sky darkens, before taking the picture.

If you turn the camera through 90° to make a vertical composition, the effect of the polarizer will go from maximum to minimum. To restore the effect just twist the polarizer through the same angle – a quarter turn.

▶ A polarizer lets you see its effect before you shoot. Then you know when to change your shooting position and the angle of the filter on the lens, to darken the sky to precisely the shade you require.

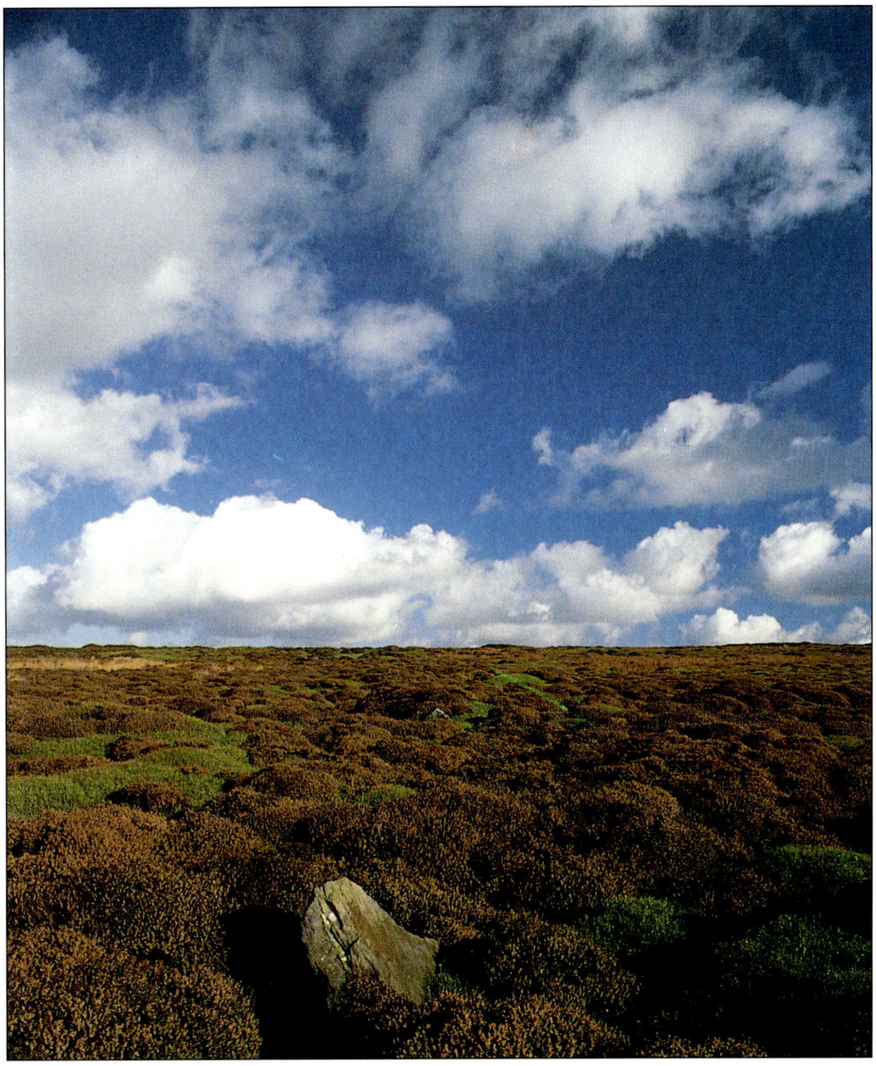

Tip: A handy hint

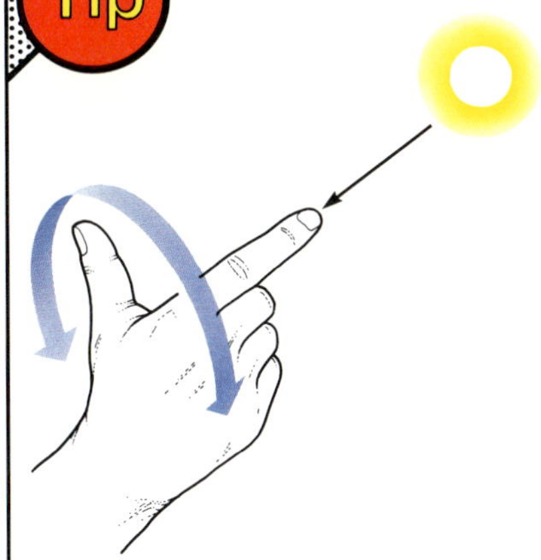

To find the area of maximum polarization on a sunny day, point your index finger at the sun and extend your thumb. Now twist your wrist. The path that your thumb traces out across the sky is the area of maximum polarization and darkening.

Bands of polarization

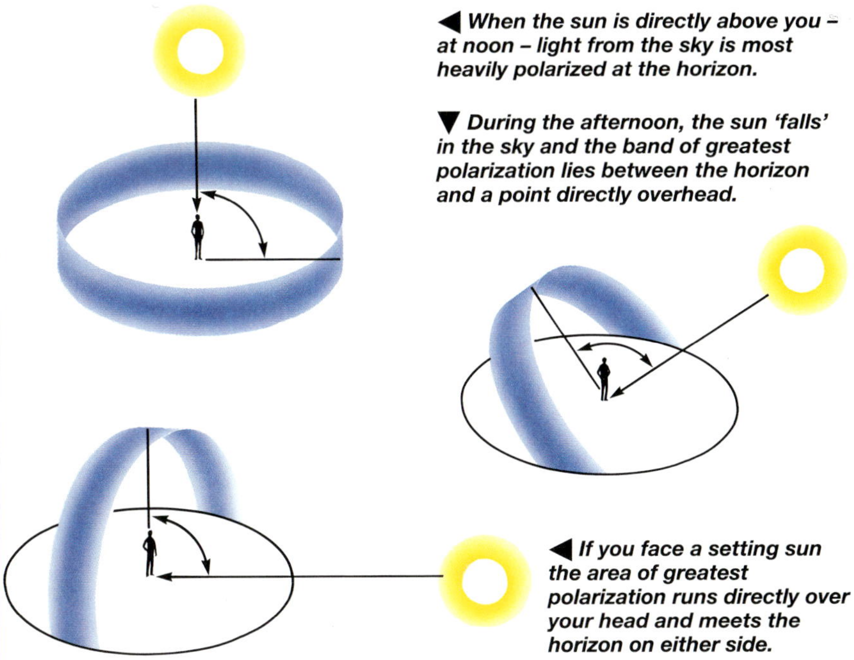

◀ When the sun is directly above you – at noon – light from the sky is most heavily polarized at the horizon.

▼ During the afternoon, the sun 'falls' in the sky and the band of greatest polarization lies between the horizon and a point directly overhead.

◀ If you face a setting sun the area of greatest polarization runs directly over your head and meets the horizon on either side.

Setting exposure

Polarizers absorb light and you usually need to give about 1⅓ stops more exposure than you would for an unfiltered picture. TTL metering takes account of the light absorbed by the filter's grey tint, but if you're using a hand held meter or flash you need to take the filter factor into consideration.

However, a TTL meter may be misled when you use a polarizer on a shot where the sky fills a large part of the frame. The polarizer darkens the sky, but the TTL meter compensates by setting a wider aperture or a slower shutter speed. The result is the same mid-blue sky and any subject included in the shot is overexposed.

The solution is simple. Fit the polarizer, and turn it so that it does not cause any darkening of the sky. Take a meter reading and either use the exposure lock, or set the controls manually. Now turn the filter until it has maximum effect, and take the picture.

Focal length

Because light from different parts of the sky is polarized to a different degree, the angle of view affects the evenness of the filter's effect.

Telephoto lenses take in just a small portion of the sky and produce a flat, even shade of blue. Wide angles cover a wider area and may record an uneven tint across the sky – depending upon the lens' focal length and angle of view. This graduated effect may work well on certain shots, but for the most even results fit a telephoto lens to your camera.

Certain cameras only work with special circular polarizers and underexpose pictures if you use an ordinary polarizer. (There is more information on page 38 about choosing the right type of polarizer for your camera.)

If you have no choice but to use an ordinary polarizer with one of these cameras, you can meter without the filter, then adjust the exposure by the filter factor.

Although they're more expensive, it's worth buying a circular polarizer, rather than a normal version, as they work well on all sorts of camera. If you change your camera, you won't have to go to the added expense of buying a new polarizing filter to fit it.

Tip

Zoom lenses

When you focus a normal fixed focal length lens, only the focusing ring turns – the filter mount at the end of the lens does not rotate. However, on a zoom lens the filter mount also turns. This changes the angle of the polarizer and alters its effect. So with a zoom lens always focus on your subject first, and then adjust the polarizer, to gain exactly the effect you are after.

▼ ***The deep blue band across the sky in this picture is a result of using a wide angle lens that takes in a view that's wider than the band of polarized light.***

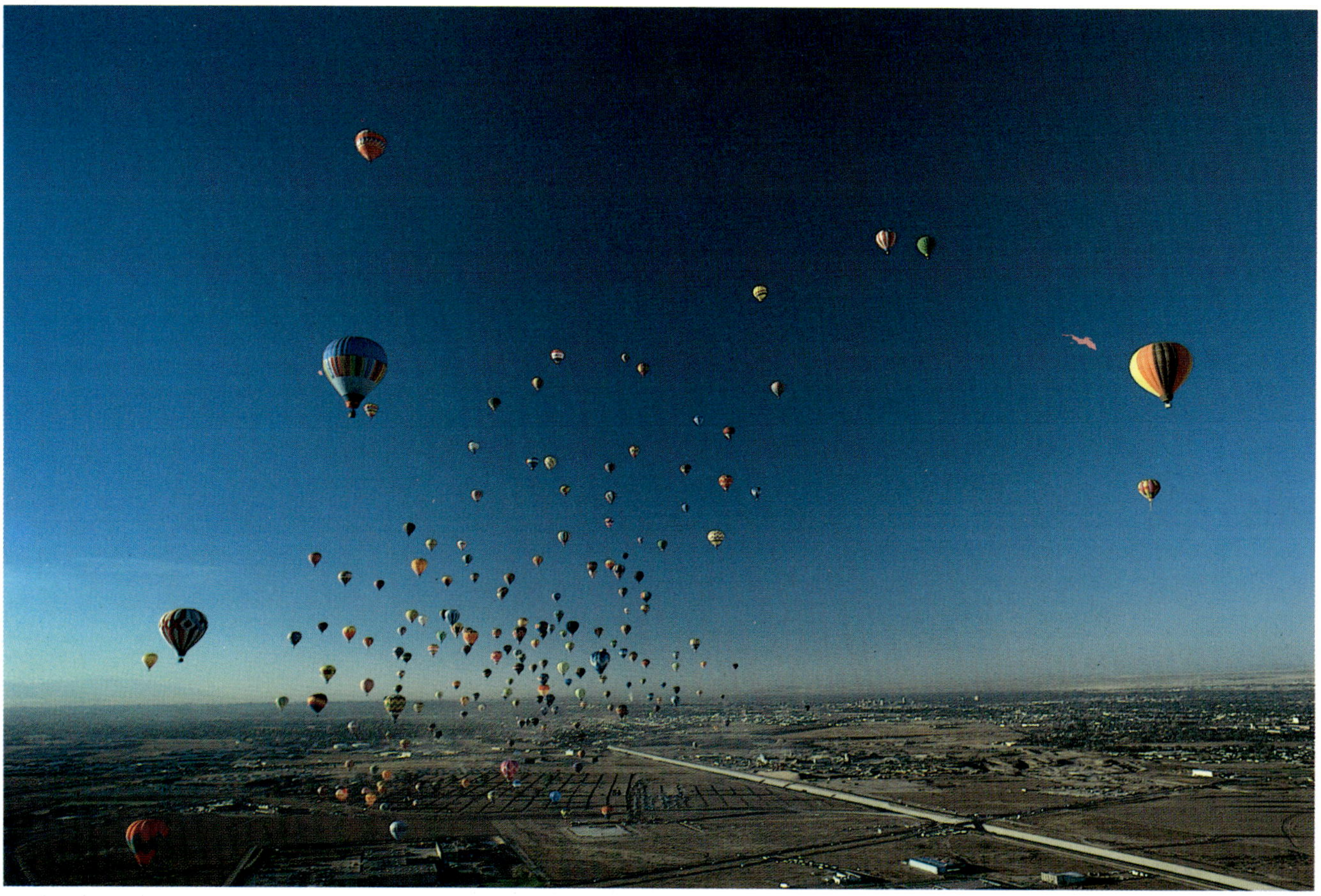

Polarizing filters 2

A polarizer's usefulness is not limited to darkening blue skies. If you want to cut out glare from shiny subjects to reveal surface detail, or you want to fill your pictures with saturated colours, a polarizing filter is the answer.

Anyone who has ever worn a pair of Polaroid sunglasses on a bright day will be able to appreciate what a difference a polarizing filter can make to a picture. Just as sunglasses cut out the glare from a rain soaked road, so too a polarizing filter over the lens on your camera can remove reflections from tarmac and water, not to mention foliage, fruit, glass, plastic, paintwork, skin and virtually any other shiny surface.

Block it out

The important factor is the shininess of the surface. Dull surfaces reflect light, but scatter it rather than polarizing it. Shiny surfaces create what are known as specular (mirror-like) reflections of the light source – or of other brightly lit objects – and polarize the reflected light. Using a polarizer lets you block out these specular reflections.

By cutting out reflections polarizing filters not only remove unsightly glare, but also reveal surface details and saturate colour. As you turn your polarizer you'll notice that colours in the scene appear much richer as the reflections disappear.

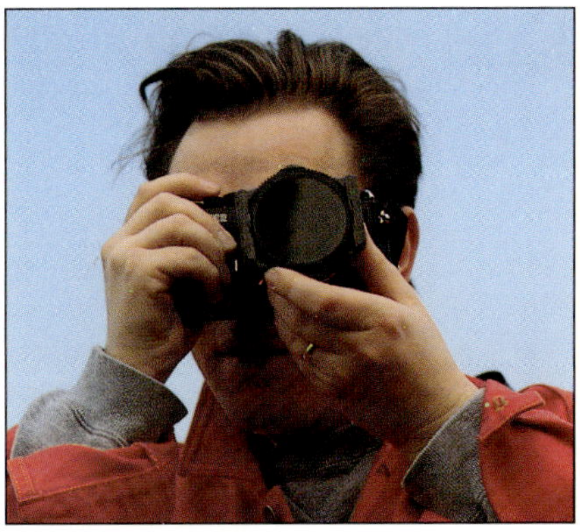

▲ Polarizers are simple to use and you can see the filter's effect before you take the shot.

▼On sunny days, reflections from water can dominate a shot. Fitting a polarizer removes the reflections and saturates colours. In this picture, the absence of reflections gives a surreal impression of the boat floating in mid-air.

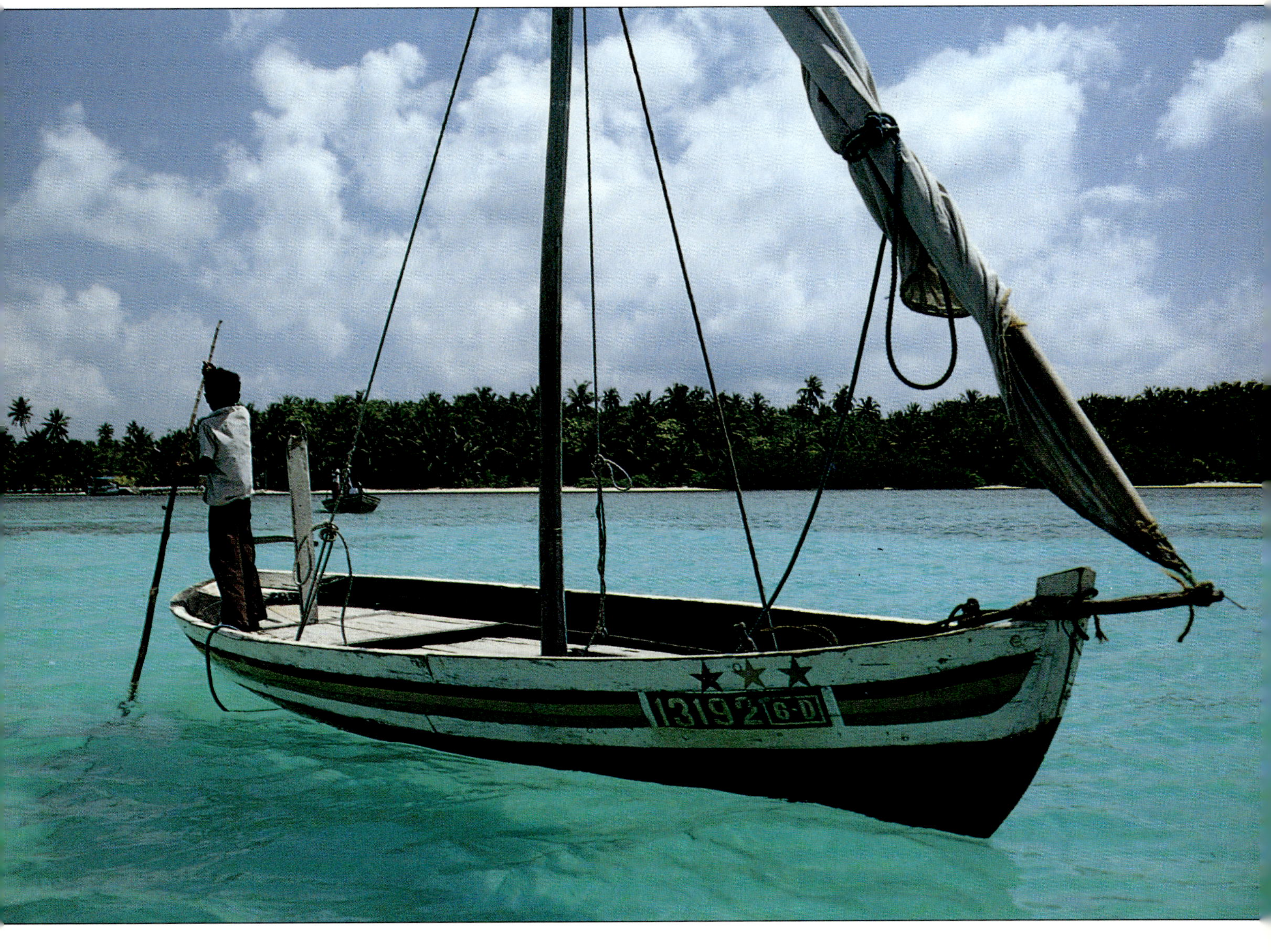

Knowing the angles

When you use a polarizing filter to remove reflections from a shiny surface, the angle between the camera's lens and the reflective surface is critical. Get the angle right and you can see the reflections disappear as you turn the polarizer. Get it wrong and the polarizer is useless.

For any reflecting surface, there is a best angle to position the camera. If you take your picture from this optimum angle the polarizing filter cuts out all, or nearly all of the reflections.

Optimum angles

So what's the optimum angle? For glass it's somewhere between 56° and 60°, for water it's 53°. However, you don't need to take out a protractor to use your polarizer effectively. Light is strongly polarized over a range of angles either side of the optimum angle. So you can start by just guessing the correct angle fairly roughly. Then when you look through the camera's viewfinder you can move around until the reflection completely disappears.

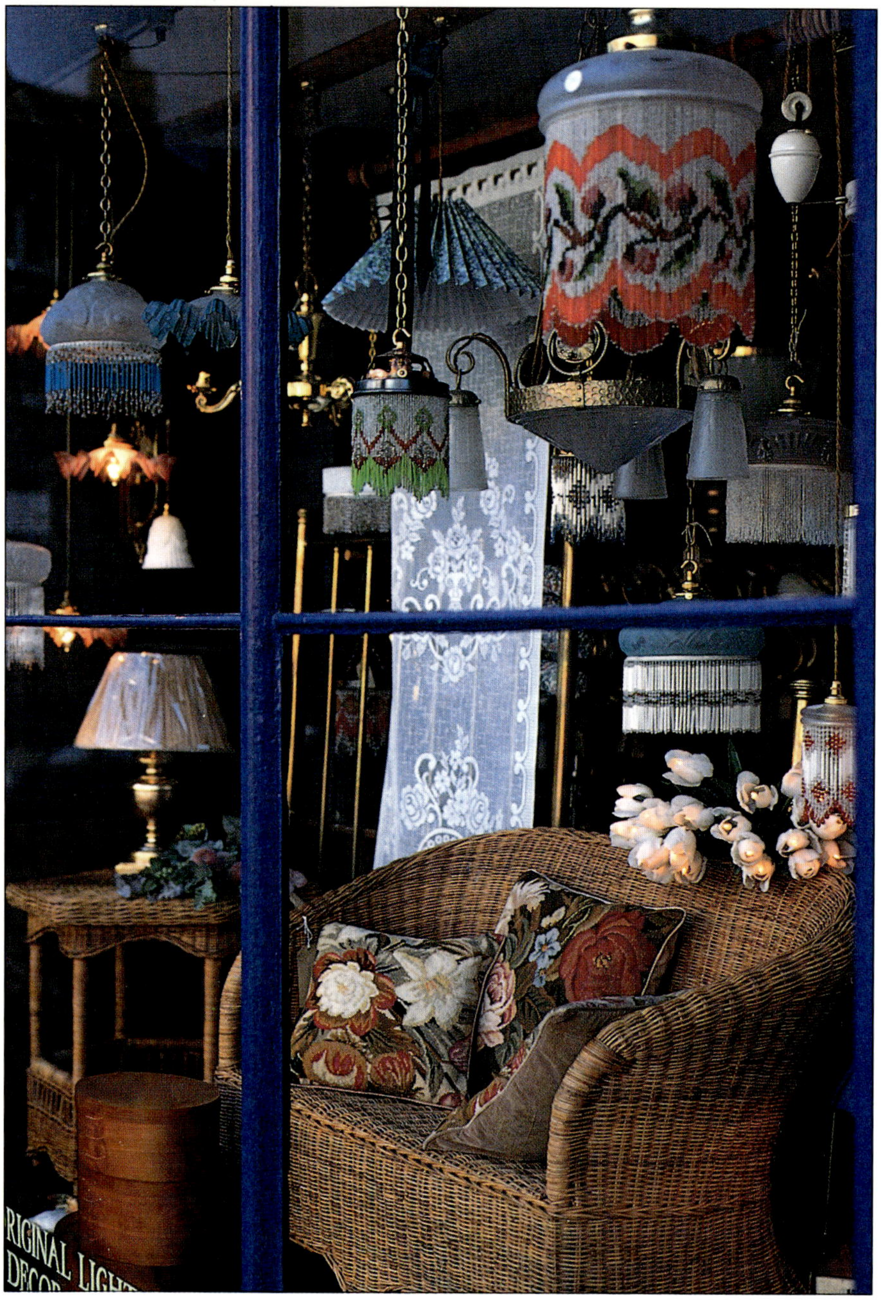

▲ ***Move round so you face the window diagonally and turn the polarizer – it now removes virtually all of the reflections.***

▼***Stand head-on to a shop window and no matter how far you rotate the polarizer you can't remove the reflections from the glass.***

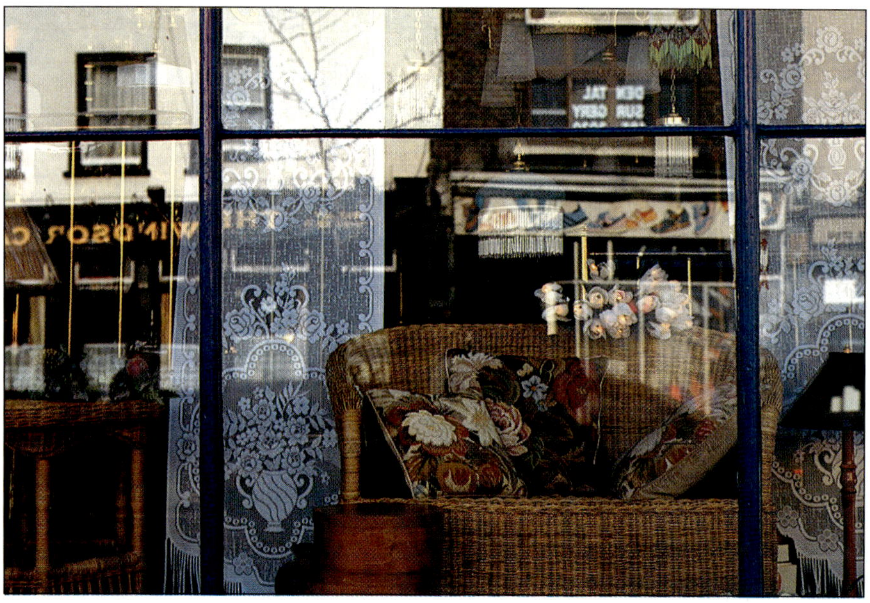

▼***Changing your position alone has no effect. It's the combination of position and a correctly angled polarizer that removes the reflections.***

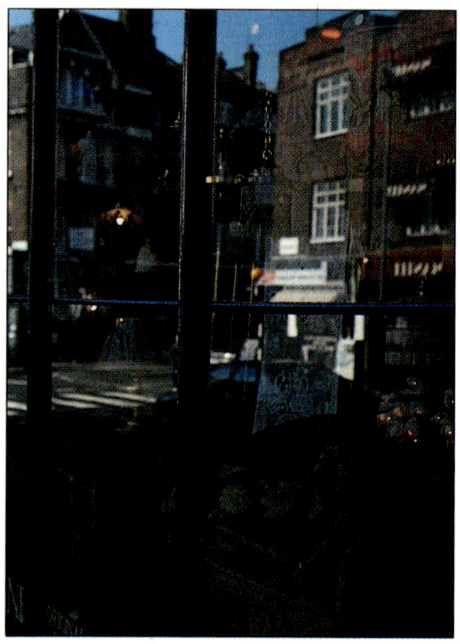

Focal length

A polarizer doesn't block all of the light reflected from a shiny surface – only those rays reflected within 15° either side of the best angle. So when you use lenses with a field of view narrower than about 30° the filter kills reflections all the way across the frame.

A 50mm lens has a field of view of approximately 45°, so at best the effectiveness of the polarizer is confined to the central two thirds of the frame. If you photograph a window which fills the frame, you'll see clearly only through the centre of the glass – reflections remain at the edges of the frame.

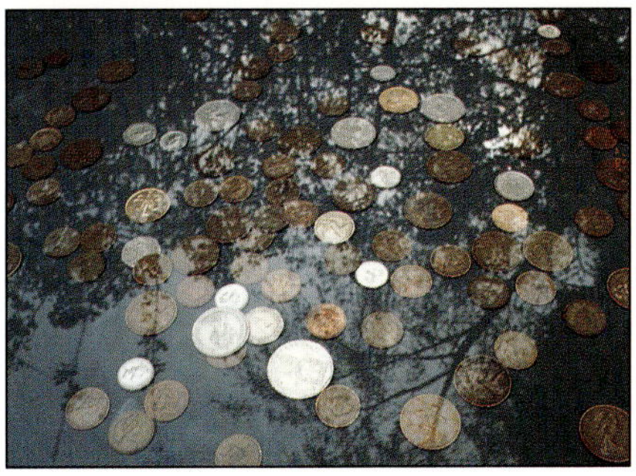

▲Without a polarizer the water's surface acts like a mirror, so that any subject above it is captured clearly and any subject below the water's surface is partially obscured.

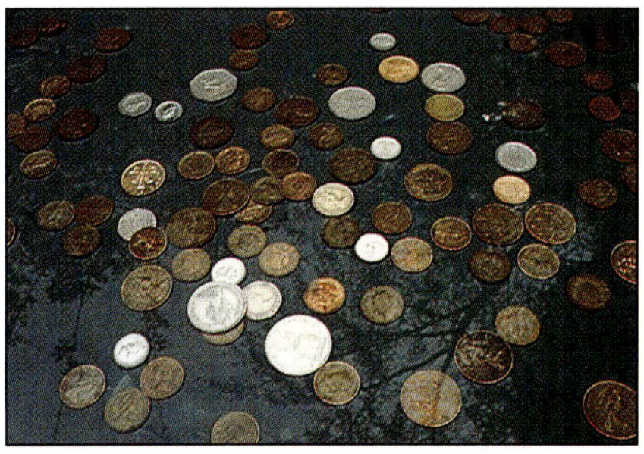

▲ With wide angle lenses, a polarizer's effect is confined to the middle of the frame. This creates what looks like a reflection-free 'hole' in the centre of a reflection-covered surface.

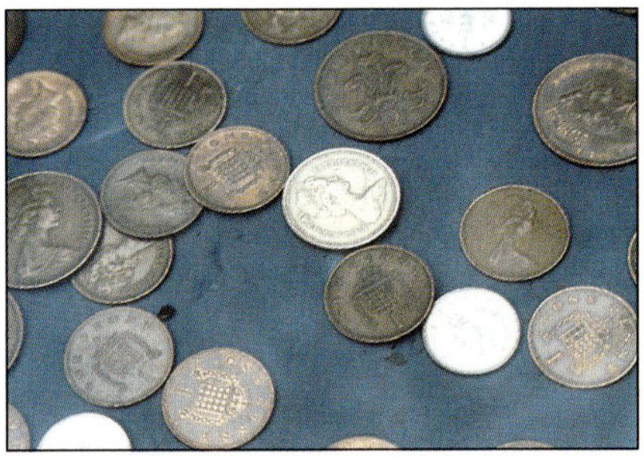

◀ If you want to make reflections disappear across the frame, fit a telephoto lens with a focal length that's longer than 100mm.

The right stuff

BACK TO BASICS

Which materials polarize light? It's easier to name materials that don't, because the list is so short: bare metal is the only surface that doesn't polarize reflected light.

If you're photographing silverware or shiny chrome work, you can't cut out the glare with a polarizer. However, light reflected by painted metal surfaces bounces off the paintwork, not off the metal, so a polarizer works well.

▼ Using a polarizer removes the reflections from the paintwork and glass on this car, but does not affect the reflections from the chrome.

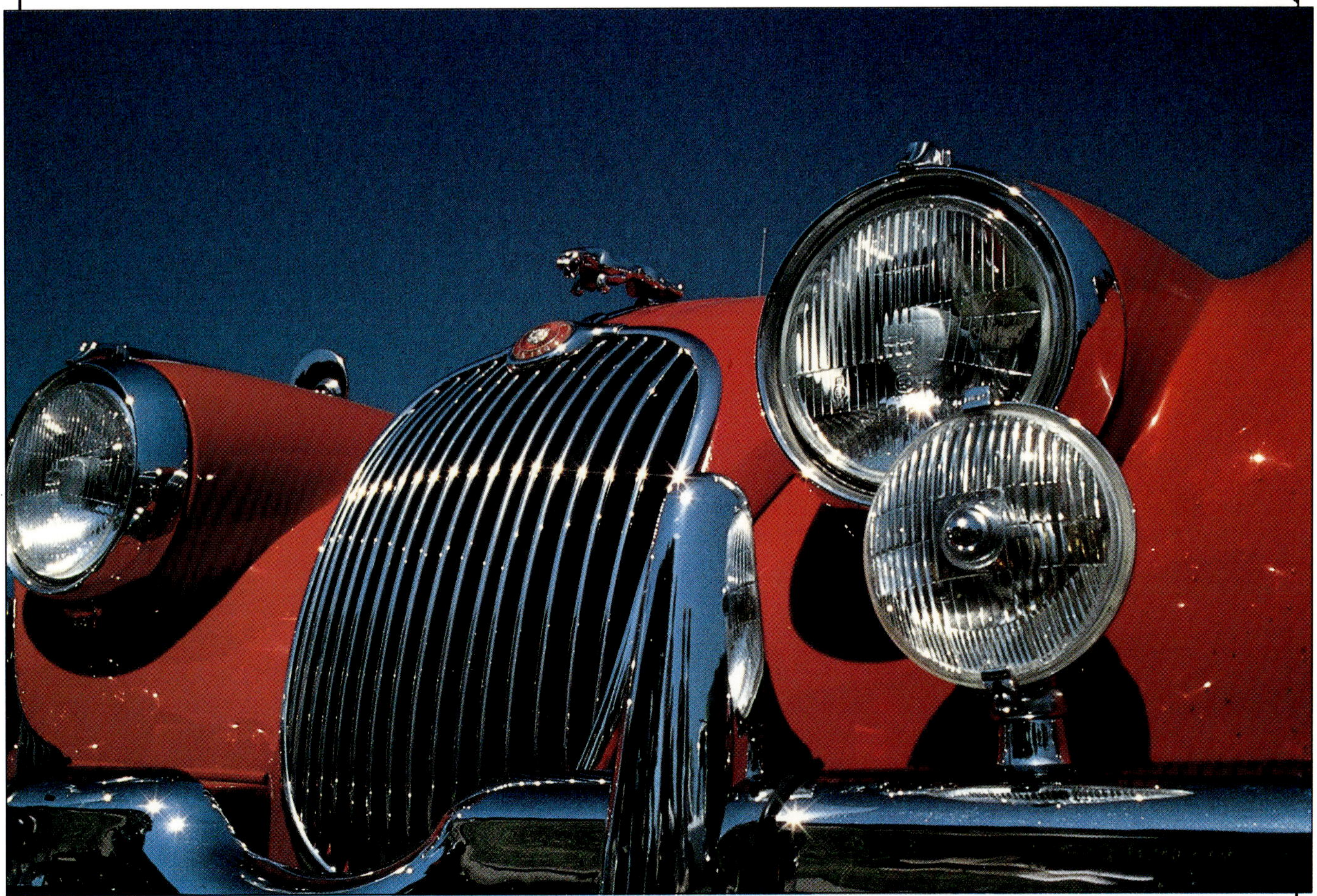

Colour saturation and glare

Reflected light doesn't just hide objects behind glass or under water – it can weaken colour as well. Similarly, polarizers are not limited to cutting out reflections from glass and water. You can also use them to remove glare and enrich colour. For example, you could use a polarizer to cut down the glare from a garden gate to reveal the rich hues of the paintwork.

Dust in the atmosphere scatters light, causing haze, but the scattering process also polarizes the light. So you can frequently use a polarizing filter to cut through haze, when you're photographing distant views. This double function – enriching colour and cutting through haze – makes polarizers invaluable for landscape photography.

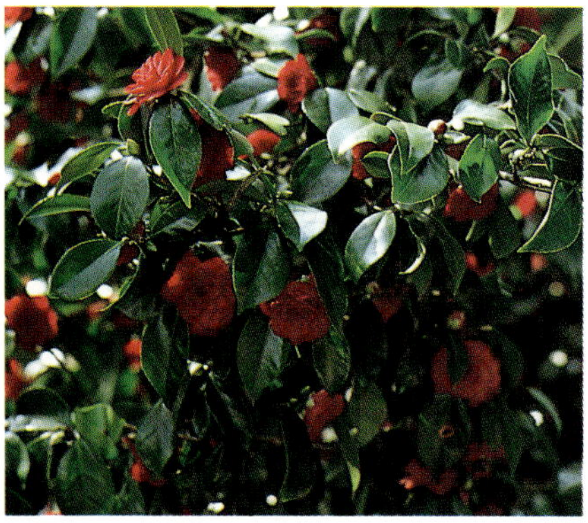

▲ *In this shot, the shiny foliage reflects the bright sunlight falling on it, weakening the colour of the leaves.*

▼ *Fitting a polarizer lets you cut out most of these reflections. You won't be able to cut out all of the reflections because the leaves all point in different directions and each leaf has its own best angle.*

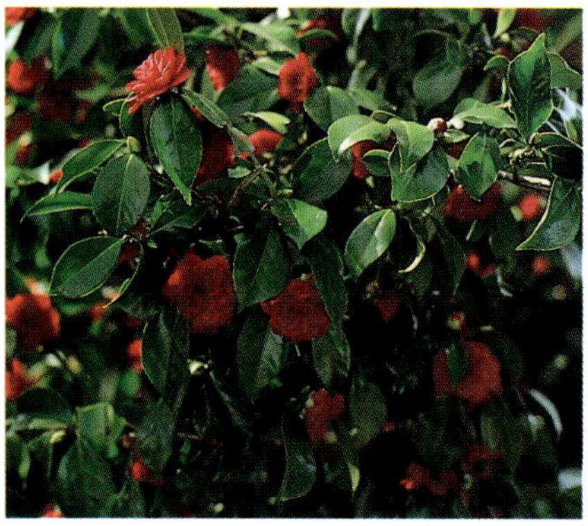

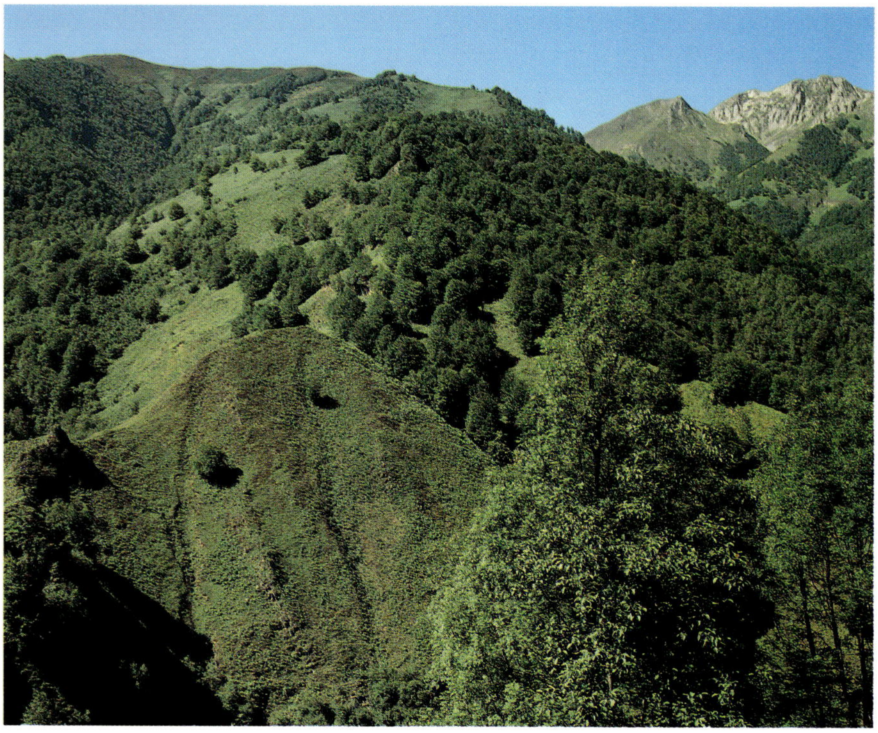

▲ *Landscape scenes usually contain numerous reflective surfaces – such as blades of grass and leaves on trees. Tiny reflections appear where the sunlight catches these surfaces. This creates a wash of polarized light across the frame which reduces colour saturation.*

▼ *The only way you can block these distracting reflections and remove the unwanted wash of polarized light is by fitting a polarizing filter over your camera's lens. This also has the effect of saturating the colours in the scene, making the grass and leaves look much greener.*

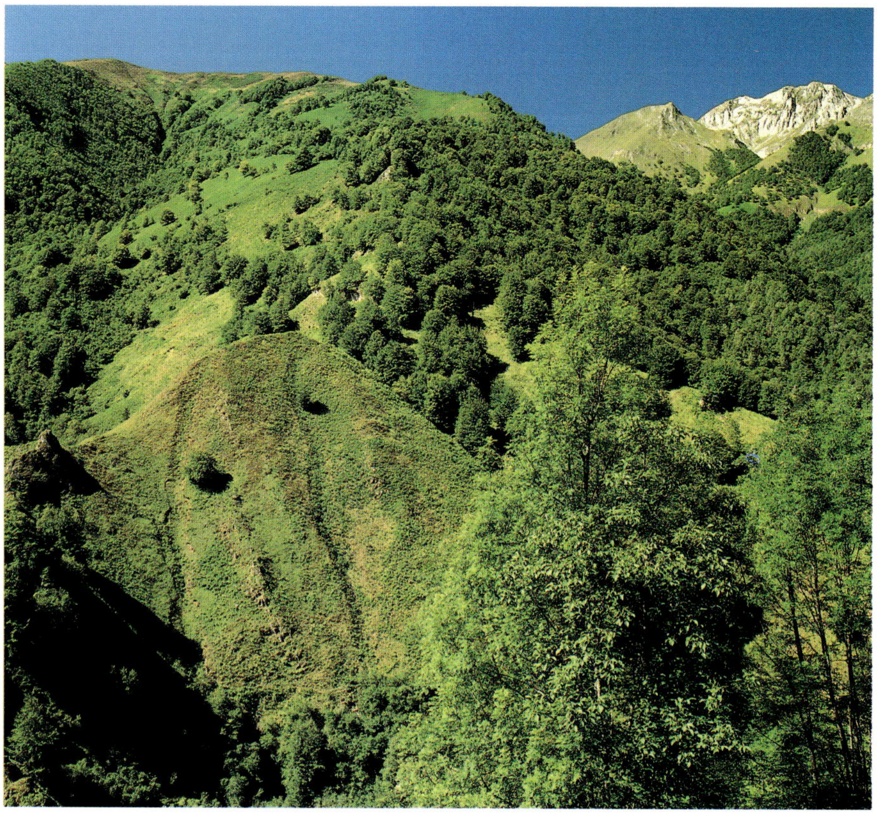

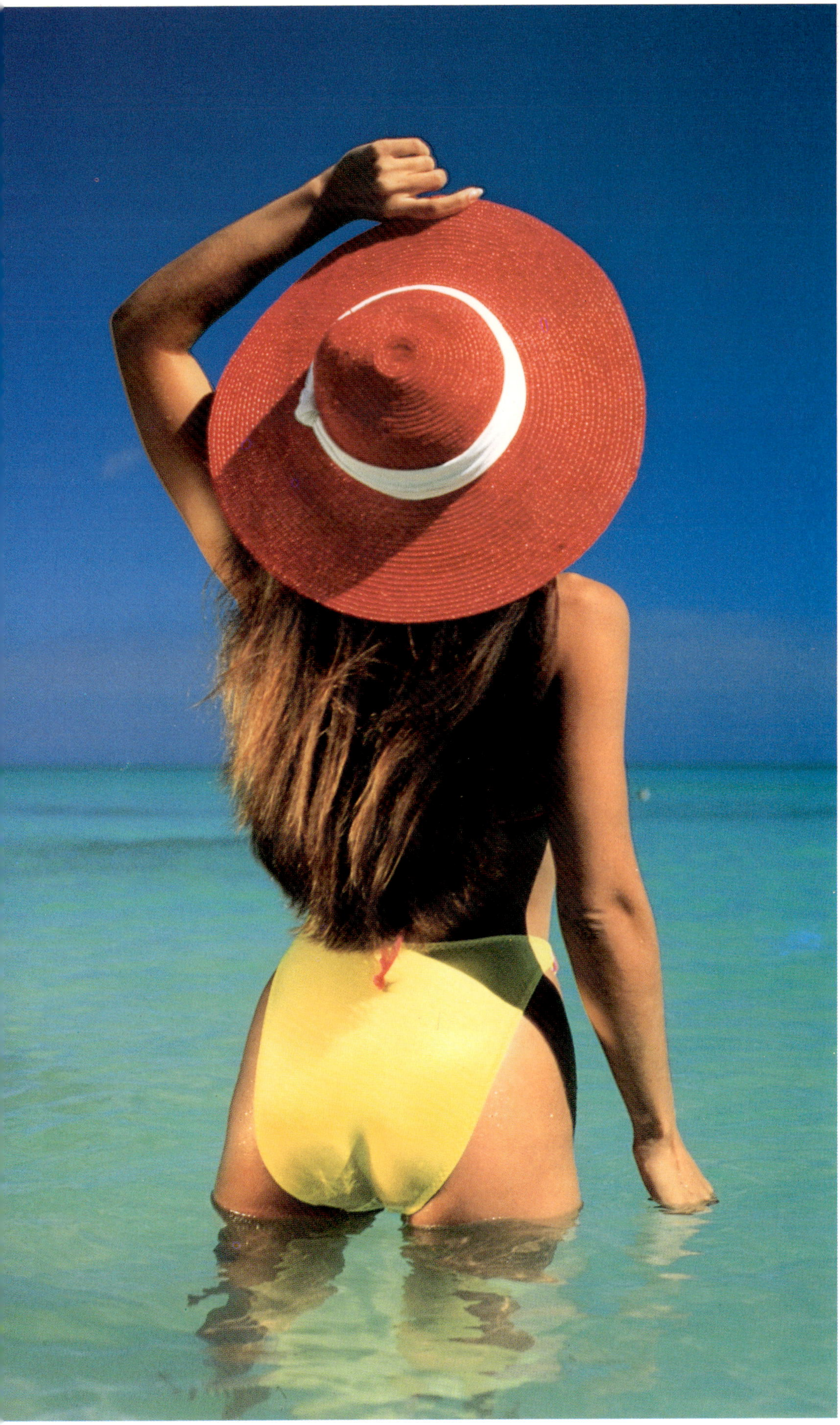

◀ *Using a polarizer over your lens on a bright sunny day lets you deepen blue skies and saturate the colours in a scene. Together, these effects are capable of producing rich, attention grabbing images.*

Tip Stacking filters

A polarizing filter is thicker than an ordinary filter, because it has to incorporate a mount and a rotating ring. This can cause problems with ultra wide angle lenses as the filter's thick mount may cut off the corners of the frame. The problem is worse if you use a polarizer with another filter. To solve it, use oversized filters, and fit them to a step-up ring screwed into the lens.

Revealing colour

Sometimes the brilliant highlights shining off irregular surfaces don't just weaken colours, but actually hide them – making the picture look almost monochromatic. The effect is most pronounced in bright sunlight – in fact, in precisely the conditions where polarizing sunglasses work best. A polarizer can cut out the glare to reveal colour and fine detail. The result is a picture which is much sharper, crisper and punchier.

Tip: Take time to reflect

Polarizers are capable of stunning effects, but don't automatically reach for one every time you're faced with reflections. Often reflections make a shot and removing them leaves you with a bland, lifeless picture. For example, the reflection of trees in water or the reflection of a blue sky in the windows of a skyscraper can create a strong, graphic image.

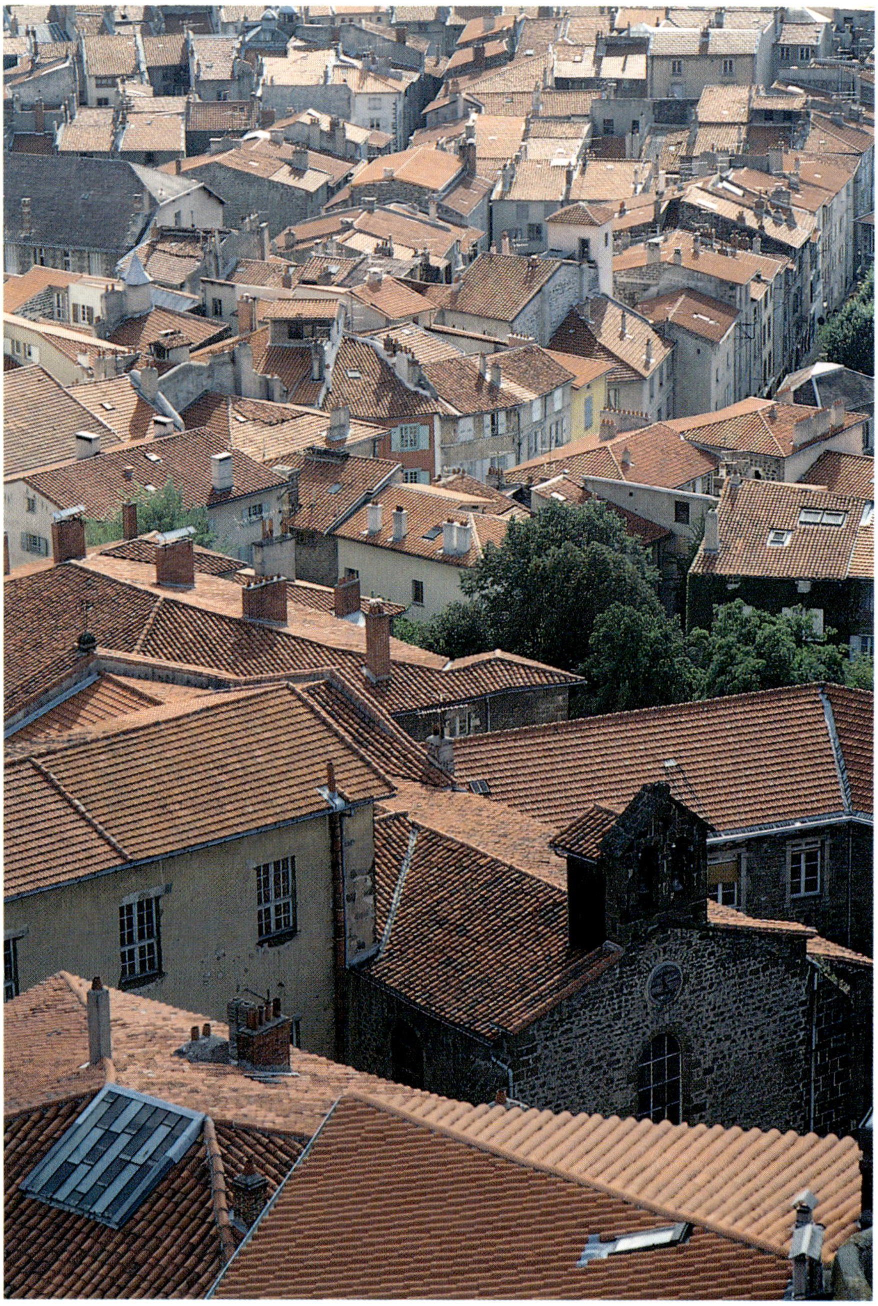

▶Using a polarizer cuts out glare from this shot to reveal the colour of the roof tiles and the buildings.

▼Without a polarizer glare obscures the colours in the shot, giving the picture a monochromatic feel.

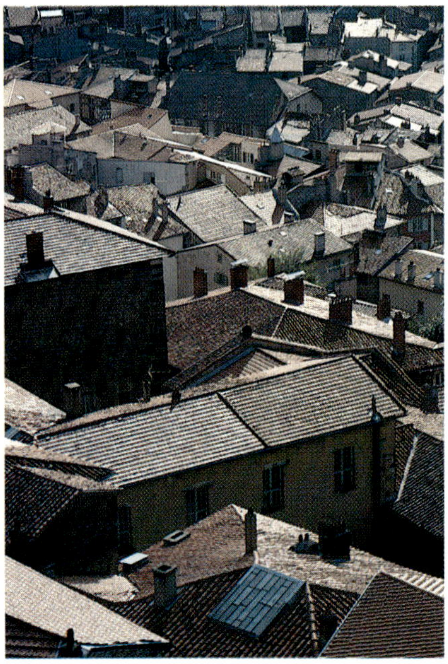

Choosing a polarizer

If your camera uses beam splitters (semi-silvered mirrors) in its AF or metering system, an ordinary polarizer can cause underexposure.

To check whether your camera suffers from this problem, fit the polarizer and point the camera at an evenly lit matt white surface. Now switch on the camera's TTL meter and rotate the filter. The meter reading should not change.

If it does, you'll need to buy a special 'circular' polarizer. This has a different construction that works well with all types of metering and autofocus systems.

Alternatively, use your ordinary polarizer, but focus manually and take it off the lens when you take a meter reading. Don't forget to take account of the filter factor – printed on the filter mount or filter box – when setting the camera's controls.

Light balancing filters

The colour of daylight varies throughout the day, which can lead to colour casts on your pictures. Learning to use light balancing filters lets you correct the colour of daylight for natural looking results.

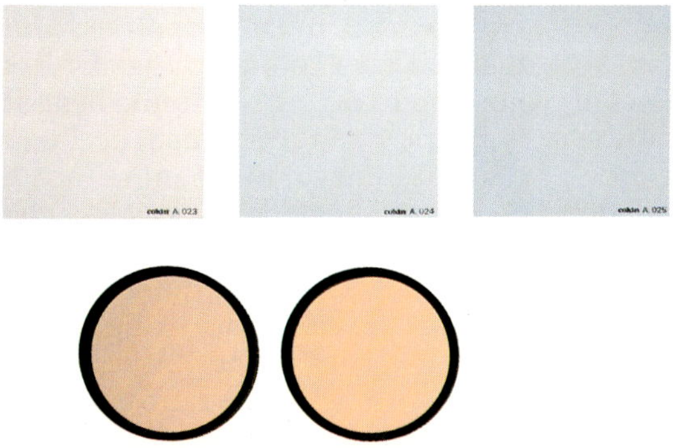

◀▲ Light balancing filters let you change the colour temperature of the light reaching the film. Filters with a blue tinge are sometimes referred to as cool down filters. They reduce the amount of yellow and orange light reaching the film. Yellow and pink coloured versions are known as warm up filters. These block some of the blue light reaching the film.

If you photograph a scene just after dawn, again at noon and then at sunset, the pictures look very different to one another. Not only does the angle and quality of the light vary, but so does its colour. In the morning the scene is bathed in a warm yellow glow, while at noon the light is whiter and the colours in the scene look more natural. By the time the sun sets, the light looks warmer again and may even appear bright orange in colour.

Different colours of daylight are described as having different colour temperatures. The bluer the light, the higher the colour temperature. The redder the light, the lower the colour temperature.

Our eyes are very good at adjusting to different colour temperatures – we tend to see light as white throughout most of the day. Daylight balanced film, however, is geared to give best results under direct summer sunlight and a clear sky, and is very sensitive to other colour temperatures.

Creating mood

Understanding colour temperature lets you take full control over your pictures. For natural looking results you must be able to judge the colour of the daylight, so that you can use an appropriate filter to balance the light to the film.

But perhaps you don't want natural looking results. Understanding colour temperature also lets you create or enhance mood. For example, a picture of an eskimo wrapped in furs might look better if you shoot in the shade under a bright blue sky. The light is bluish and adds to the cold feel of the shot. Similarly, the warm light of sunset is likely to enrich a picture of a romantic couple.

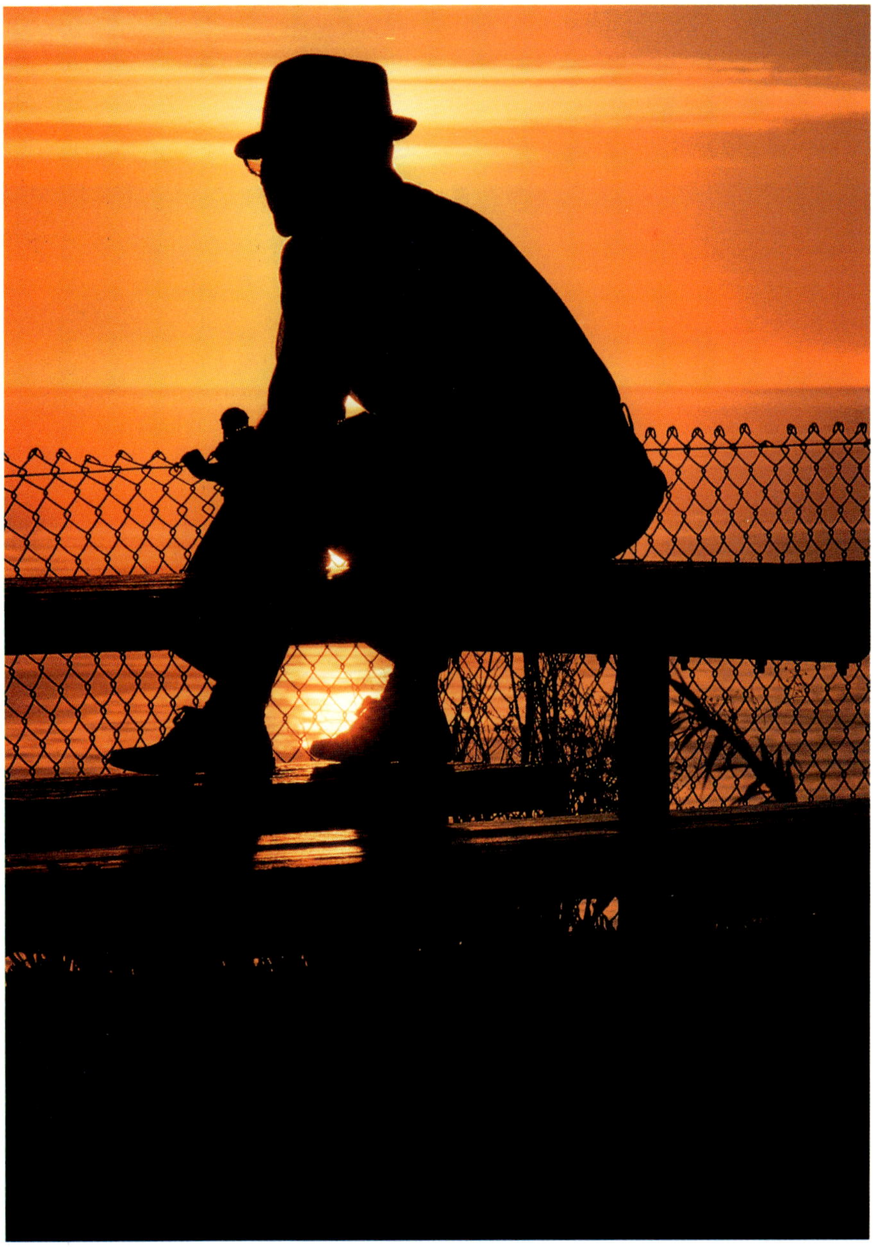

▶ The light at sunrise has a low colour temperature, which means it contains a high proportion of yellow and red coloured light. This gives the picture a warm, romantic feel.

Colour temperature

Light can be any colour, but daylight ranges from a reddy orange through yellow and white to blue. Each different colour of daylight has its own colour temperature, which is usually measured in degrees Kelvin (K).

The idea that different colours of light have different temperatures may seem odd at first, but the theory is actually very simple and the colour temperature scale works well in practice. It is based on the fact that colour changes of daylight match the colour changes of a material when it is heated. For example, imagine heating the dull, black ring on an electric cooker – when it's heated, the ring begins to glow red. Its colour then changes to bright orange as the heat is increased. If you heat it to a high enough temperature the metal will turn yellow and then white and, assuming that it doesn't melt, will eventually turn blue in colour.

Scattered light

However, it must be pointed out that the blue colour in the sky has nothing to do with extreme heat. It is a happy and convenient accident that daylight colour changes match those of heated materials. The changes in the colour of daylight are, in fact, a result of the scattering of short wavelengths of light (see 'Back to basics', page 42).

The reason for using the colour temperature scale is to place a measurement on each colour. This makes it easier to choose light balancing filters when you want to correct the colour of the light reaching the film to ensure natural looking pictures.

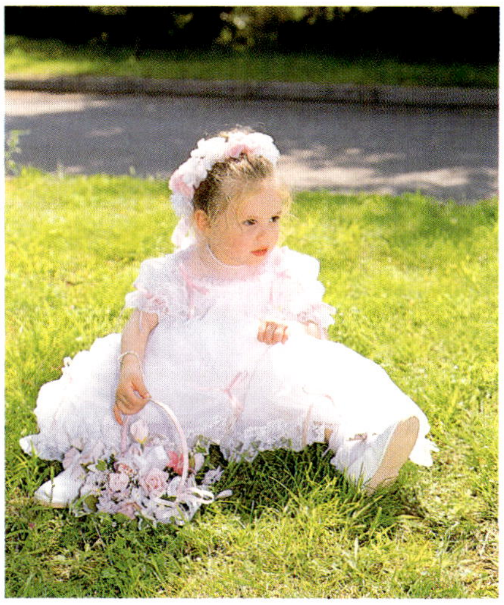

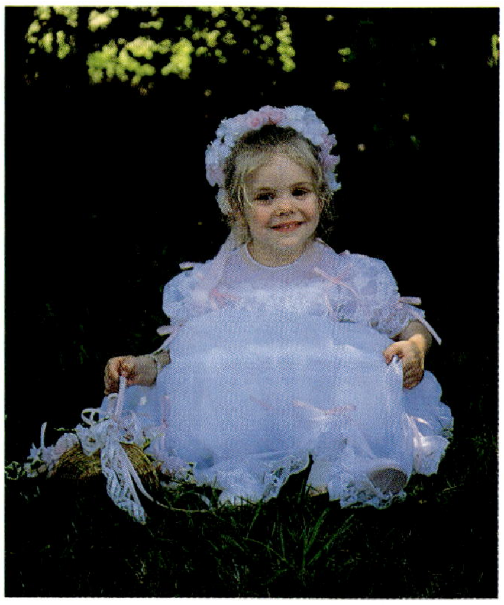

▲ *The colour temperature of direct sunlight at noon on a sunny summer day is about 5,500K. The light looks white to the eye, and gives neutral coloured results when it is recorded on film.*

▲ *Shaded areas are illuminated by skylight – light from the sky when direct sunlight is blocked – and have a higher colour temperature (at least 6,500K). This gives pictures a distinctive blue cast.*

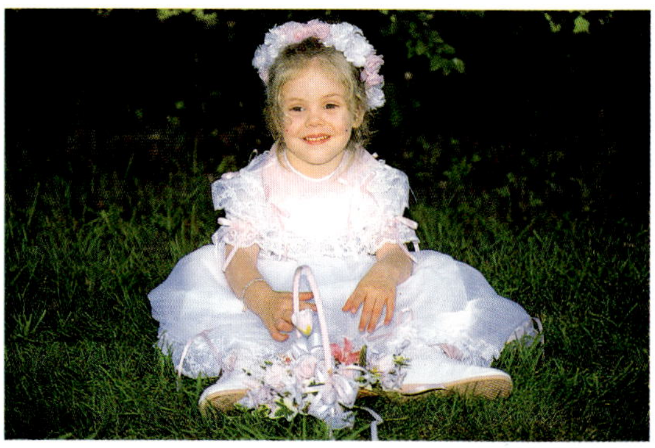

▶ *Using an appropriate light balancing filter over your lens gets rid of the blue cast to give neutral coloured results. Alternatively, you can use fill-in flash. Light from your flashgun has the same colour temperature as noon daylight – 5,500K.*

Temperature scale

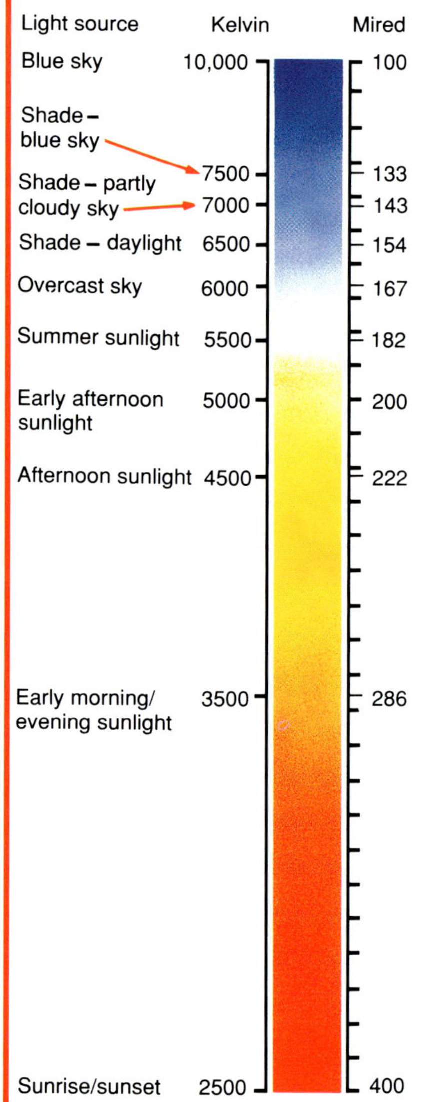

Kelvin scale and mireds

Although the Kelvin scale is a useful way of measuring the colour of light it has its drawbacks, especially when it comes to choosing light balancing filters. The main problem is that the Kelvin scale is not linear. This means that a light balancing filter doesn't shift the colour temperature by a fixed amount at every point on the scale.

The mired (micro reciprocal degree, pronounced my-red) scale gets around the problem. Measured in mireds, a filter causes an identical colour temperature shift, regardless of the original colour temperature.

To calculate a mired value (M) just divide the colour temperature in Kelvins into 1,000,000.

Using warm up and cool down filters

Daylight balanced slide films record colours accurately in light with a colour temperature of 5,500K (182M). If you shoot under light of a different colour temperature you end up with pictures showing various shades of yellow or blue, depending on the lighting conditions.

But all is not lost: you can achieve natural looking pictures simply by placing an appropriate light balancing filter over your lens. Daylight balanced colour print films also record accurate colours in light with a colour temperature of 5,500K. But colour casts are less of a problem as they can be removed at the printing stage.

Light balancing filters for daylight come in two types – warm up and cool down. Warm up filters are yellow, so they block the amount of blue light reaching the film, making the image appear warmer. Cool down filters are blue, so they block the amount of yellow light reaching the film, making the images look cooler.

Kodak's Wratten filters are the most commonly used filters for balancing the colour temperature of daylight. The 81 series – 81, 81A, 81B, 81C, 81D, 81EF – are yellow coloured warm up filters. The 82 series – 82, 82A, 82B, 82C – are blue coloured cool down filters. If you are buying another make, ask for filters corresponding to those manufactured by Kodak.

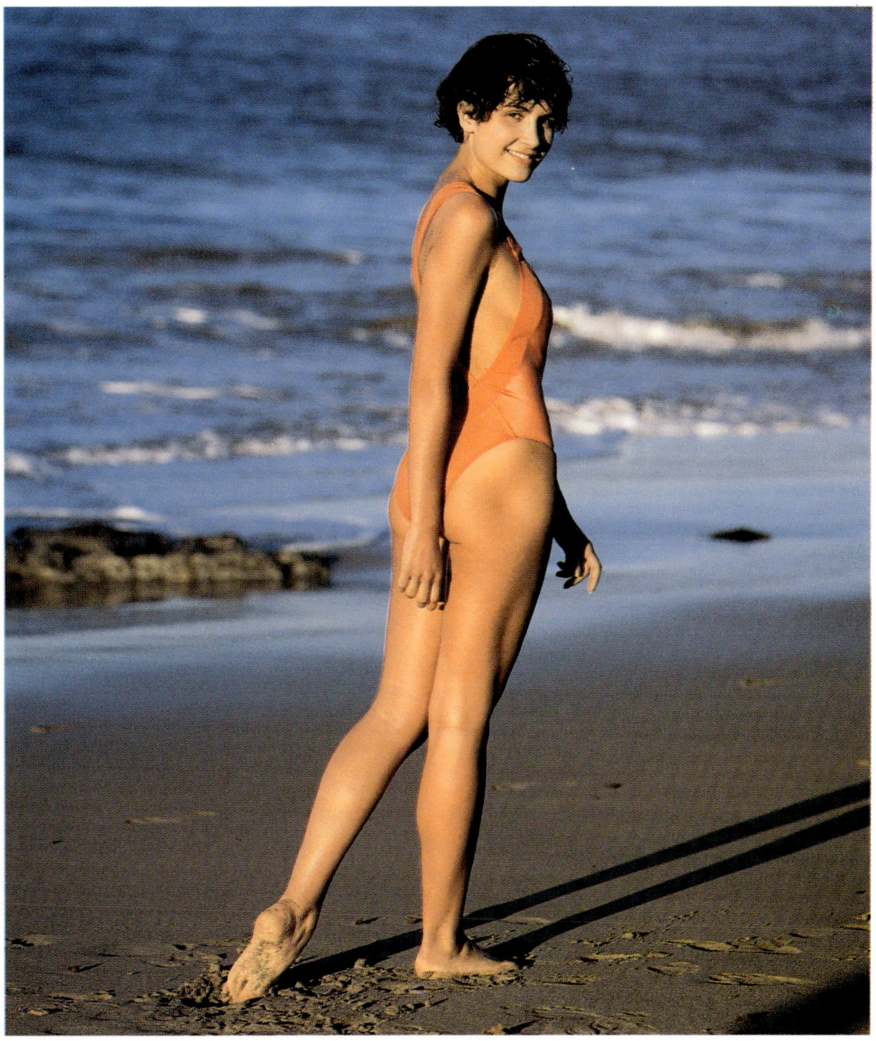

▲ On a sunny day the late afternoon light has a soft, flattering quality. However, it also has a low colour temperature. If you don't want to record the light's distinct yellow-orange colour, fit an 82C cool down filter over your camera's lens. This raises the colour temperature of the light reaching the film to 5,500K, which gives a natural looking effect.

Warming up

Warm up filters are the most useful light balancing filters for daylight. Warm colours look more natural than cold colours, because the eye is used to seeing yellow and orange light at sunrise and sunset. So it's more likely that you will want to correct the cold blue colour caused by blue skies and overcast conditions, than the warm glow of early morning or late evening.

Learning to choose an appropriate warm up filter helps you achieve natural looking results under a wide range of lighting and weather conditions.

Kodak Wratten Filters

81EF

shade under a blue sky

81D

shade under partly cloudy sky

81C

deep shade under daylight

81B

shade under daylight

81A

overcast sky

81

noon daylight - to warm up skin tones slightly

Creative use of colour temperature

Just because you have a set of light balancing filters in your camera bag, it doesn't follow that you have to use them. By choosing carefully the time of day you shoot, and the weather conditions you shoot under, you can leave the light unfiltered and use colour temperature creatively to enhance the mood or feel of a photograph.

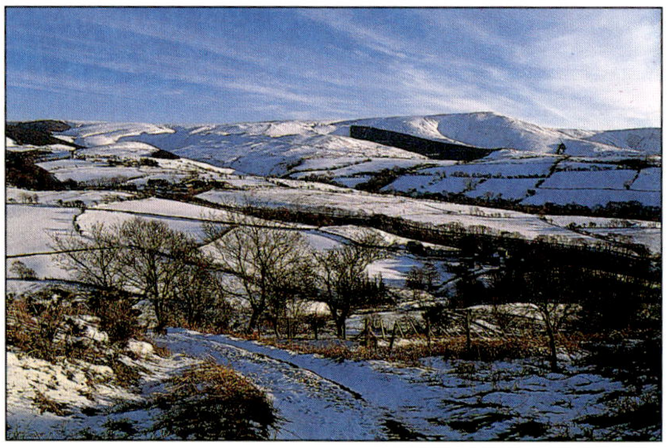

◀ *Photographing a snowy landscape on a sunny day, under a blue sky enhances the cold feel of the shot. You can exaggerate the chilly feel by including areas of shade. These areas have a higher colour temperature than the areas in direct sunlight and take on a blue colour cast. This cast is a result of the blue sky acting like a large blue reflector – bouncing blue light into the shadow areas.*

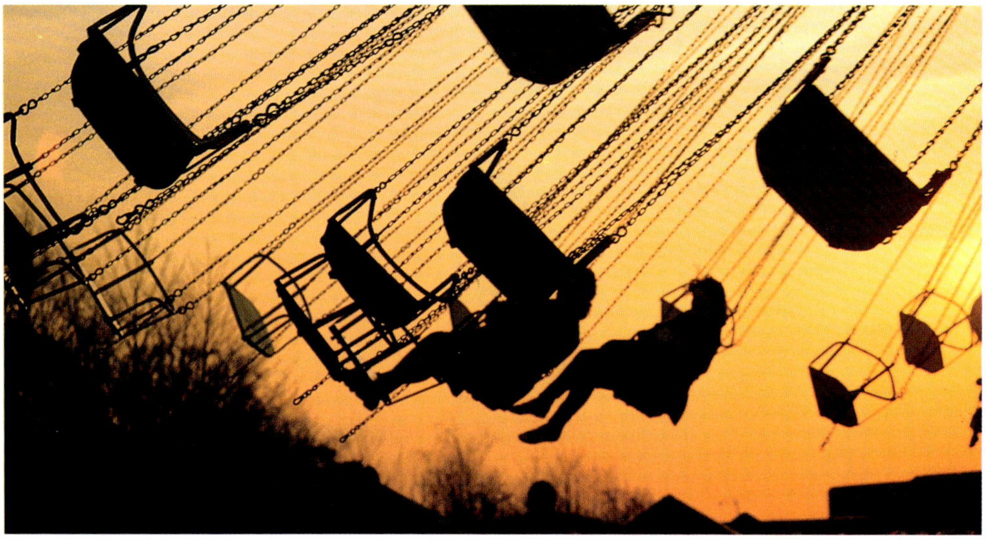

◀ *Photographing at sunset lends a warm feel to your pictures that suits many subjects. If you shoot a city scene, the pollution in the atmosphere scatters most colour temperatures – so only red and orange sunlight reaches the subject. The scattered light may also give a glorious, purple-coloured sky, (see 'Back to basics').*

Why does daylight change colour?

BACK TO BASICS

Sunlight is made up of a range of colours of light known as the spectrum. Seen together, the different colours all appear as white. But when the sunlight reaches the Earth's atmosphere, air molecules scatter some of the colours. It is this scattered light that gives the *sky* its colour.

Blue light is most easily scattered, so it is scattered first when sunlight enters the atmosphere. If you look away from the sun on a clear day, you'll see a blue sky made up of this scattered blue light. Red light is scattered the least.

As the sunlight continues its path through the atmosphere other colours of light are also scattered. So the colour of sunlight reaching the Earth depends on the thickness of the atmosphere it passes through – the thicker the atmosphere, the more scattering takes place, and the redder the colour of the sunlight.

At noon, the sun is overhead and the sunlight has less atmosphere to pass through – so only blue light is scattered. Similarly, at high altitudes sunlight has only passed through a thin section of atmosphere and the sky is bluer than at lower altitudes.

At sunrise and sunset, however, the sunlight passes through a greater thickness of atmosphere and more colours of light are scattered – resulting in a redder light.

The lower levels of the atmosphere have the greatest scattering effect. This is due to the atmosphere being denser. Pollution in the air also scatters light. If the air is heavily polluted you may even see a yellow sky at noon, because so much light is scattered by the pollution. However, generally you can see the effect of pollution most clearly at sunrise and sunset.

The blue-purple colour of the sky opposite the sun is made up of the scattered colours of light.

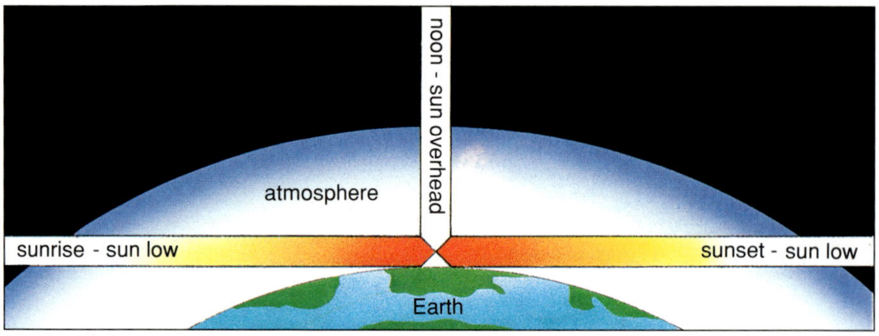

Colour conversion filters

If you photograph under artificial lighting, you're likely to find strong colour casts on your pictures. Fitting an appropriate colour conversion filter over your lens is a simple solution to the problem.

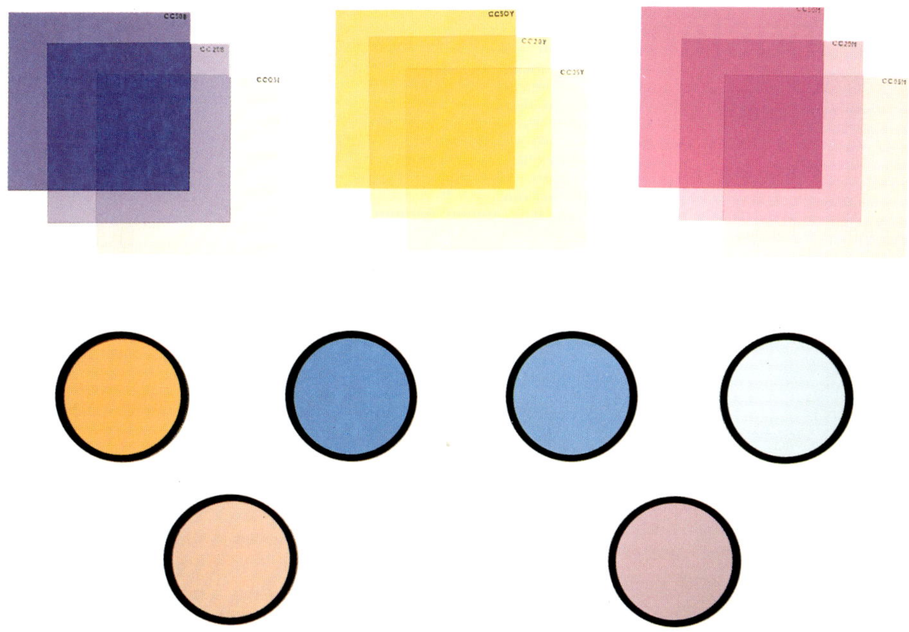

Light balancing filters are invaluable for correcting the different colour temperatures of sunlight to give natural looking results on daylight balanced film. But sunlight isn't the only light source that can produce colour casts on your pictures. Tungsten bulbs and fluorescent tubes also produce colour casts – and these are generally stronger than those produced by sunlight.

Green and orange casts

The light from tungsten photographic lights and domestic light bulbs gives photos a strong orange cast. Fluorescent strip lights, on the other hand, give a rather sickly green colour cast.

To correct these colour casts, you need to use much stronger light balancing filters, known as colour conversion filters.

One of the advantages of using flash light is that it has the same colour temperature as noon sunlight. This means that you don't need to use any filtration to obtain natural looking colours on film.

▲ There are different types of colour conversion filters available. The widest range is available as thin gels – these are inexpensive, but fragile. Glass versions are more robust, but they are also more expensive.

▼ The photographer deliberately recorded the colour casts from the artificial lights in this picture. The two colours balance each other and add to the shot.

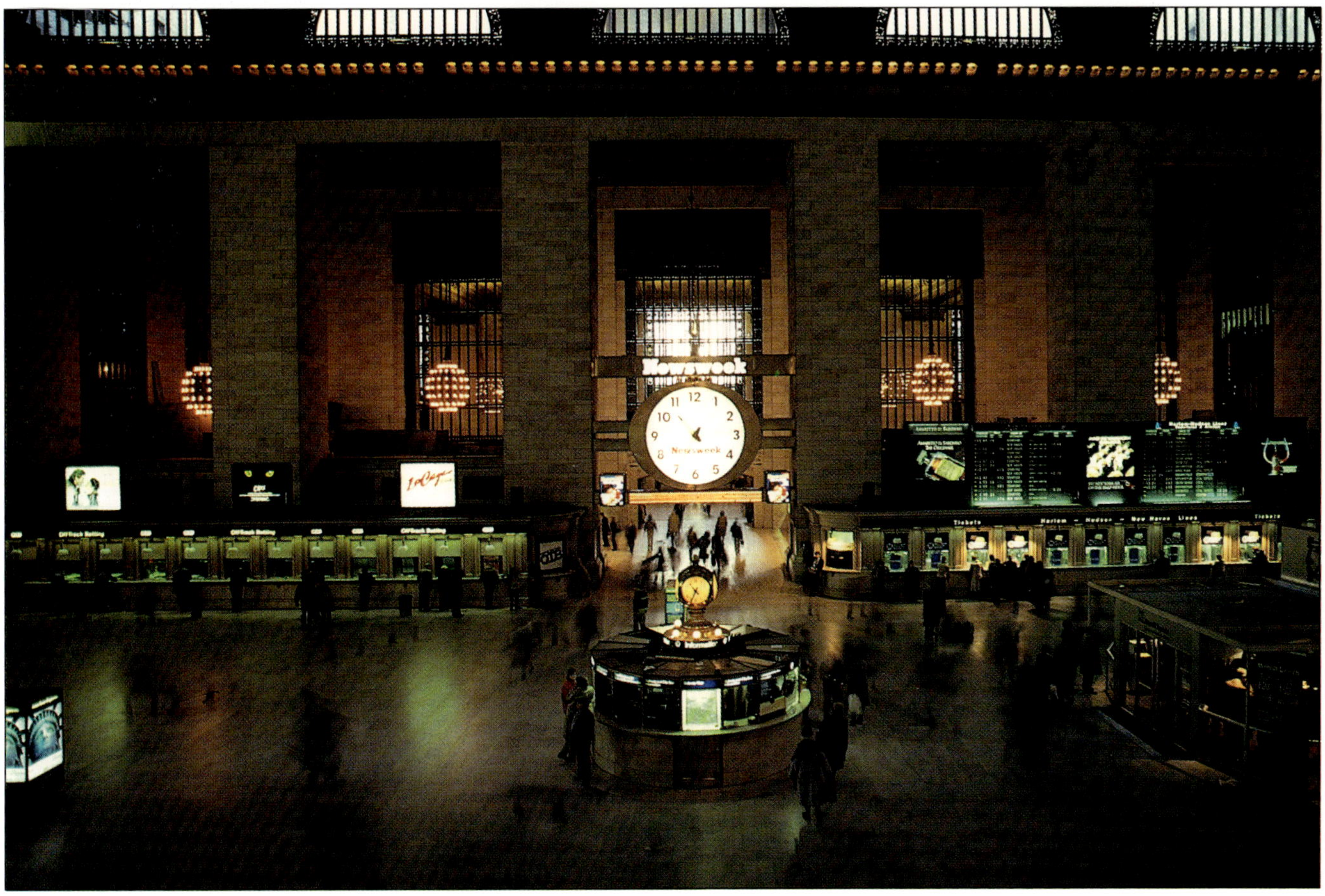

Tungsten lighting

In the centre of a tungsten light bulb is a metal filament. This heats up when an electrical current is passed through it. When it's heated the filament begins to glow and emits light.

Some photographic tungsten bulbs have a blue coating. This raises the colour temperature of the light to match that of daylight. However, most of them emit light with a low colour temperature. This gives pictures a distinctive orange cast. To correct this you need to place a deep blue coloured filter over your camera's lens.

The filter you need depends on the type of tungsten light you use. Tungsten studio lamps require an 80A filter, tungsten photofloods require an 80B filter and household bulbs require an 80B and an 82C filter, used together.

Tip Tungsten balanced film

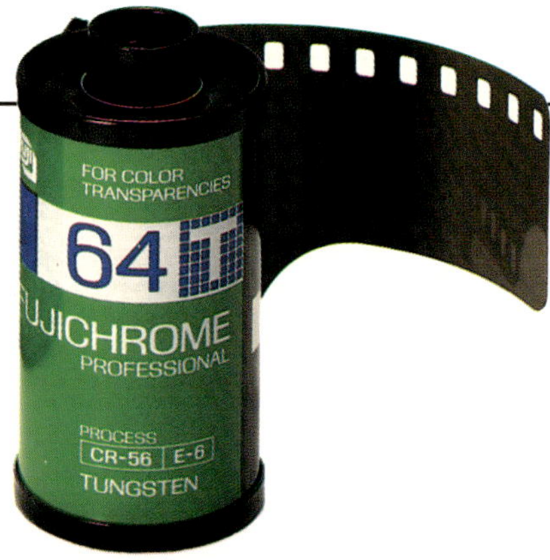

Amateur tungsten lights aren't very powerful, which means you often require long exposures. Placing a filter over the camera's lens blocks some of the light, which means you have to use an even slower shutter speed. This can lead to blur, and very long exposures may even lead to reciprocity failure.

An alternative to using a colour conversion filter is to load up with tungsten balanced film, which gives natural looking results under tungsten lighting. There are two varieties – Type A, for use with tungsten photofloods (which have a colour temperature of 3,400K) and Type B, for use with tungsten studio lamps (which have a colour temperature of 3,200K). However, Type A tungsten balanced film is now virtually obsolete – though an 81A warm up filter bounces light from a photoflood to type B film.

The advantage of using tungsten balanced film is that you don't need to use a filter. This means that you can set faster shutter speeds.

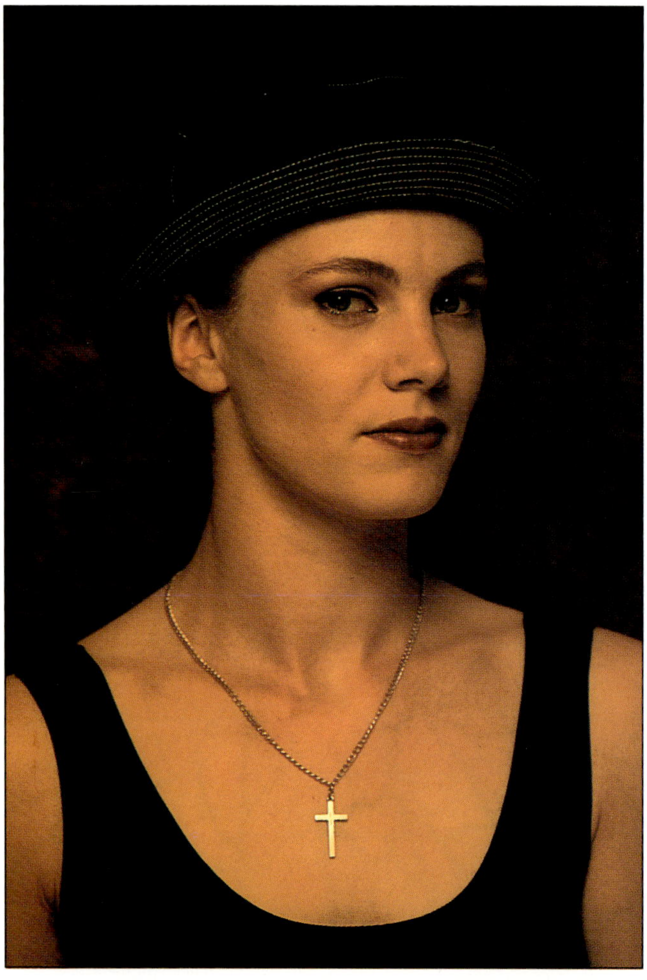

▲ Pictures taken on daylight film under tungsten lighting show a strong orange colour cast. This is most noticeable in the lighter areas of the frame.

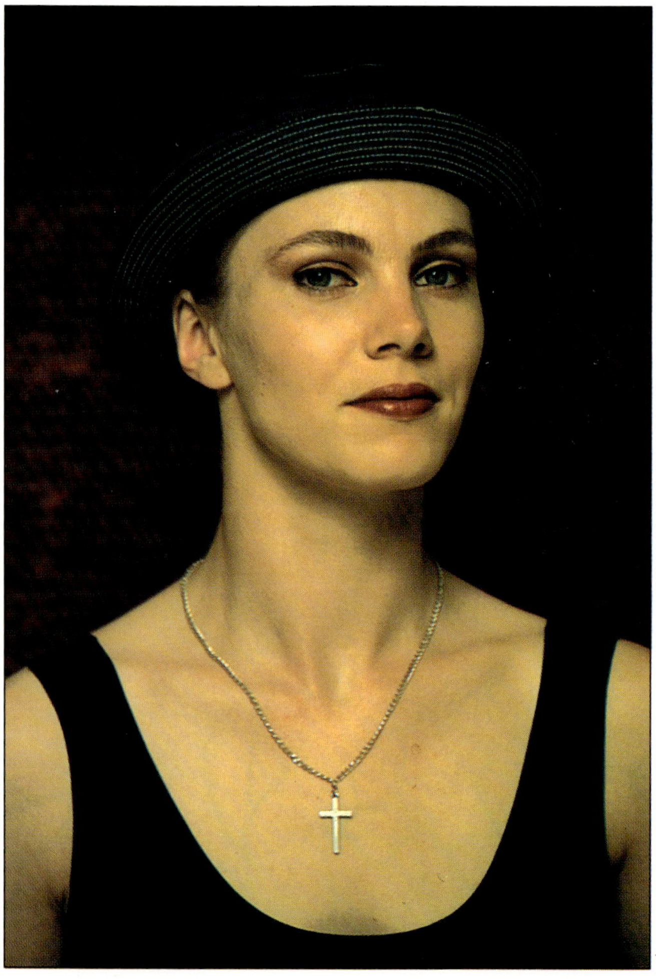

▲ Fitting a blue 80A filter over your camera's lens corrects the orange colour cast from the tungsten bulb and gives natural looking colours.

Fluorescent lighting

The strip lighting found in many offices and public places uses fluorescent tubes. These are not hot light sources – like tungsten. Instead, they produce light by passing electricity through vapour inside a glass tube. This causes the fluorescent coating on the inside of the glass to glow. Light from fluorescent tubes appears white to the eye, but gives pictures taken on daylight film a green colour cast.

The colour cast produced by fluorescent lighting can be removed using magenta coloured filters. However, the colour of the cast varies between different types of tube and each type of tube requires specific filters to achieve a neutral result on film.

The problem is that it's next to impossible to judge which filters you need by eye. Using a colour temperature meter is an expensive solution. Alternatively, you can use a Kodak Wratten CC30 magenta filter. This filter gives fairly neutral looking results under most fluorescent lighting.

Some filter manufacturers make a specific filter for correcting colour casts from fluorescent strip lighting. These are similar to Kodak's CC30 magenta filter, but they tend to warm up the colours in the image slightly.

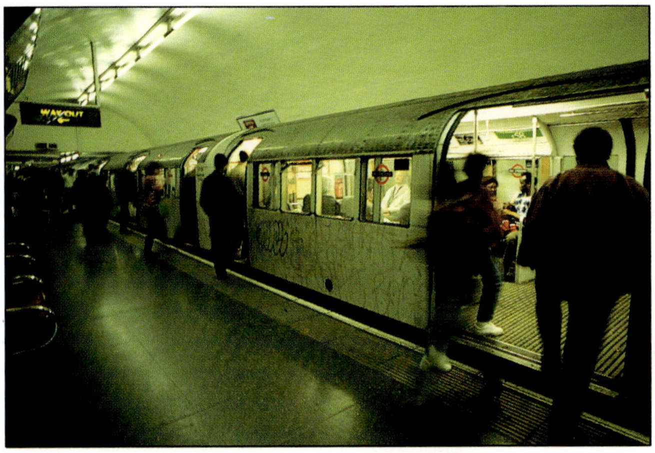

▲ ***If you photograph under fluorescent lighting using daylight balanced slide film, your pictures show an unnatural-looking green colour cast.***

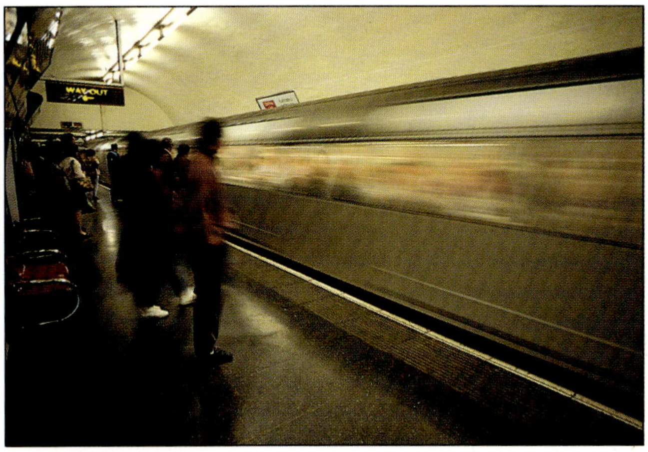

▲ ***Fitting a Kodak Wratten CC30 magenta filter over the camera lens removes most of the green light, and improves the shot.***

Colour temperature meters

The most accurate way to determine which filters are needed to correct colour casts – from natural and artificial light – is to use a colour temperature meter. There are two types – two-way colour and three-way colour.

Two-way colour temperature meters measure the redness or blueness of the light. So they can give accurate readings under daylight and tungsten lighting.

Three-way colour temperature meters have three silicon photocells, which measure the levels of blue, green and red light striking the meter. So they can also measure the colour of light from fluorescent tubes.

Colour correction is measured on a red-blue scale and a green-magenta scale. The figure that's displayed on the meter's LCD panel can be translated into filter values using a table on the back.

▼ ***Colour temperature meters cost as much as a mid-range SLR, but they are the only way to measure the colour of light accurately.***

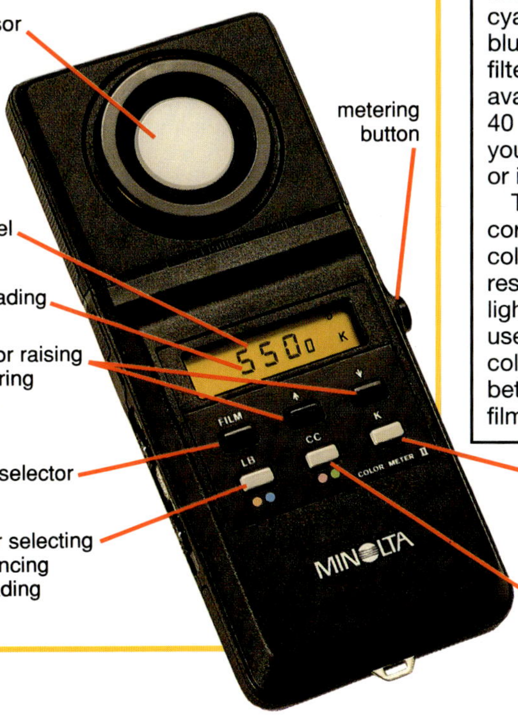

Filter colour

The Kodak Wratten CC (colour compensating) filter range is made up of cyan, yellow, magenta, blue, green and red filters. Each colour is available in 5, 10, 20, 30, 40 and 50 strengths, and you can use them singly, or in combination.

These filters let you correct even slight colour casts, for neutral results under any lighting. They are also useful for correcting colour differences between batches of slide film.

Filters for light sources

Fitting a filter over your camera's lens isn't the only way to balance different colours of light to your film. You can also filter the light source – colour conversion filters for light sources are available as thin coloured plastic sheets.

This technique is useful when you're mixing different types of light sources. For example, an effective studio lighting technique is to use a long exposure and mix flash and tungsten lighting for the studio equivalent of slow-synch fill-in flash. Moving subjects are frozen by the flash, but surrounded by blur from the long exposure using tungsten light. However, while flash gives neutral colours on film, the tungsten lighting gives the blurred parts of the image an orange colour cast.

The solution to the problem is simple – place a blue filter sheet over the tungsten light.

Tip

Mix and match

A useful method for correcting the green colour cast from fluorescent lights is to aim tungsten studio lamps at the fluorescent tubes. The orange cast from the tungsten lights cancels out the green cast from the fluorescent tubes, giving approximately natural colours on the film.

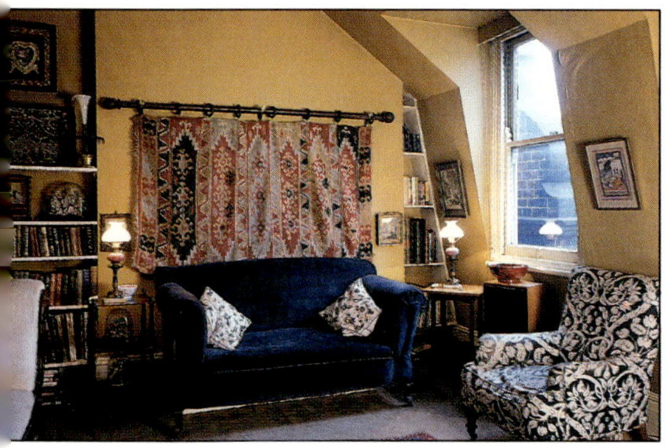

▲ ***The photographer used tungsten studio lamps to light the interior of this room. Shooting on daylight balanced film would have resulted in a strong orange colour cast from the tungsten lamps, so he loaded up with tungsten balanced film instead. However, the sunlight pouring through the window on the right is not balanced to the tungsten film and gives that area of the image a distinct blue cast.***

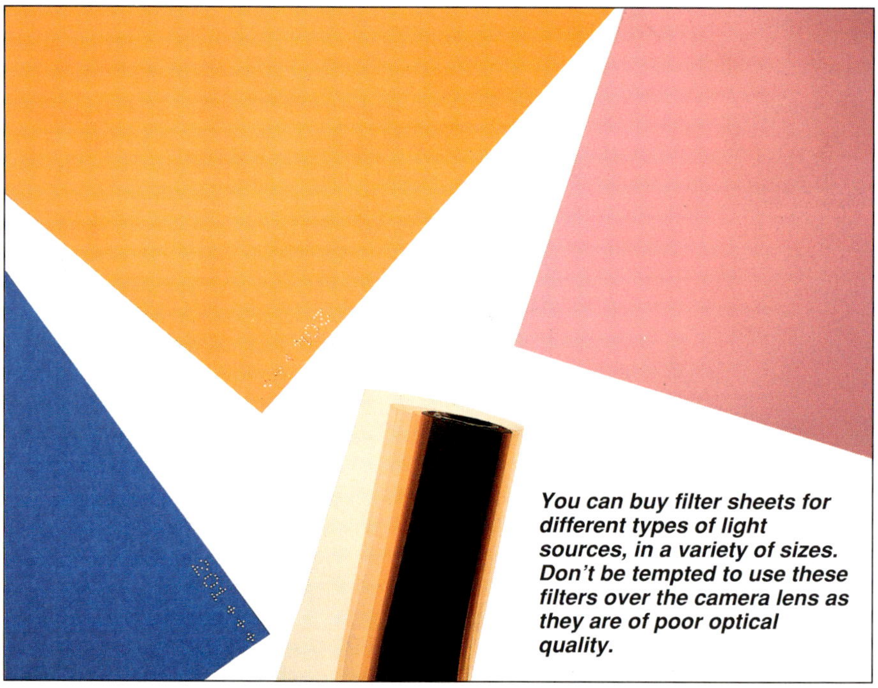

You can buy filter sheets for different types of light sources, in a variety of sizes. Don't be tempted to use these filters over the camera lens as they are of poor optical quality.

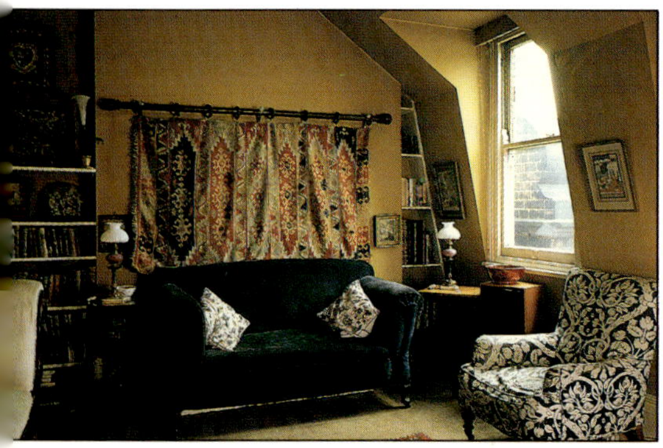

▲ ***The solution was to switch to daylight balanced film and place a blue filter sheet over each light. The filters balanced the colour of the tungsten light to the film. Using daylight film meant the sunlight from the window gave neutral colours. An alternative would have been to leave the lights unfiltered and shoot on tungsten film, but place amber coloured filters over the windows to balance the sunlight to the film.***

Which filter?

BACK TO BASICS

The filter you need to correct colour casts depends on the type of light you're shooting under, and the type of film you're shooting on. The chart provides an at-a-glance guide to which filters give natural results under different artificial light sources – on both daylight balanced and tungsten balanced film. For example, the filter required for shooting under a 60W domestic light bulb using household tungsten balanced film is an 82C cool down filter.

LIGHT SOURCE	DAYLIGHT BALANCED FILM	TUNGSTEN BALANCED FILM
Flash	–	85B
Tungsten studio lamp	80A	81
Tungsten photoflood	80B	81B
60 watt domestic bulb	80B + 82C	82C
Cool white fluorescent tube	30M	60R
Daylight fluorescent tube	40M + 40Y	85B + 40M + 40Y

Graduated filters

If you're fed up with washed out skies and underexposed foregrounds, make room for a set of graduated filters, or 'grads', in your camera bag. You can use them to control the brightness of the sky, or liven up dull areas of the frame with a splash of colour.

Types of grad

Graduated filters are available in two varieties – as mounted glass filters, and oversized, square acrylic filters.

The acrylic filters are the most versatile, as you can vary the height of the tinted area.

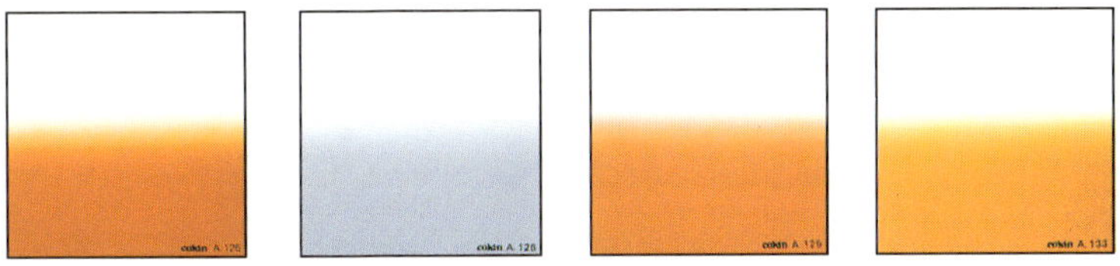

square acrylic filters slot into a system filter holder

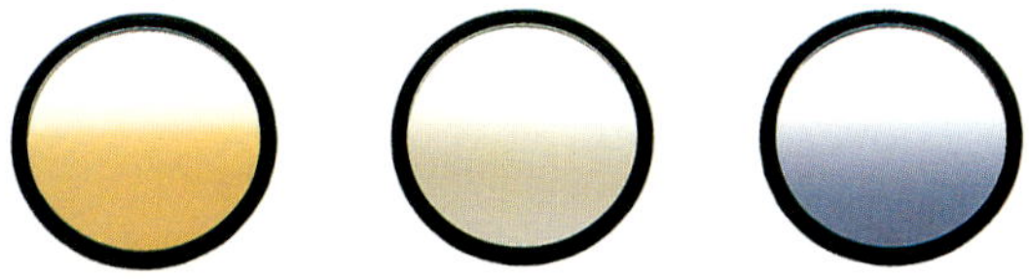

mounted glass graduated filters screw straight on to the end of your lens

Bright skies test your exposure skills to the limit. If you meter from the sky, the ground can turn out underexposed, but if you expose for the ground you are quite likely to end up with a washed out sky. Graduated filters (usually referred to as grads) offer a convenient solution to the problem.

The top area of these filters is tinted with a dye. The tint fades gradually into a clear area at the bottom of the filter. The tinted area blocks some light, while the clear area lets the incoming rays through to the film. If you position the tinted area carefully, you can block some of the light from the sky, so that the exposure for the sky and the ground is the same. This way, both the ground and the sky are recorded correctly.

You can choose whether you want the tinted area to be coloured or a neutral grey. Filters with grey tints are known as neutral density (ND) grads. Coloured grads are available in a variety of colours and change the colour of the scene covered by the tint – neutral density grads do not.

The most popular use for graduated filters is to reduce the brightness of the sky. But there's no reason why you shouldn't use them to balance any bright and dimly lit areas in a scene. Otherwise, you can use the coloured versions to pep up dull areas in the frame.

▼ A strong orange graduated filter is useful if you want to boost the colour and intensity of a sunset. This adds to the picture's romantic atmosphere and enhances the late evening feel of the shot.

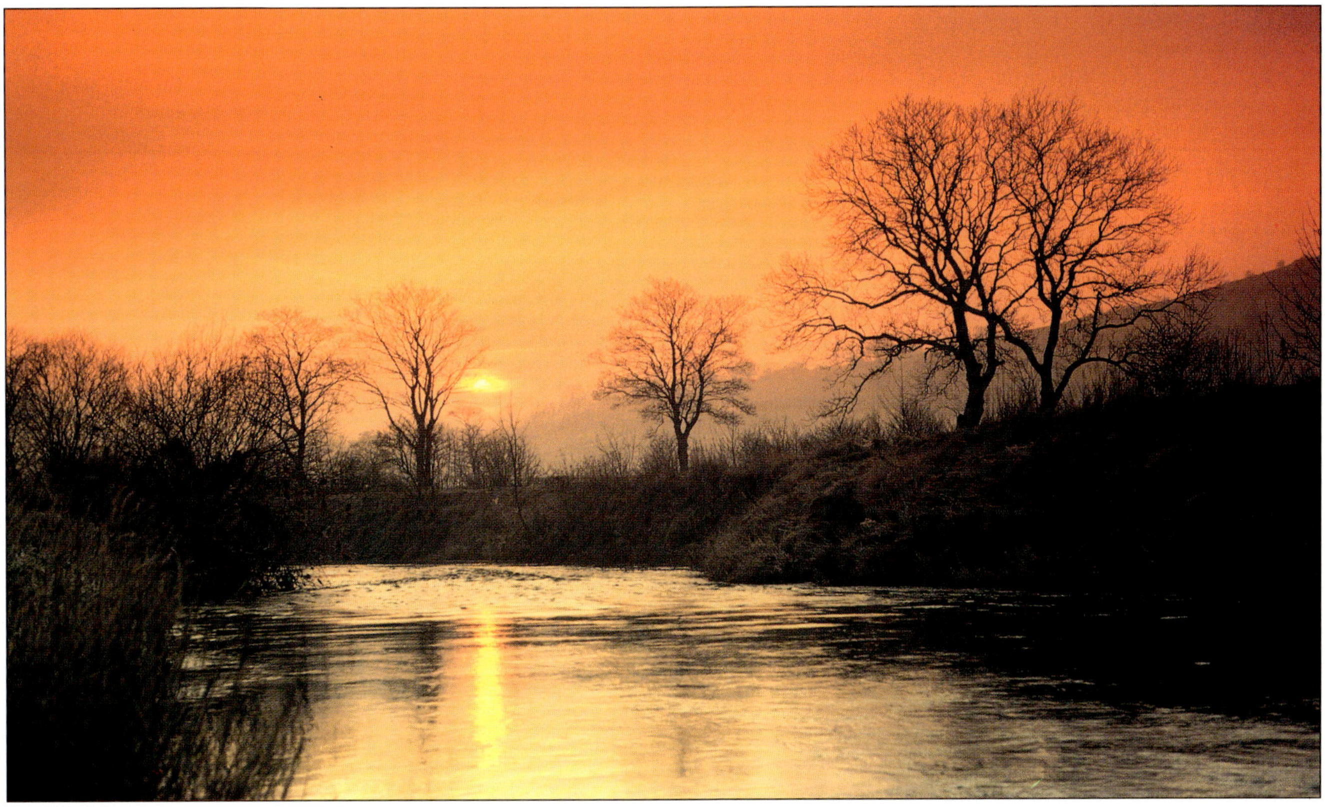

Neutral density grads

If you want to balance the brightness of the light from the sky and the ground without altering the colours in a scene – choose a neutral density grad. The grey tinted area blocks equal amounts of all wavelengths of light, so the colour of the light reaching the film is unaffected by the filter.

Neutral density grads are available in several different strengths to help you to cope with the differing brightness of the sky. The strength of the tinted area – how much light it blocks – is indicated as a factor on the side of the filter itself or on the filter box.

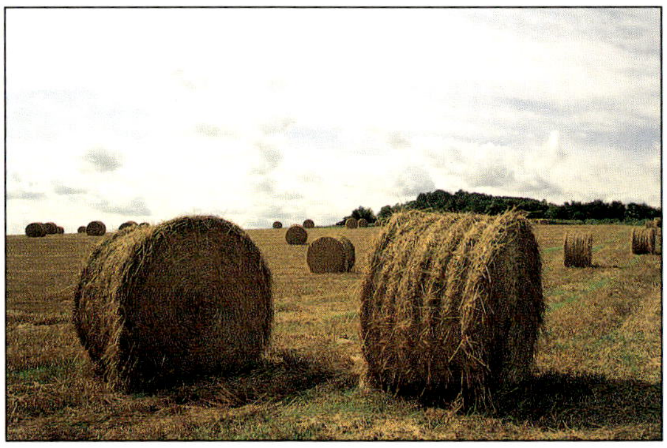

◀ *In this scene the light from the sky is brighter than that from the ground. Setting a correct exposure for the ground means that the sky is overexposed – it looks washed out and cloud details are obscured.*

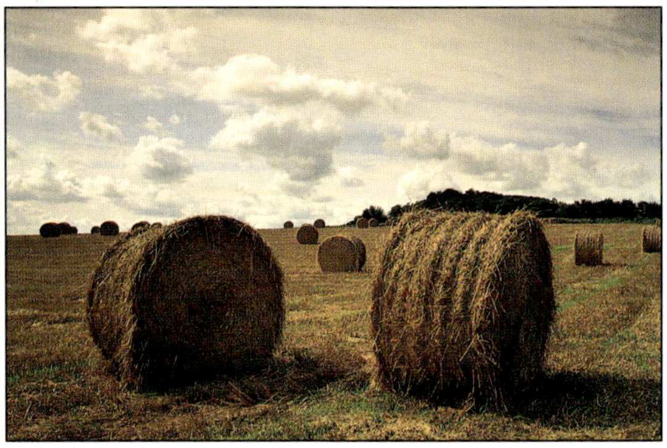

◀ *Fitting a 2X neutral density graduated filter over the lens blocks one stop of light from the sky. This balances the brightness of light from the sky and the ground. Detail is now visible in both areas of the picture.*

Blocking Light

The tinted area on a 2X neutral density grad blocks one stop of light. This means that it reduces the exposure by one shutter speed setting or one f stop. For example, if a meter reading from the sky gives an exposure of 1/125th at f8 and a reading from the ground gives an exposure of 1/60th at f8, this means that the sky is one stop brighter than the ground.

Fitting a 2X neutral density grad blocks one stop of light from the sky, which means that setting the correct exposure for the ground – 1/60th sec at f8 – correctly exposes the sky as well. A 4X neutral density grad blocks two stops of light.

Exposure

When you're using a grad you need to pay careful attention to exposure. If you use your camera's TTL meter, it's best to take a reading without the grad in place. Point the camera at the ground – or the area that will be covered by the clear area of the filter – and take a reading. Then lift the camera up and point it at the sky – or the area that will be covered by the tinted area – and take a second reading.

The difference between the two readings tells you how much brighter the sky is than the ground. Set the exposure for the ground and fit a grad to balance the sky to this exposure. However, you may not want a balanced exposure – for example, why not darken the sky further for a stormy look.

Aperture and focal length

BACK TO BASICS

When you're using a grad, you have to take care over the focal length of the lens you choose, the aperture you set and the distance you focus from the camera. These factors affect depth of field, which influences the filter's effect on the image.

Wide depth of field means the boundary between the tinted and the clear areas can be seen very distinctly. Narrow depth of field means the boundary is more likely to be blurred so you gain a softer, more graduated effect.

Be especially careful when you use a graduated filter with a wide angle lens for landscape pictures. The lens' characteristic depth of field, together with the narrow apertures and wide depth of field used for landscape photography, means that your pictures may have a distinct line running across them where the tinted area fades into the clear area. If your camera has depth of field preview use it to check the effect you will get on film. Open up a stop or two if you want a more graduated effect.

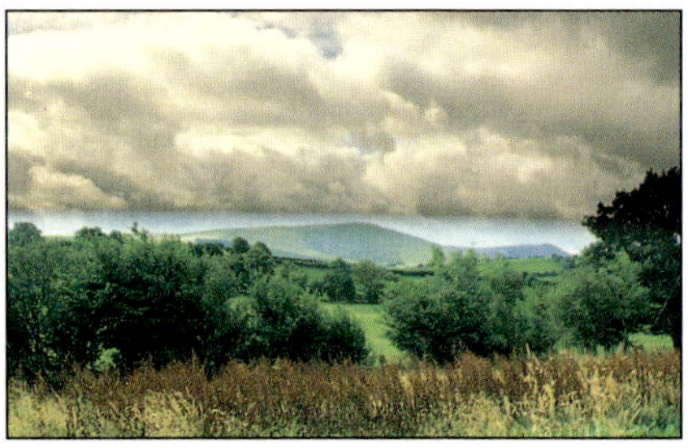

▲ *A small aperture on a wide angle gives wide depth of field. This keeps the filter in fairly sharp focus, so the boundary between the tinted and clear areas is clearly defined.*

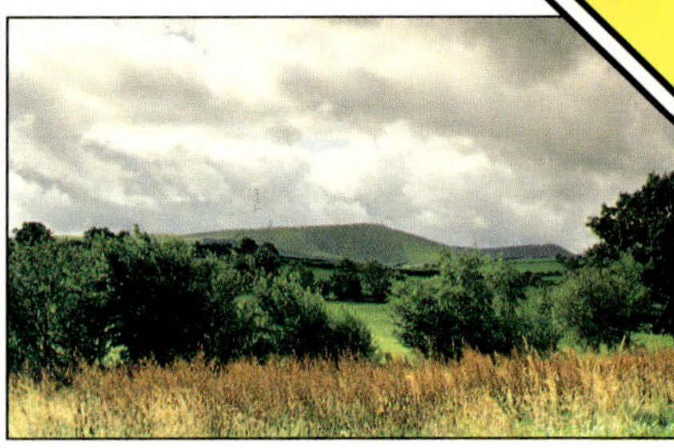

▲ *Setting the lens to a wider aperture gives less depth of field. This throws the filter out of focus and blurs the boundary between the tinted and clear areas for a more acceptable result.*

Coloured grads

If you want to add a dash of colour to a grey sky, or change the colour of a brightly lit foreground, fit a coloured grad over your lens. The tinted area on these filters is made up from a coloured dye, which fades gradually into the clear bottom half of the filter.

There is a wide range of coloured grads available, which gives you maximum control over the look of your final images. For example, using an orange grad on a sunset boosts the natural yellow-orange colour of the sky, whereas fitting a purple grad changes the entire feel of the shot – giving a more sombre feel.

Coloured grads can be used to dramatic effect, but you should fit them sparingly. Individual shots lose their impact if you fill your photo album full of pictures with technicoloured skies. Also, you should be selective about when you use these filters. While creative use of coloured grads can turn an ordinary shot into a masterpiece, used unwisely they can have the opposite effect, and ruin an otherwise good photograph.

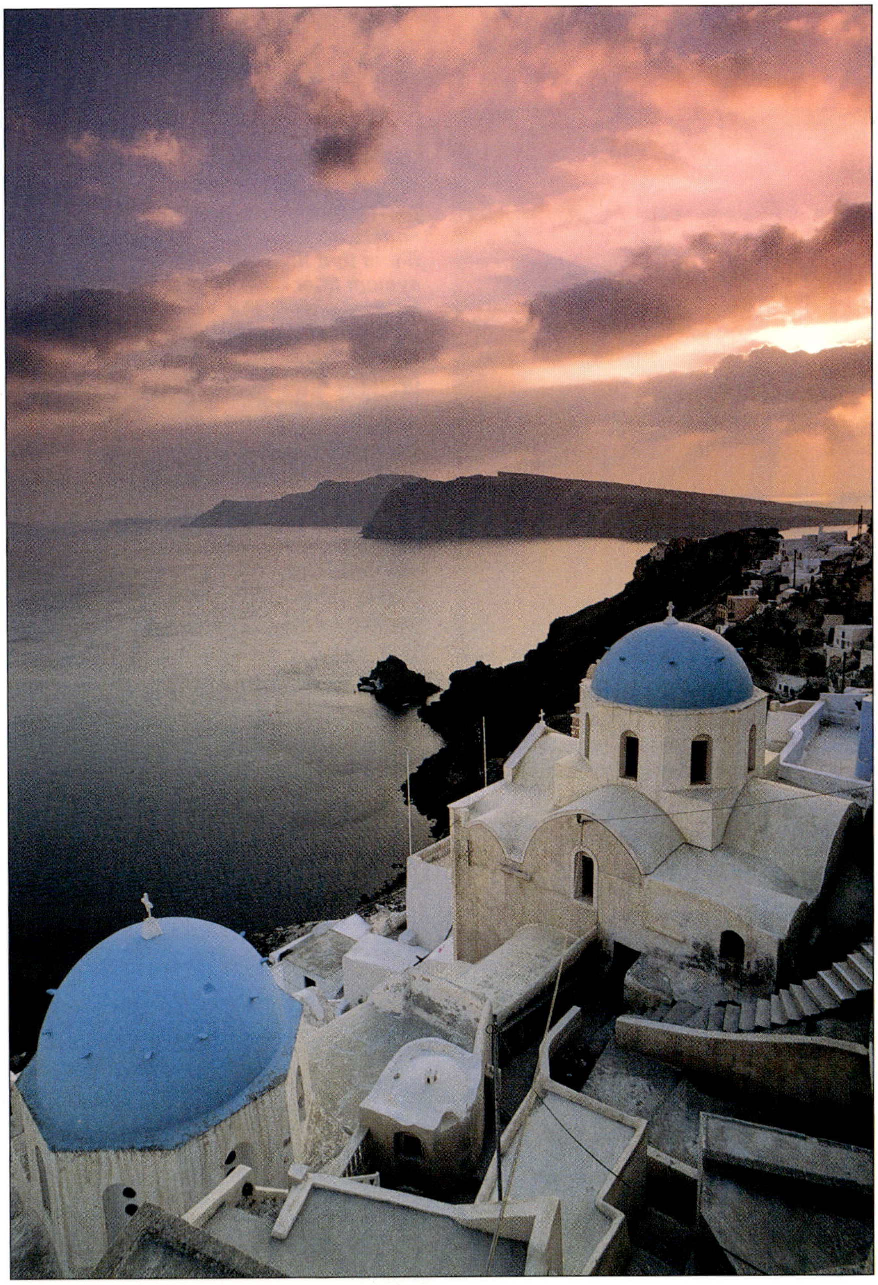

▶ ***You don't have to use a graduated filter to balance areas of sky and ground. In this shot, a coloured one was used to underexpose the sky and bring out the clouds, to create a moody atmosphere.***

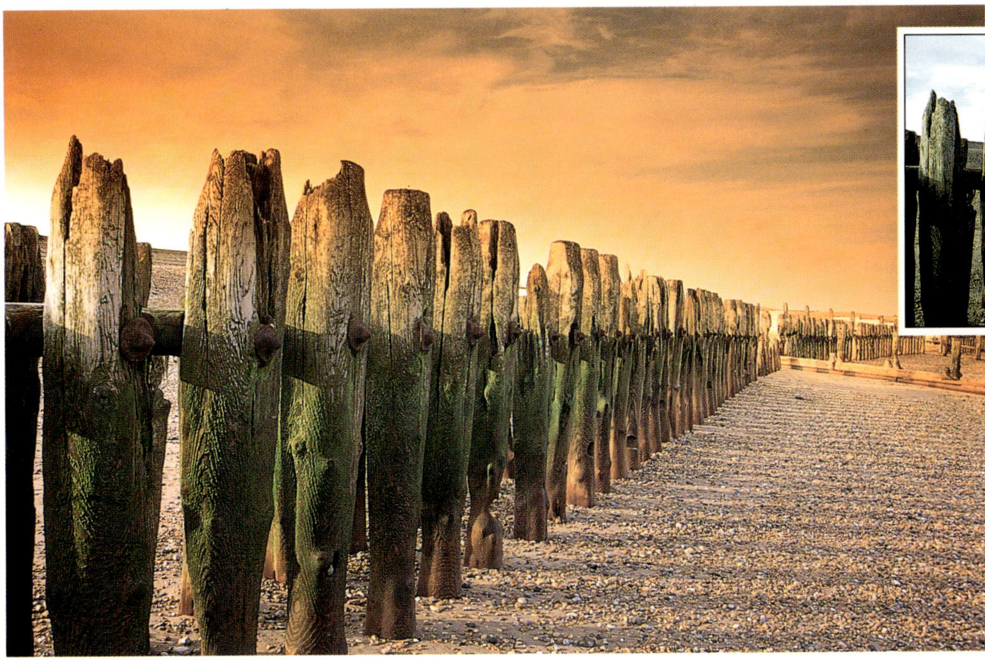

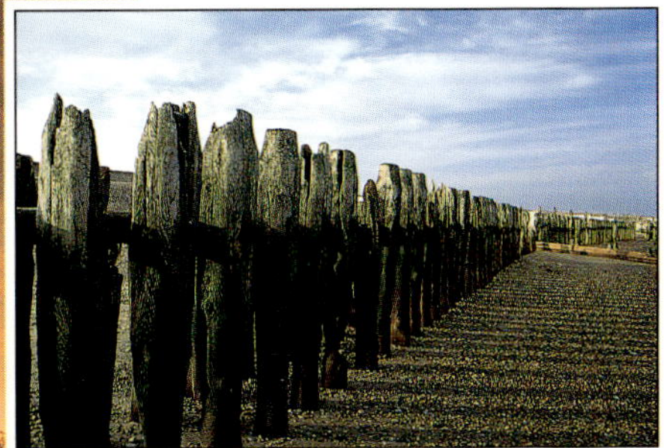

◀▲ ***You can lift an ordinary picture to create an attention-grabbing image by fitting two graduated filters over the lens at the same time. Here, the photographer fitted a tobacco one over the sky in the normal way, and then positioned a mauve one upside down, so that it covered the foreground.***

Subjects for backlighting

Backlighting can be very useful for portraits, giving an attractive halo effect to the subject.

It also solves a problem that can occur with frontlighting, where the subject may squint and frown because the sun is shining directly into their face.

When direct sunlight casts strong, unwanted shadows across the subject's face, putting the sun behind them will send their whole face into shadow. Expose for the shadows so you can see the detail of the features. There will be no strong highlights and the overall effect will be softer and with more detail showing.

Backlighting is also a good choice for trees and other plants. It lights up every detail and the colours appear richer and darker than in a frontlit picture.

It is particularly effective for translucent subjects like petals and leaves – it emphasizes each vein and hair.

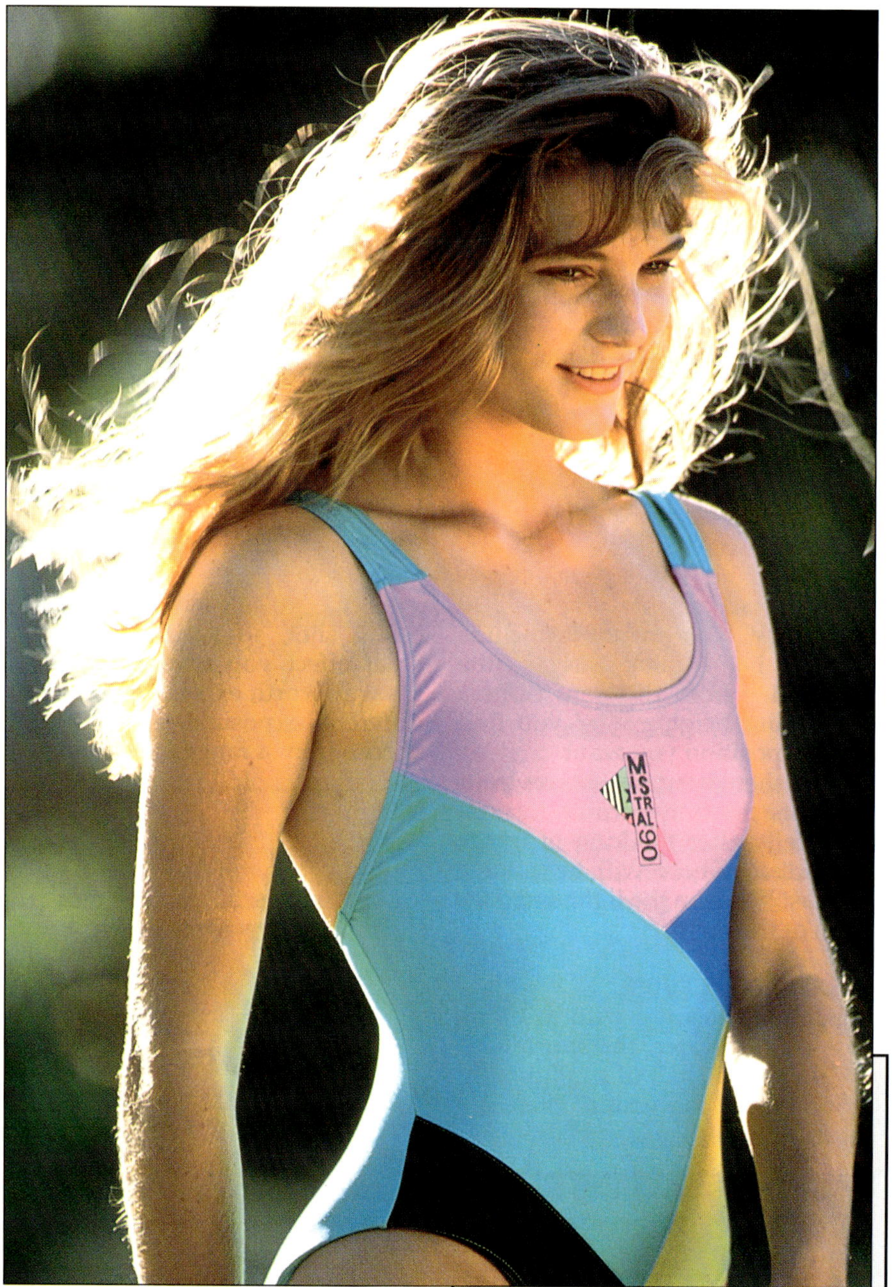

▶ HIGHLIGHTING HAIR
This picture is exposed for the shadow areas of the face and body, so the backlit hair acquires a bright, pleasingly overexposed halo.

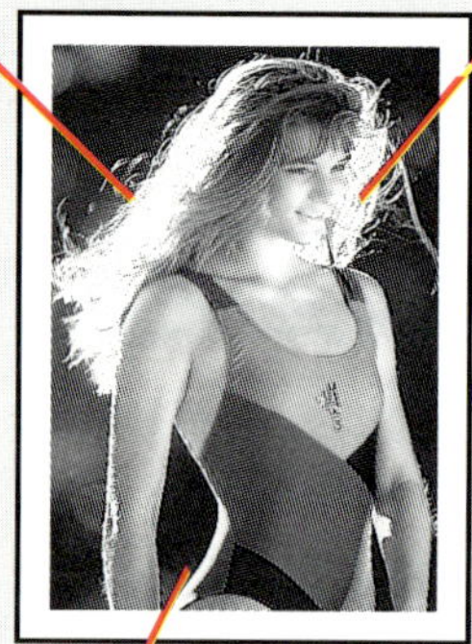

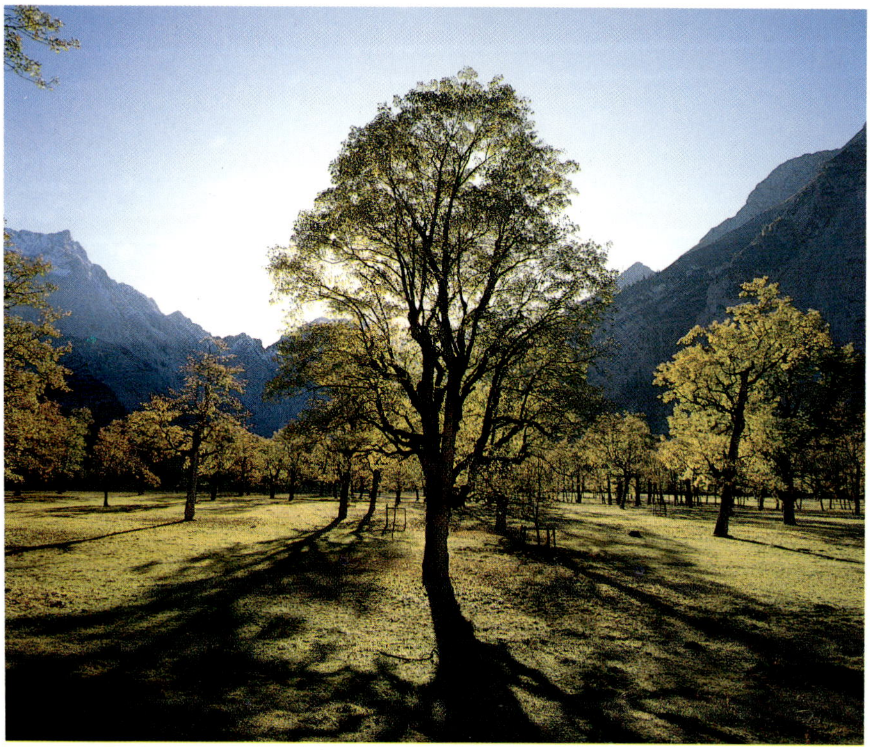

◀ NATURAL BEAUTY
Nature provides some beautiful subjects for backlighting. The sun shining through the leaves adds a rim of glowing highlights. In contrast, the dramatic shadows add a dark pattern which echoes the outline of the mountains.

Coloured grads

If you want to add a dash of colour to a grey sky, or change the colour of a brightly lit foreground, fit a coloured grad over your lens. The tinted area on these filters is made up from a coloured dye, which fades gradually into the clear bottom half of the filter.

There is a wide range of coloured grads available, which gives you maximum control over the look of your final images. For example, using an orange grad on a sunset boosts the natural yellow-orange colour of the sky, whereas fitting a purple grad changes the entire feel of the shot – giving a more sombre feel.

Coloured grads can be used to dramatic effect, but you should fit them sparingly. Individual shots lose their impact if you fill your photo album full of pictures with technicoloured skies. Also, you should be selective about when you use these filters. While creative use of coloured grads can turn an ordinary shot into a masterpiece, used unwisely they can have the opposite effect, and ruin an otherwise good photograph.

▶ You don't have to use a graduated filter to balance areas of sky and ground. In this shot, a coloured one was used to underexpose the sky and bring out the clouds, to create a moody atmosphere.

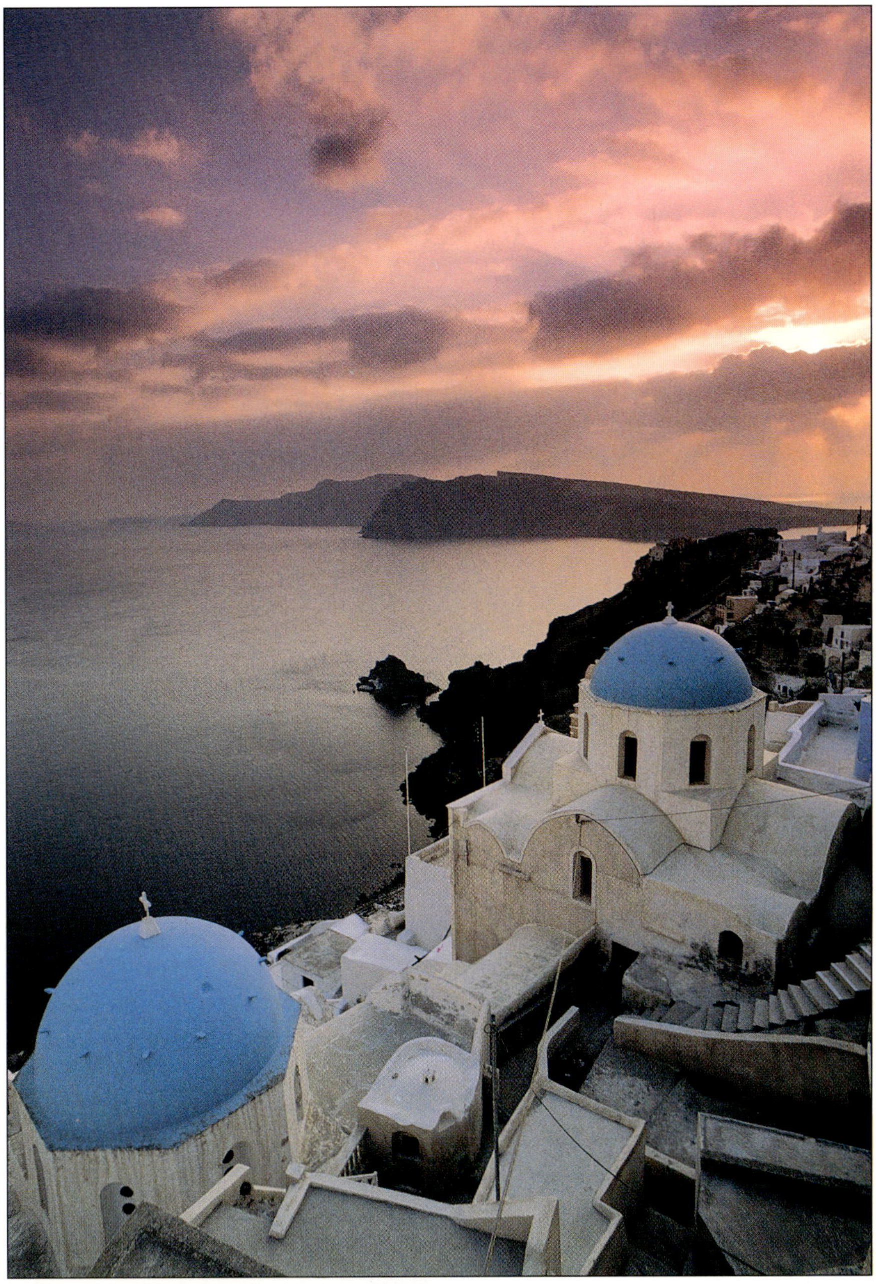

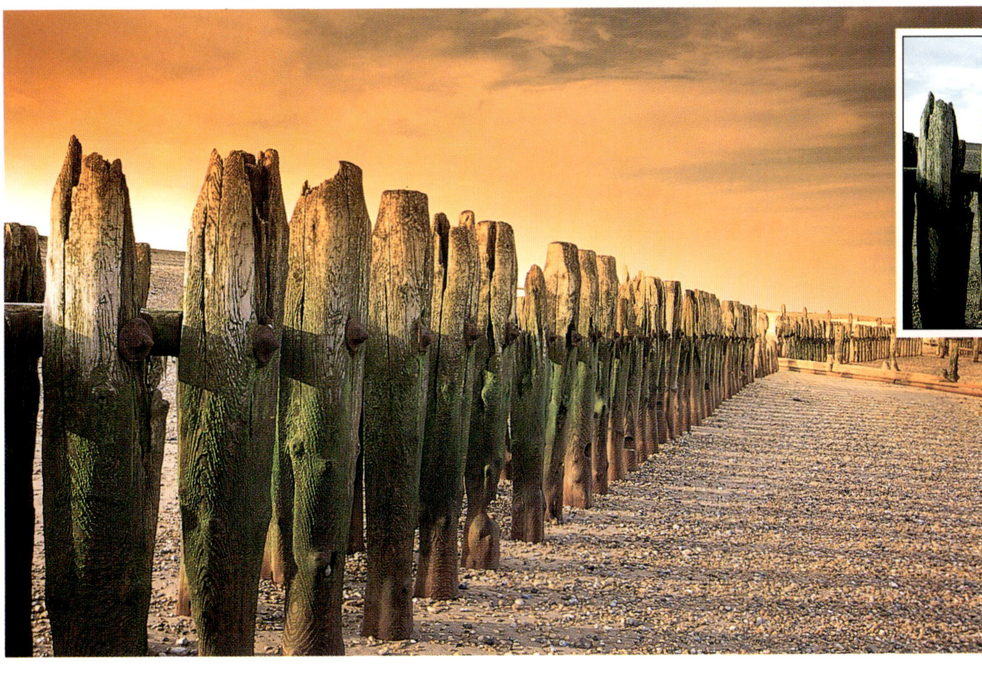

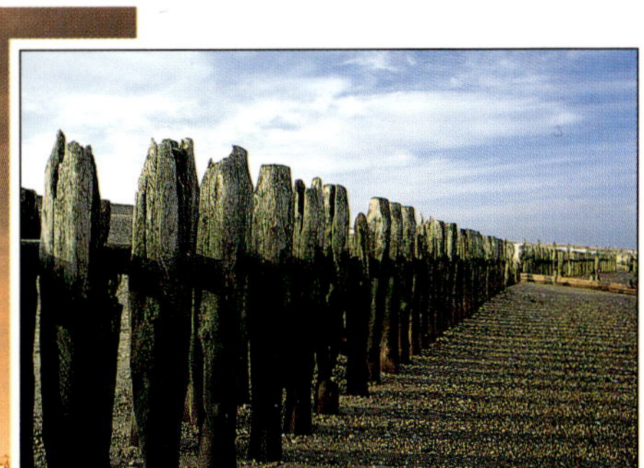

◀ ▲ You can lift an ordinary picture to create an attention-grabbing image by fitting two graduated filters over the lens at the same time. Here, the photographer fitted a tobacco one over the sky in the normal way, and then positioned a mauve one upside down, so that it covered the foreground.

Positioning a grad

Glass graduated filters are mounted on a rotatable mount, similar to that used on polarizing filters. This lets you alter the angle of the boundary between the tinted and clear areas of the filter to match the angle of the horizon.

For example, imagine photographing one face of a vertical mountain-side, with sky on one side of the frame. Using the filter in its horizontal position would darken only half of the sky as well as half of the mountain. Twisting the filter so the tinted area lies over the sky gets around this problem and allows you to make a correct exposure.

Square, acrylic filters can be twisted in different directions, and they can also be moved up and down in the filter holder to alter the height of the tinted area in the frame. For example, if you want to place the horizon low in the frame, you simply move the filter downwards to the correct position. If you want the horizon high in the frame, do the opposite. This makes these types of grads more versatile than the glass mounted varieties.

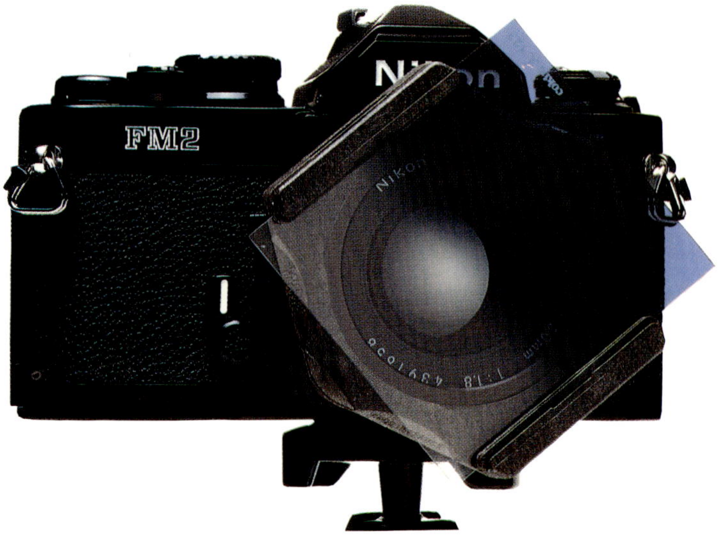

▶ ***The oversized, square acrylic filters that fit system filter holders are versatile and easy to use. You can twist the filter to match the angle of the horizon. They also let you alter the height of the graduated tinted area within the frame, so you can cope with high and low horizons.***

Watch the foreground

The most important thing to bear in mind when using a grad, especially a coloured grad, is that the tinted area affects everything that it covers in the scene – not just the sky. This can cause problems, especially when there is a subject in the foreground of your shot. For example, if you fit a blue grad over your lens for an outdoor portrait you are likely to come up with a rich blue sky in the background, but the shot will be ruined because part of your subject's face will also take on a blue tint.

If you want to include a foreground object, position it in the part of the frame covered by the clear area of the filter. Otherwise, use two angled filters – one on either side of the subject.

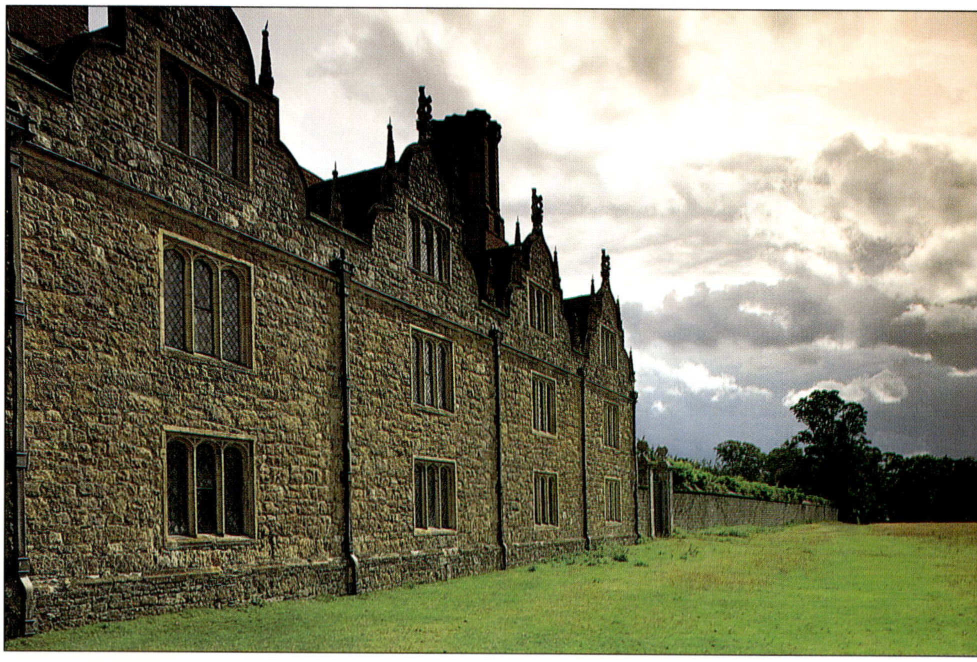

▲ ***To balance the exposure for the sky and the building, the photographer twisted the filter so that the boundary between the tinted and clear areas was positioned to line up with the rooftop.***

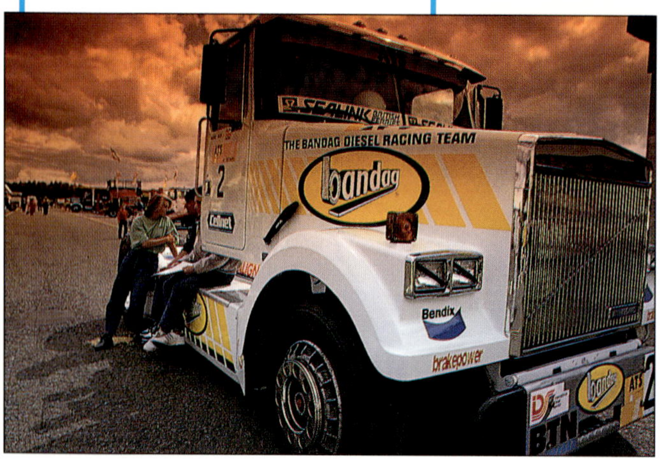

◀ ***This wide angle shot is a perfect example of how not to use a graduated filter. The colour of the filter looks unnatural and doesn't suit the subject matter. Wide depth of field means there's a distinct line between the coloured and clear parts of the picture and the photographer has positioned the filter so that it covers part of the subject.***

Shooting into the sun

Backlighting a subject, by shooting towards the sun, produces stunning effects. You can create a halo or rim of light around a subject or throw it dramatically into silhouette.

Photographing into the sun opens up a whole range of creative choices. The first decision you need to make is whether or not to include the sun itself. Look through the viewfinder from different camera angles and heights until you find the composition you want.

You then need to choose your exposure carefully because this can drastically alter the kind of image you create. There will be a huge contrast between the light and dark areas of the picture.

The choice is yours

Imagine a seascape with a sailing boat on the water, the sun low in the sky and a shaft of sunlight glittering across the water. There are several choices you can make about how to expose the picture.

You could measure exposure so that the sun shining through the sail is the main feature. The sea would appear black and the shaft of light mid grey.

If you correctly expose the boat, the sea will be severely burnt out (overexposed). And if you measure exposure for the sea, the boat is thrown into silhouette and the emphasis is on the glimmering water.

Each exposure will give an interesting shot, so you must decide what effect you want to achieve. It's well worth experimenting with different exposures so you can choose from a range of results.

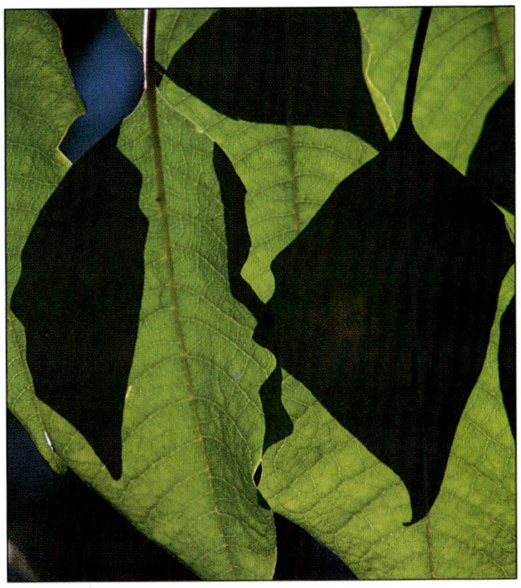

▲ SHINING THROUGH
Plants become almost transparent when backlit and leaf veins show up as the sun shines through them.

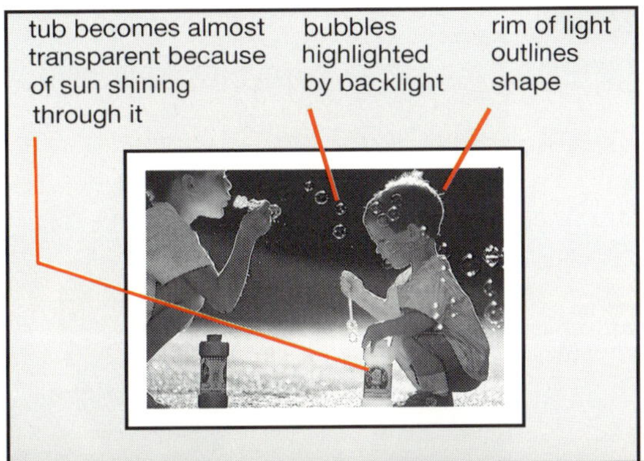

▼ BACKLIT BUBBLES
By crouching, the photographer frames the children against the shadow area. The 'halo' effect would not be seen from a higher viewpoint, which would frame the children against the sunlit paving.

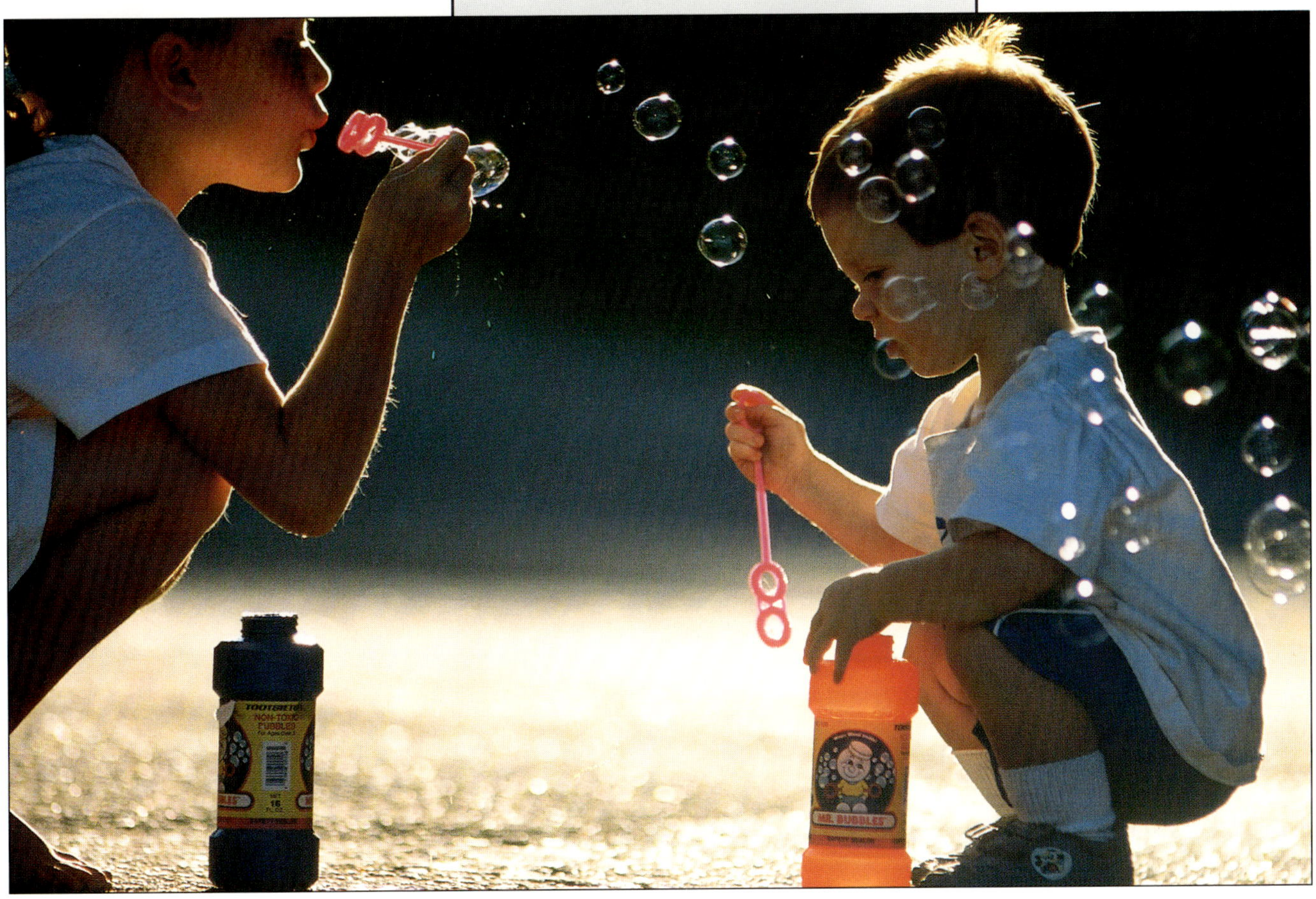

Subjects for backlighting

Backlighting can be very useful for portraits, giving an attractive halo effect to the subject.

It also solves a problem that can occur with frontlighting, where the subject may squint and frown because the sun is shining directly into their face.

When direct sunlight casts strong, unwanted shadows across the subject's face, putting the sun behind them will send their whole face into shadow. Expose for the shadows so you can see the detail of the features. There will be no strong highlights and the overall effect will be softer and with more detail showing.

Backlighting is also a good choice for trees and other plants. It lights up every detail and the colours appear richer and darker than in a frontlit picture.

It is particularly effective for translucent subjects like petals and leaves – it emphasizes each vein and hair.

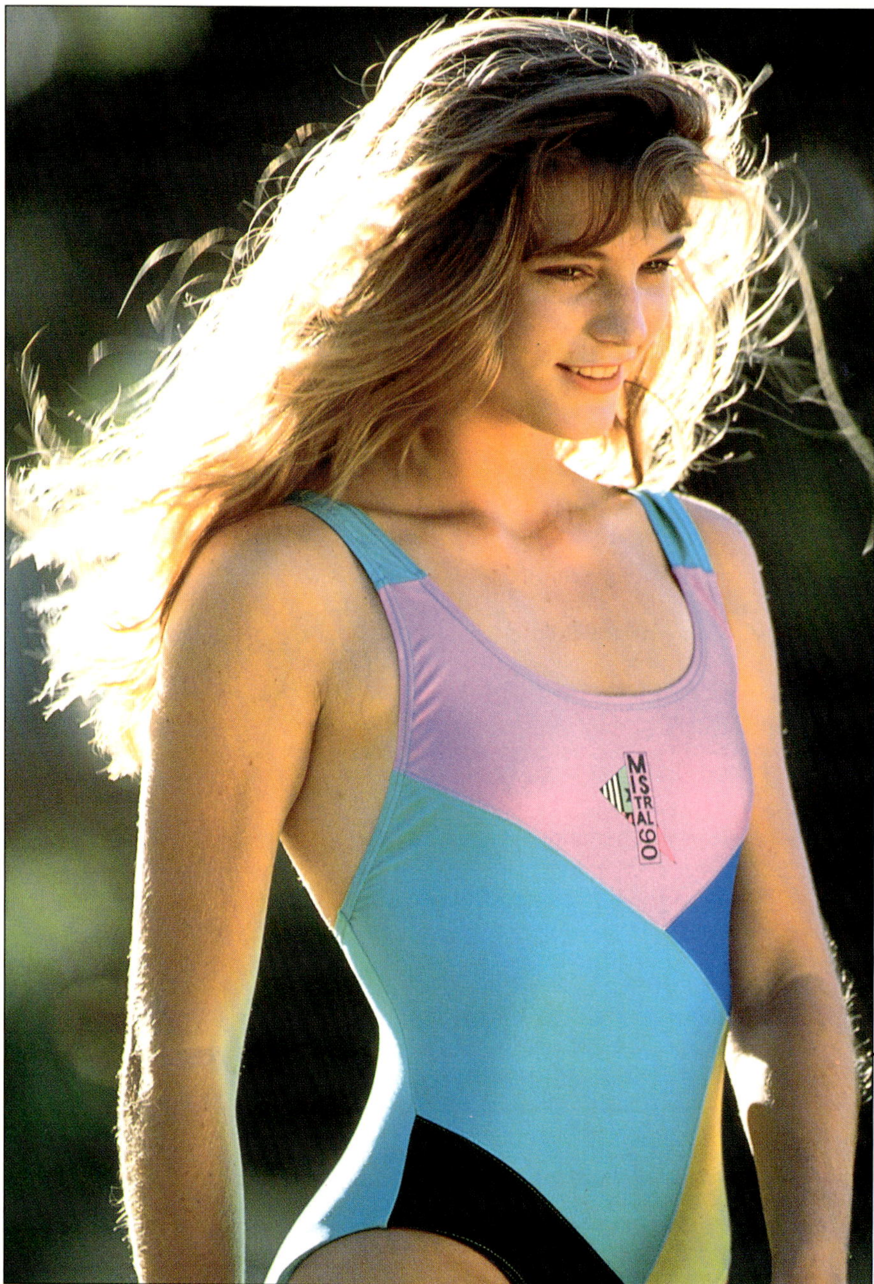

▶ **HIGHLIGHTING HAIR**
This picture is exposed for the shadow areas of the face and body, so the backlit hair acquires a bright, pleasingly overexposed halo.

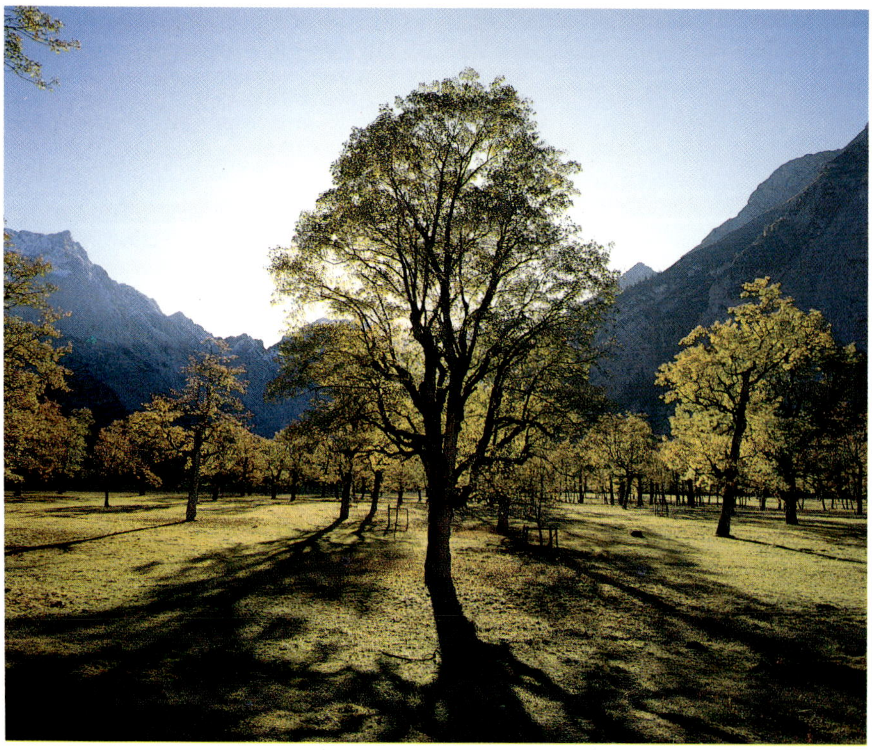

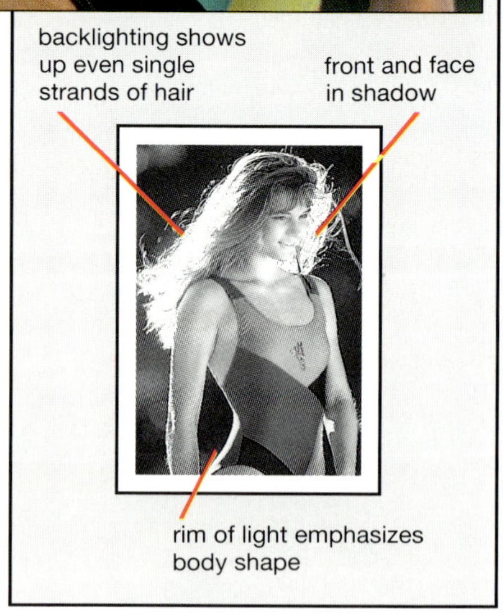

◀ **NATURAL BEAUTY**
Nature provides some beautiful subjects for backlighting. The sun shining through the leaves adds a rim of glowing highlights. In contrast, the dramatic shadows add a dark pattern which echoes the outline of the mountains.

Creative flare

Shooting into the sun can present problems which you normally try to eliminate. However, sometimes you can use them to your advantage. If the light is shining straight into the lens it creates 'ghost' shapes, known as flare, in a variety of colours and sizes on the photo. This is not generally desirable.

To avoid flare, you can shade the lens with your hand or a lens hood. To be on the safe side, try to make sure the sun is not directly in view but is hidden behind a natural barrier such as a tree.

Flare can also appear in the photo simply as a pale misty area rather than in definite shapes. This can sometimes add atmosphere to a picture.

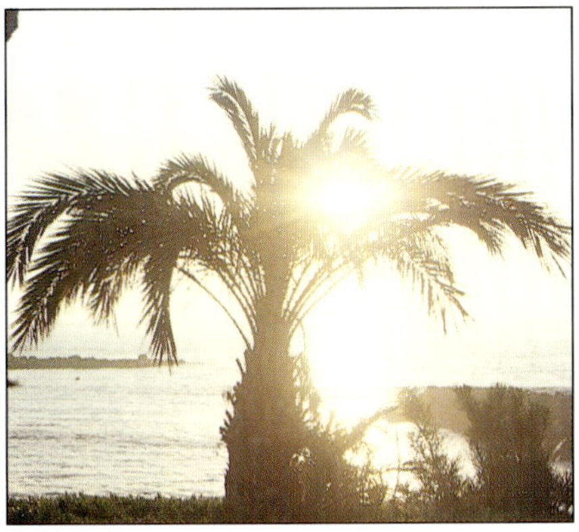

▲▼ USING FLARE
The flare 'burns out' too much of the tree (above). By changing the camera angle slightly to put more of the tree in front of the sun, the flare is reduced (below).

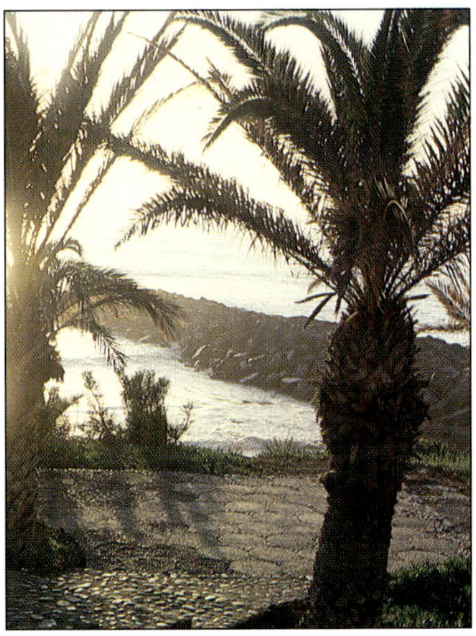

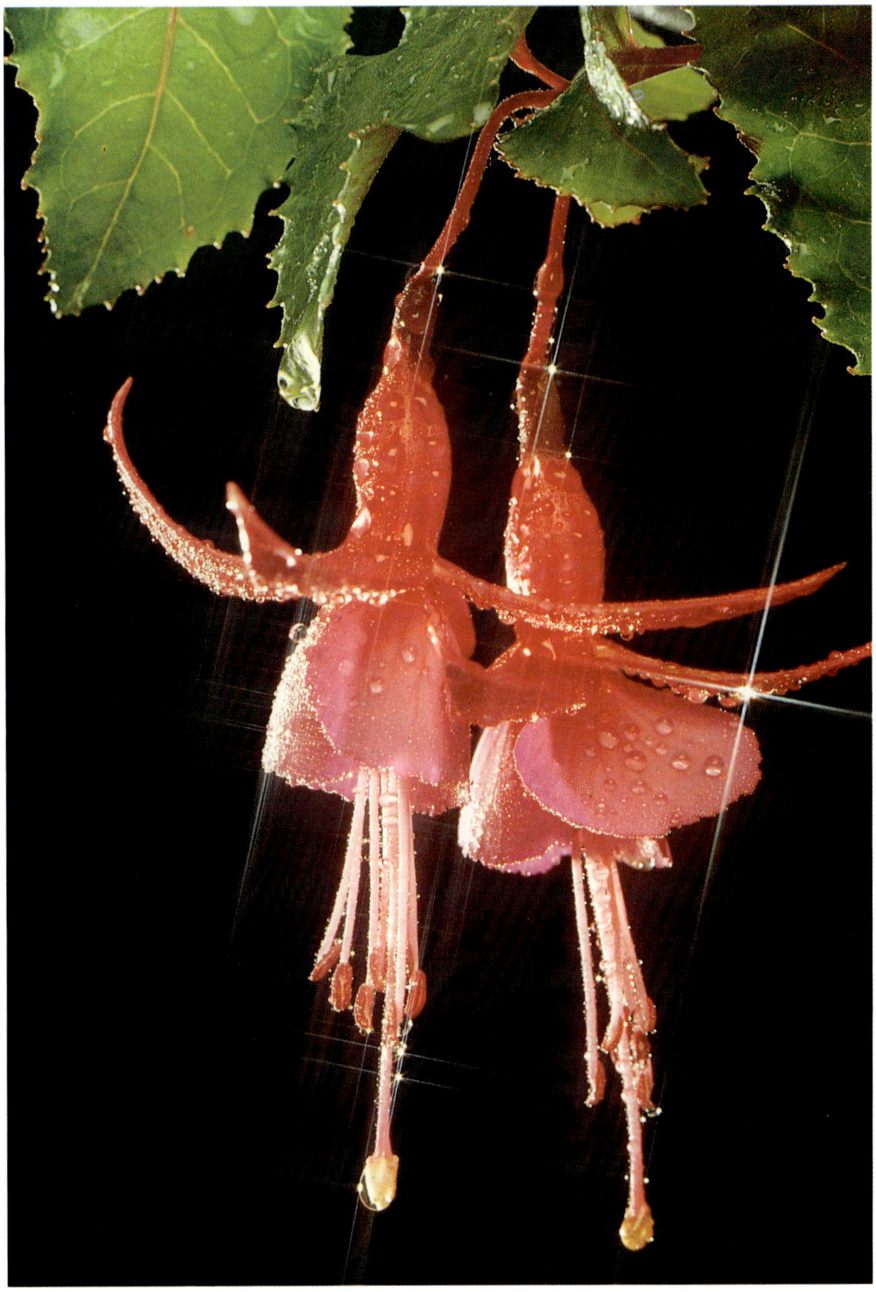

▲STARBURST FILTER
This filter combines well with backlighting. It exaggerates highlights and freshens delicate subjects like flowers. Here the highlights on the water droplets are streaked into star-like lines by the filter.

Filters and flare

With clever use of filters you can improve your backlit pictures, and even exaggerate flare so it becomes a feature rather than an eyesore.

A starburst filter One way of making use of flare is to fit a starburst filter over the lens. This has a square pattern etched on a clear piece of glass, and creates lines streaking out in the shape of a star from the centre of the flare.

Starbursts are best with subject matter that's not too 'solid' – for instance leaves, flowers or ripples on water rather than buildings or figures. As well as the colours glowing from backlight, you can give the specks of light a twinkle.

A skylight filter is also worth considering for any backlit picture. It doesn't alter flare, but gives a slightly pink warmth to shadows, which tend to pick up a bluish tinge if the sky is blue.

Tip: Overcoming exposure problems

A general rule for exposure control for subjects against the light is to give an extra one and a half stops on top of that indicated on the meter. However, under extremely bright conditions you may have to give up to four times the exposure indicated. Some cameras have a backlight button which does this for you.

Silhouettes

One great joy of the light at sunset and sunrise is that the sun produces an attractive orange or red colour cast. The warm glow of the light gives an atmospheric feel to what might otherwise be a dull picture.

Including a silhouette shape such as a boat, a tree or a building adds drama and interest to a sunset picture. Choose a solid, clearly outlined shape which will look effective as a silhouette.

Take a meter reading from the sky just as the sun has gone below the horizon. Then backlit subjects are thrown into shadow and they become silhouettes.

The light changes so quickly at sunset that you must check exposure almost continuously. Within just one minute the exposure can have changed by a whole f stop, so keep shooting before it's pitch dark.

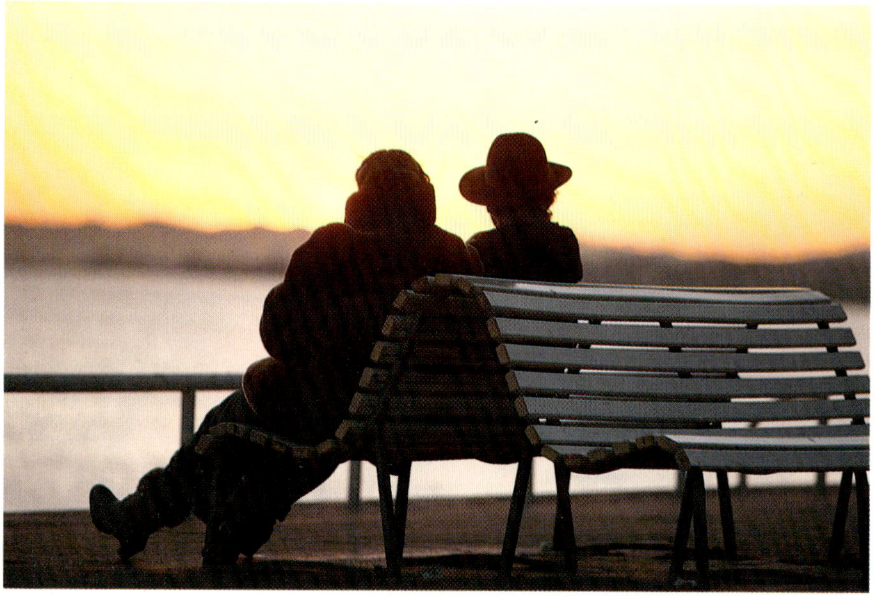

Tip

Danger!

You could seriously damage your eyes by looking through a telephoto lens at the sun. It is safe to do so only if the sun is weak enough for you to look at it with the naked eye without blinking. If possible, note where the sun is when you're composing and don't look in that area.

◀ FOREGROUND SILHOUETTES
The dark, backlit shapes made by the man's hat and the woman's coat give a solid, motionless feel to the scene. The figures invite you to admire the pink outline rim on the backlit hills.

▶ SUN ON SEA
Exposing for the glittering waves turns the intricate shape of the pier into a delicate silhouette, and the picture becomes almost monochromatic. The distance between subjects adds depth to what would otherwise be a rather flat image.

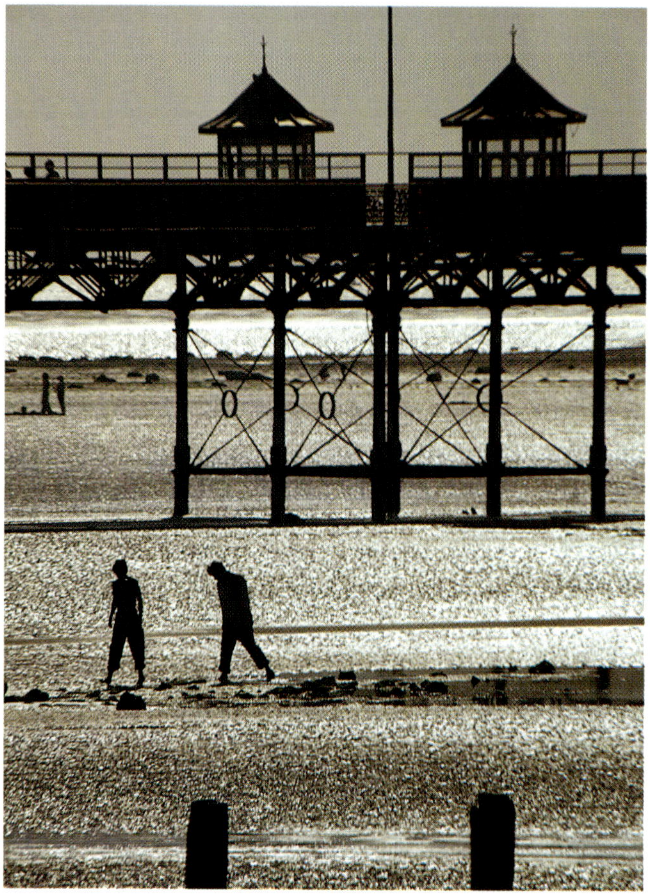

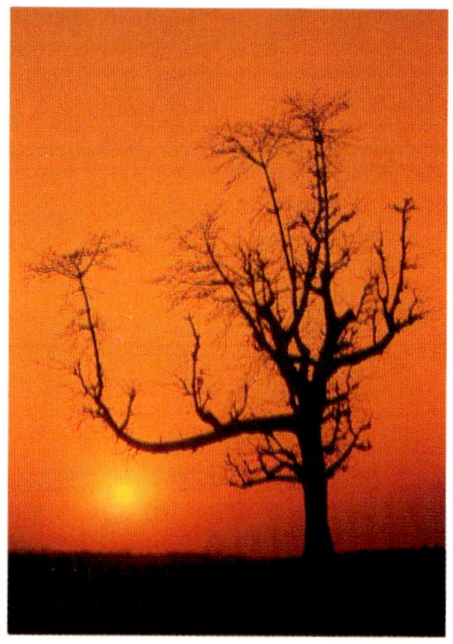

▲ SUNSET AND SIMPLICITY
Exposing for the sky emphasizes the stark foreground silhouette. The photographer chooses a camera angle that's low enough to leave out everything except the tree but still includes the hazy setting sun.

CHECK IT! ✓

When using backlighting you need to:

- ❑ avoid unwanted flare by shielding the lens or changing the angle of the shot.
- ❑ decide what part of the picture to use to measure exposure.
- ❑ remember *never* to look straight at the sun, particularly with a telephoto lens.

Capturing reflections

From the crystal clear to the abstract, the sharp to the distorted, reflections offer the imaginative photographer a great deal of scope for producing some stunning, and often unusual, pictures.

The first step in taking pictures of reflections is teaching yourself to notice them – this isn't quite as simple as it seems because we tend to ignore the reflections around us in everyday life.

In photography, reflections are often avoided because of their confusing effect on the subject of an image. But reflections can make interesting pictures in their own right. Think of bright, neon lights reflected in a puddle, your own face in a mirror or a sunset reflected in a window.

Mirrors, glass, polished silver and chrome, water and even glossy paint all reflect images of the world around them; and by varying your viewpoint you can choose whether to include both the subject and its reflection or just the reflection itself.

Ways with water

Water relies on reflections to give it colour and substance. Time affects the 'colour' of water too, because as the day progresses and the light shifts from blue, through neutral, to red, so its surface reflects these changes in tone.

This enables you to get several quite different shots of the same subject by waiting for the lighting to change. Think of the blue tones of a lake in early morning light or the orange hues on the same lake at sunset.

Movement also affects reflections in water. When the water is still you will get an almost perfect mirror image, but when it is disturbed by a breeze, say, a more abstract, rippled effect results. Or create ripples of your own by throwing a stone into water.

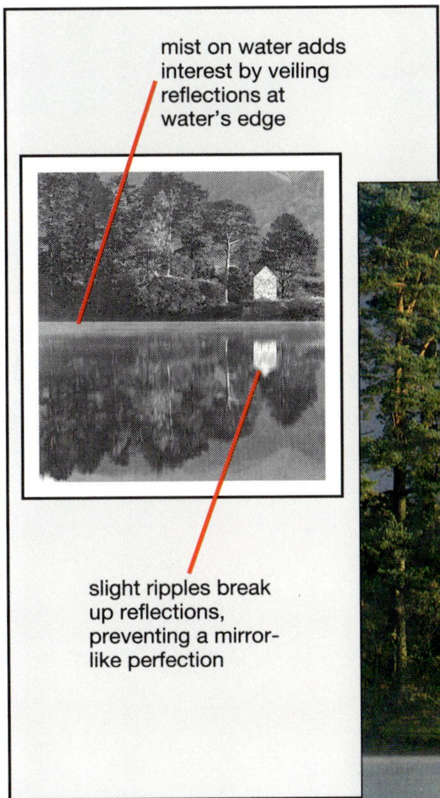

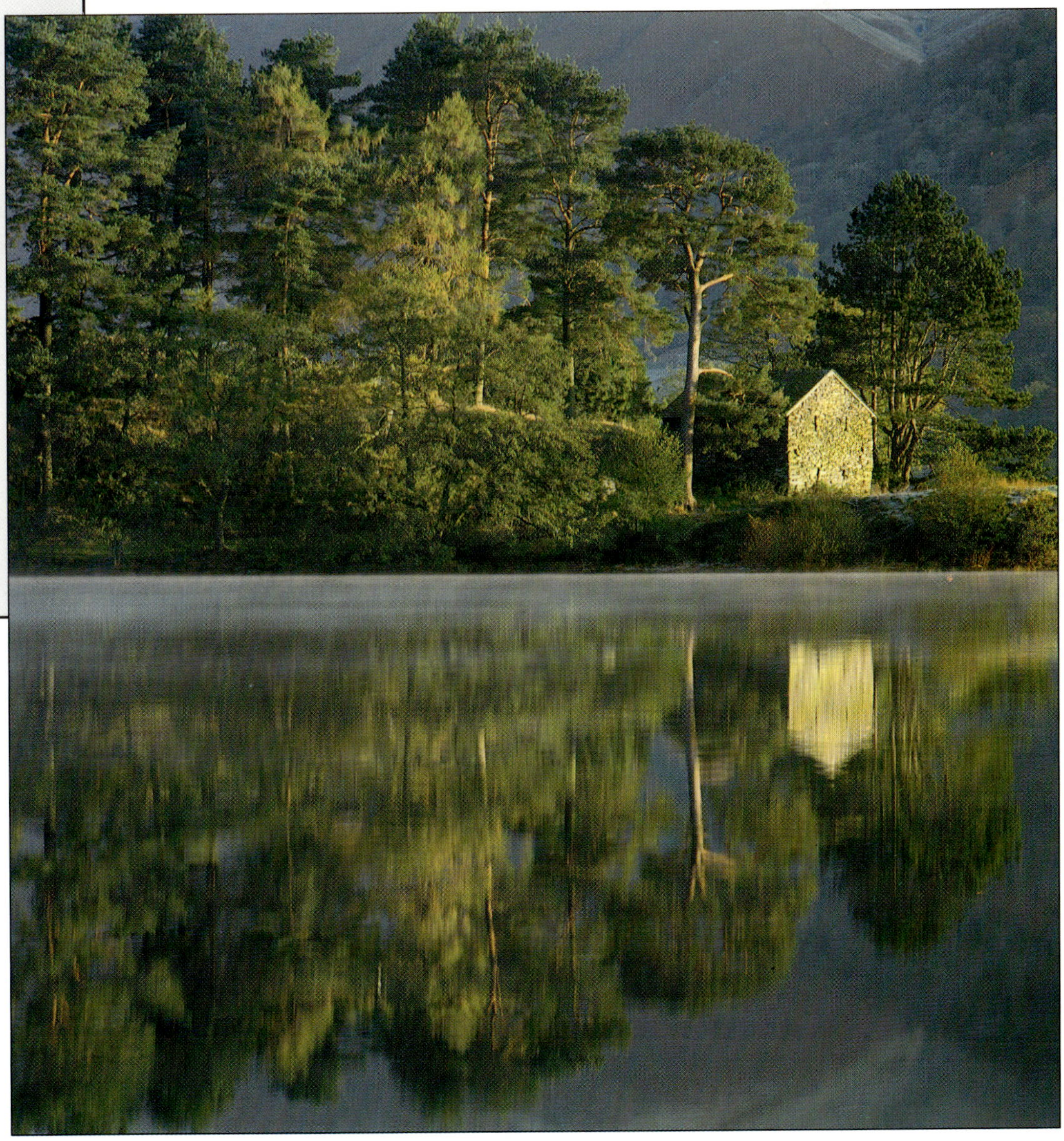

▶ **ON THE WATERFRONT**
Think of reflections and most people usually imagine mountains and trees mirrored in a lake – it's the classic shot. The photographer waited for late afternoon sunlight to highlight the barn and surrounding trees, giving a wide range of hues.

Using mirrors

Mirrors are perhaps the most obvious source of reflections, and because they form a natural frame around a subject they are ideal for portraits. But remember that the distance between your camera and the subject is not the same as the distance between your camera and the mirror.

So to keep the mirror and subject sharp you need to make sure that the depth of field is sufficiently large to keep both planes in focus.

However, many successful pictures are taken of mirrors where the mirror frame is sharp but the reflection is out of focus. For this, romantic, effect you should aim for as narrow a depth of field as possible and focus on the mirror.

Multi-mirrors

Using more than one mirror produces some clever pictures, too. For example, by adding another angled mirror you can reflect a second view of your subject, so that their face and profile are in the same shot.

This technique is also useful when shooting interiors since it allows you to show part of a room not covered by the camera's angle of view. Seek out reflections in the wing mirrors of cars or in shop windows. Or capture your friends in distorted mirrors at fairgrounds for some amusing results.

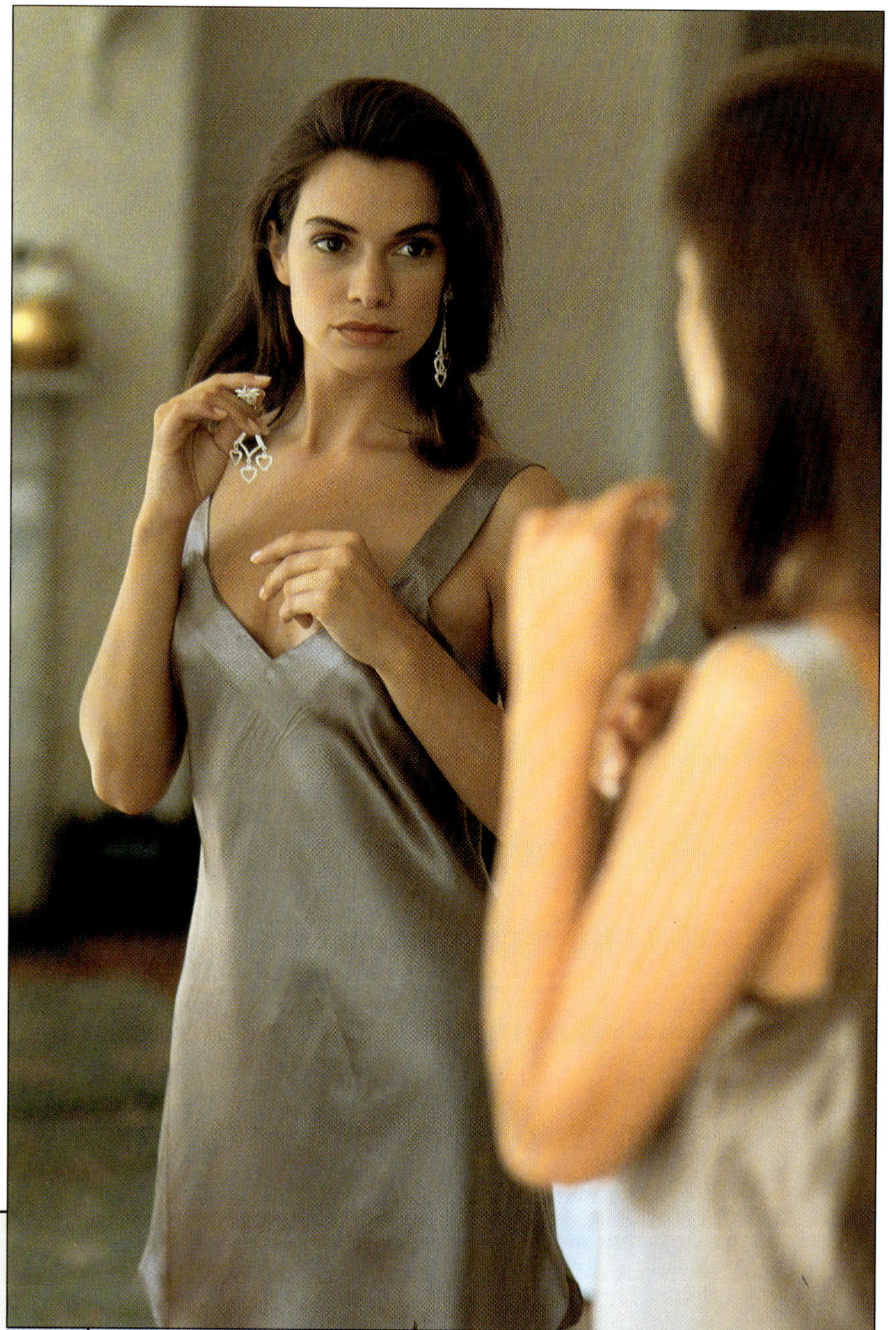

▲ **WHO'S THE FAIREST?**
Mirrors are a classical way of shooting fashion images, whether you decide to concentrate on the reflection or include the subject too, as in this example. To obtain a sharp picture of the reflection, the photographer has focused on the image in the mirror and thrown the subject herself out of focus.

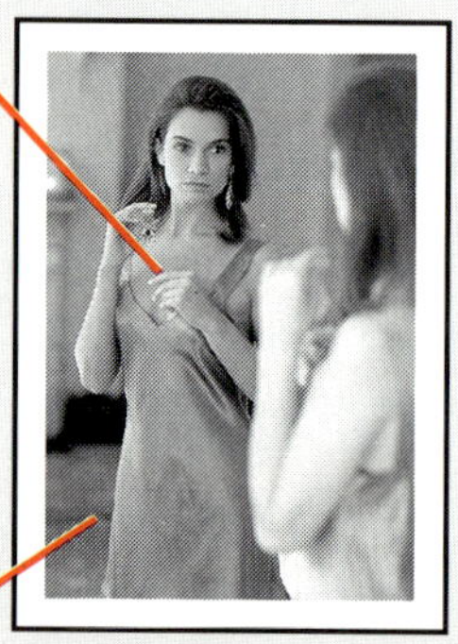

Tip

Preventing burn

Don't fire flash at highly reflective surfaces such as mirrors or glass. They bounce light away so efficiently that parts of the picture can be 'burnt out' and the exposure greatly altered. To prevent this happening, soften the light from the flash by bouncing it off a ceiling or wall.

Reflections in glass

With its transparent quality, glass allows you to capture either a partial or total reflection, depending on the strength of the light on either side of the glass. Total reflections occur when the exterior light is much stronger than that inside.

Partial reflections allow you to add extra information to a scene and they occur when both sides of the glass are equally lit. For example, windows in restaurants or cafes can be used to add clouds or a street scene to a portrait.

Modern glass buildings often benefit from reflecting their surroundings. If the glass is smooth and flat, the reflection is perfect; but if the glass has any flaws, the effect is distorted.

For a really dramatic shot wait for the golden light of early morning or late afternoon sun to be reflected. Or try to capture a person's face or a landscape in a pair of mirror sunglasses.

Think small

Smaller, more unusual, objects such as knives, salt cellars and even Christmas tree baubles, all reflect their surroundings, and with some thought can be worked into a larger composition.

Depending upon the effect you want, it's worth bearing in mind that silver coloured metals tend to reproduce colours more accurately than reflections in brass or copper surfaces.

▶ THROUGH THE ROUND WINDOW
Reflections can be found in the most unusual places. Here the photographer used a traffic mirror to capture a country cottage and its idyllic surroundings. The window frame helps to balance the scene and also reveals the purpose of the mirror.

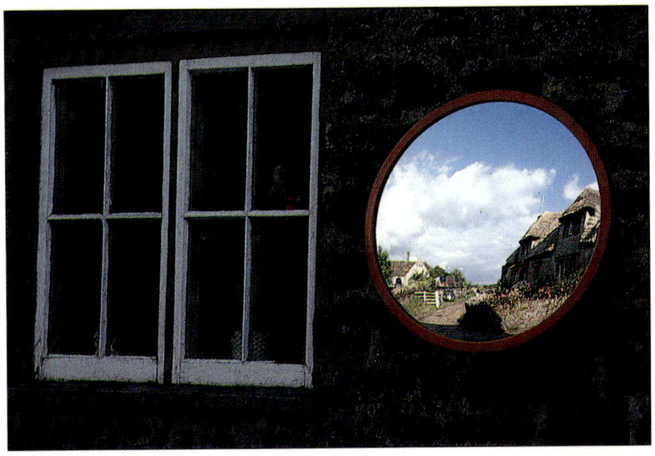

▼ PALM PRINTS
The reflection of the palm trees is very sharp in this image because the glass in the modern office building is smooth and even. The clear, blue sky provides a plain backdrop which helps to keep the overall image simple.

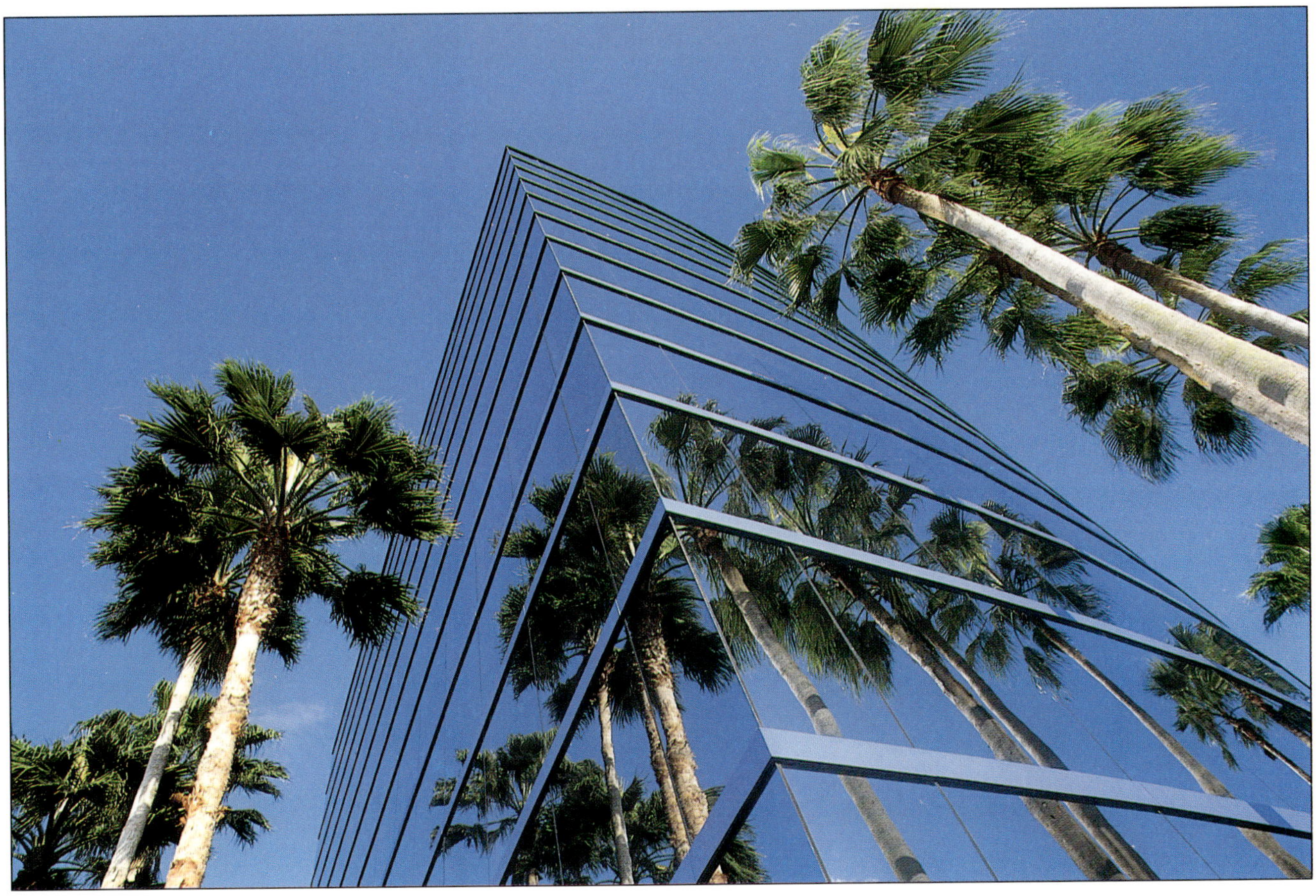

Abstract ideas

If you want to create more impressionistic, abstract pictures try looking for more unusual sources of reflections. For example, shallow puddles or a wet pavement can contain a mass of shimmering colours. Such images look particularly stunning at night when street lights and neon signs create impressionistic shapes across dark streets.

Polished metals, such as chrome and brass, are also excellent for abstract images, especially if the surface is curved. For example, the roundness of a car hubcap creates a wide angle distortion, similar to the effect made with a fisheye lens.

You can use abstract reflections to give a completely new slant on a much photographed subject, too. Concentrating on the distorted reflection in water of a famous bridge, for example, or moving in on just a small section of the image, can create an interesting shot.

Shooting abstracts with a telephoto lens allows you to focus on even the smallest design.

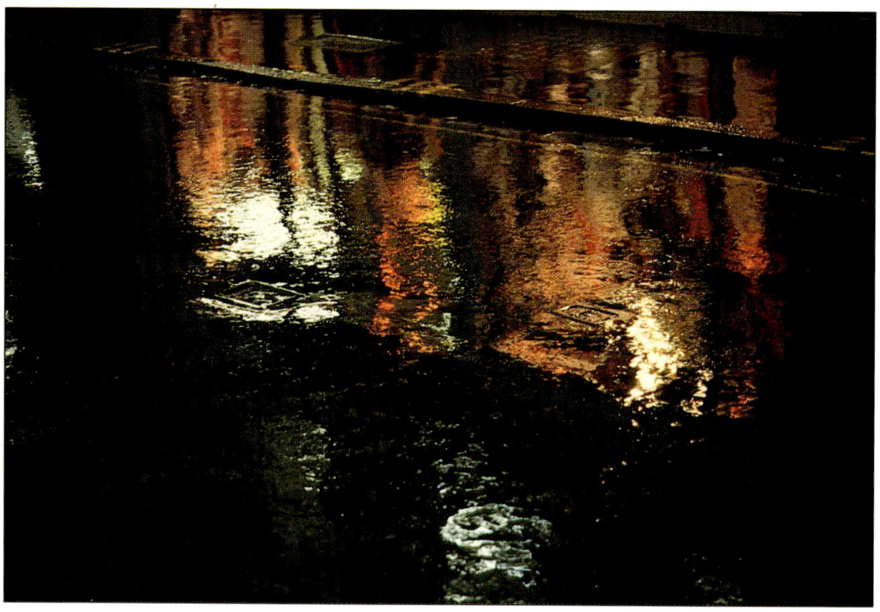

▲ SHIMMERING LIGHTS
You don't need a large body of water in order to capture a reflection in it. In this case the photographer captured the bright street lights and those in a shop window on a rainwashed road. The effects of the gleaming, impressionistic lights are enhanced by the shot being taken at night. The lights were kept bright with minimal exposure.

▼ CLEAR WATERS
Reflections in water create unique images because changes in light and ripples in the water alter their design from one minute to the next. Here, the photographer waited until the water was absolutely still in order to capture a crystal clear image of the boat's reflection. Excluding the boat itself made the image even more abstract.

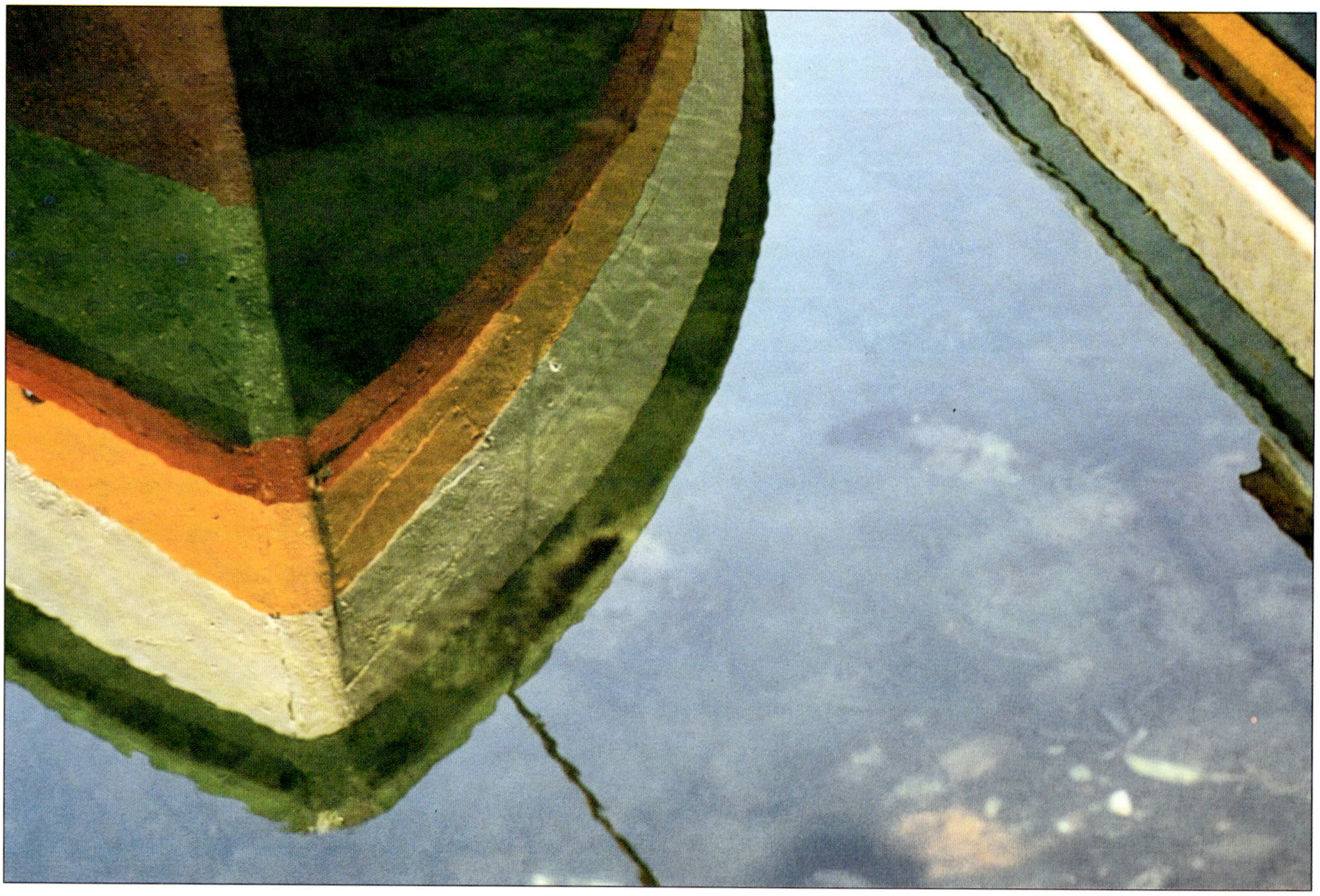

Reflective surfaces

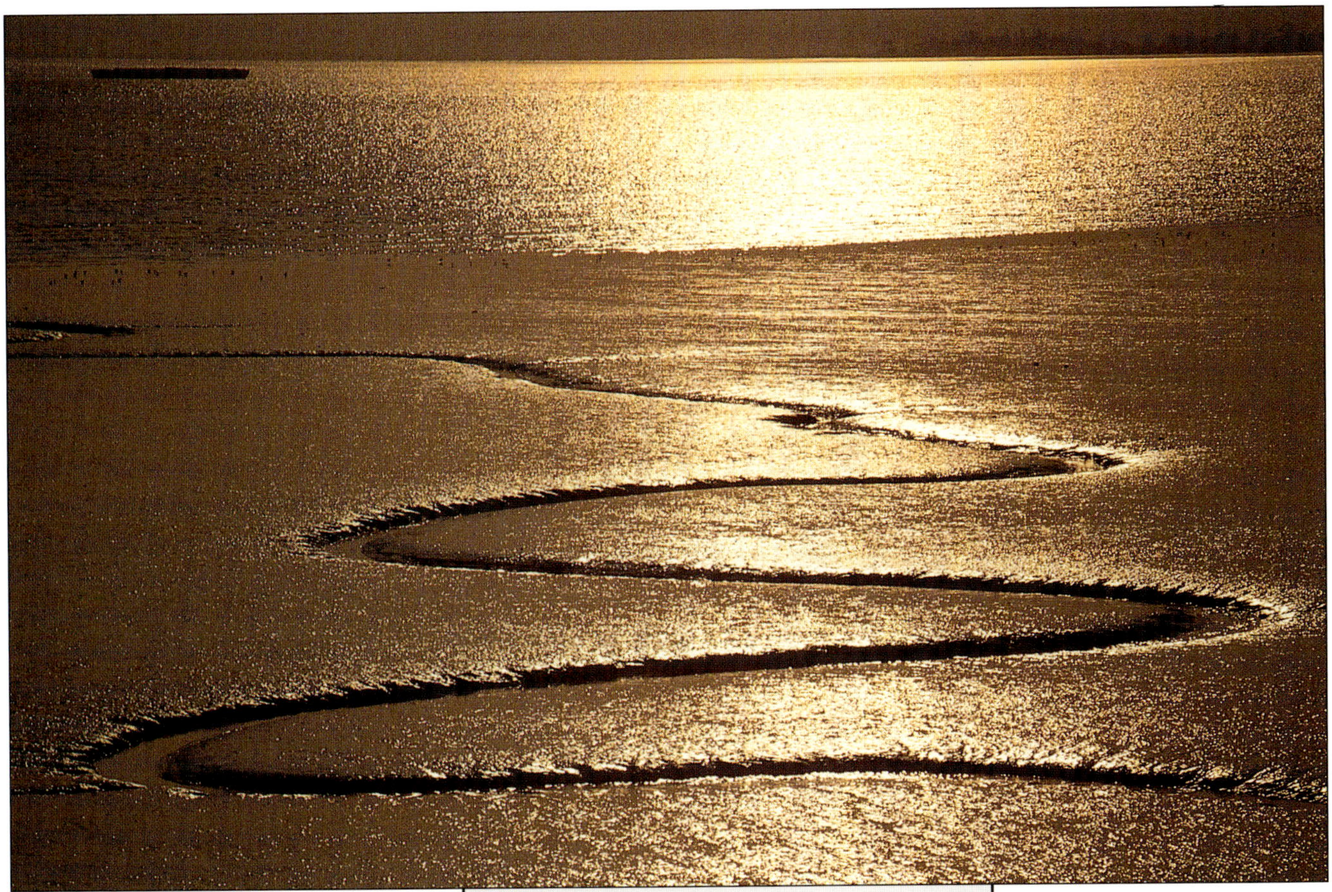

Unlike matt surfaces which scatter light, shiny ones reflect it in one direction only. By learning how light affects glossy objects you can show them to their best advantage or even enhance them for greater creativity.

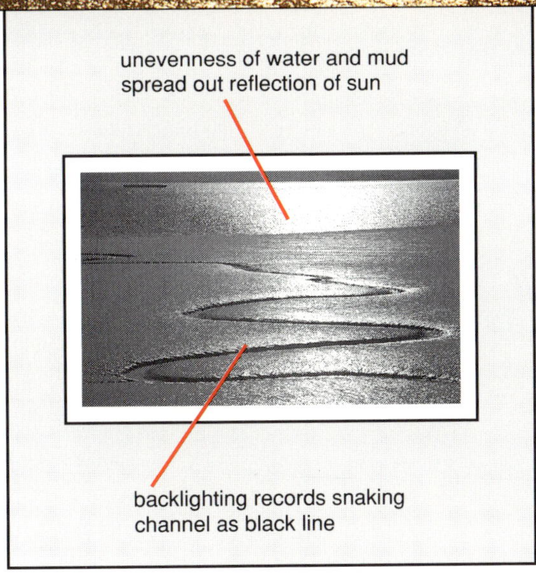

▲ **RAKING LIGHT**
Low angled sunlight grazes the water's surface producing hundreds of tiny highlights. These tiny points of light reveal the estuary's glimmering, smooth surface.

Reflective surfaces, such as polished silver, chrome and tinfoil have always been regarded with a certain amount of fear by photographers because they are tricky to record accurately.

In the past, people have tried a variety of methods to eliminate reflections from shiny objects. In old photography manuals the advice was to spray milk on to the surface or roll the object(s) in plasticine to get rid of the unwanted sheen.

But it is these very reflections which give shiny objects their character; and pictures which emphasize an object's glossiness are well worth capturing.

There is no instant formula for lighting shiny surfaces – it all depends what information you want to convey to the viewer. You need to decide whether you want to enhance the colour, texture or form of your subject.

Positioning the light

Shiny objects need highlights positioned on them to reveal their shape and texture. On flat, shiny surfaces, such as wet cobblestones or the sea, low-angled backlighting produces the strongest highlights. (Side and toplighting give some highlights on shiny objects, while frontlighting shows detail but conceals texture.)

While light can easily be skimmed over flat surfaces, curved objects are only partly illuminated. Take advantage of this by positioning the light so that the highlight(s) falls on an area where it is most useful – the flared bell of a trumpet or the headlamp of a car, say.

Quality of light

The size and strength of the lighting you use governs the nature of the reflections (or highlights) from glossy objects. Depending on the effect you want, there are two basic types of lighting generally used:

Small, hard lighting

Sources – sun, direct flash, domestic and studio lamps.
Highlights – small, bright, hard.
Advantages – emphasizes brilliance and smoothness of shiny objects; keeps colours saturated; injects life into simple, plain objects.
Disadvantages – doesn't reveal form (highlights are too small to follow contours of objects); points of light confuse detailed objects.

Large, diffused lighting

Sources – cloudy or overcast sky, white sheet in front of lamp, window light diffused by tracing paper, strip lighting.
Highlights – broad, soft.
Advantages – reveals form well (highlights distort to match the contours of glossy objects, enhancing their roundness); keeps detail in complicated surfaces.
Disadvantages – desaturates colours (highlights are reflections of the light source and so don't contain colour – using reflectors of the same hue as the object restores some colour); simple objects can look rather dull as texture is not so well emphasized.

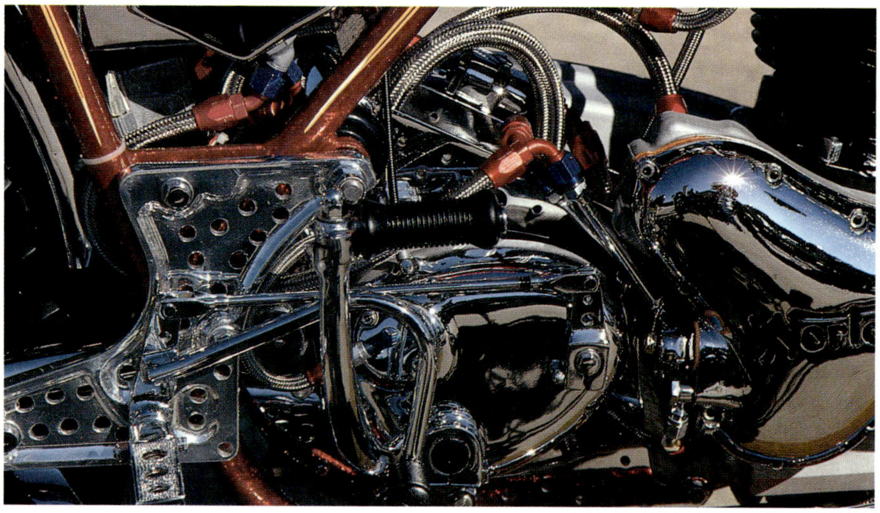

▲ NITTY GRITTY
To create sharp highlights on reflective surfaces, make the most of hard, direct light such as that on a sunny day. Here, pinpoints of light dance over this motorcycle engine.

▼ SHAPELY BODY
When you want to emphasize the form of a shiny object use large, diffused lighting. Here, the broad reflections on the bonnet and wheel guards of the car match the contours of its body.

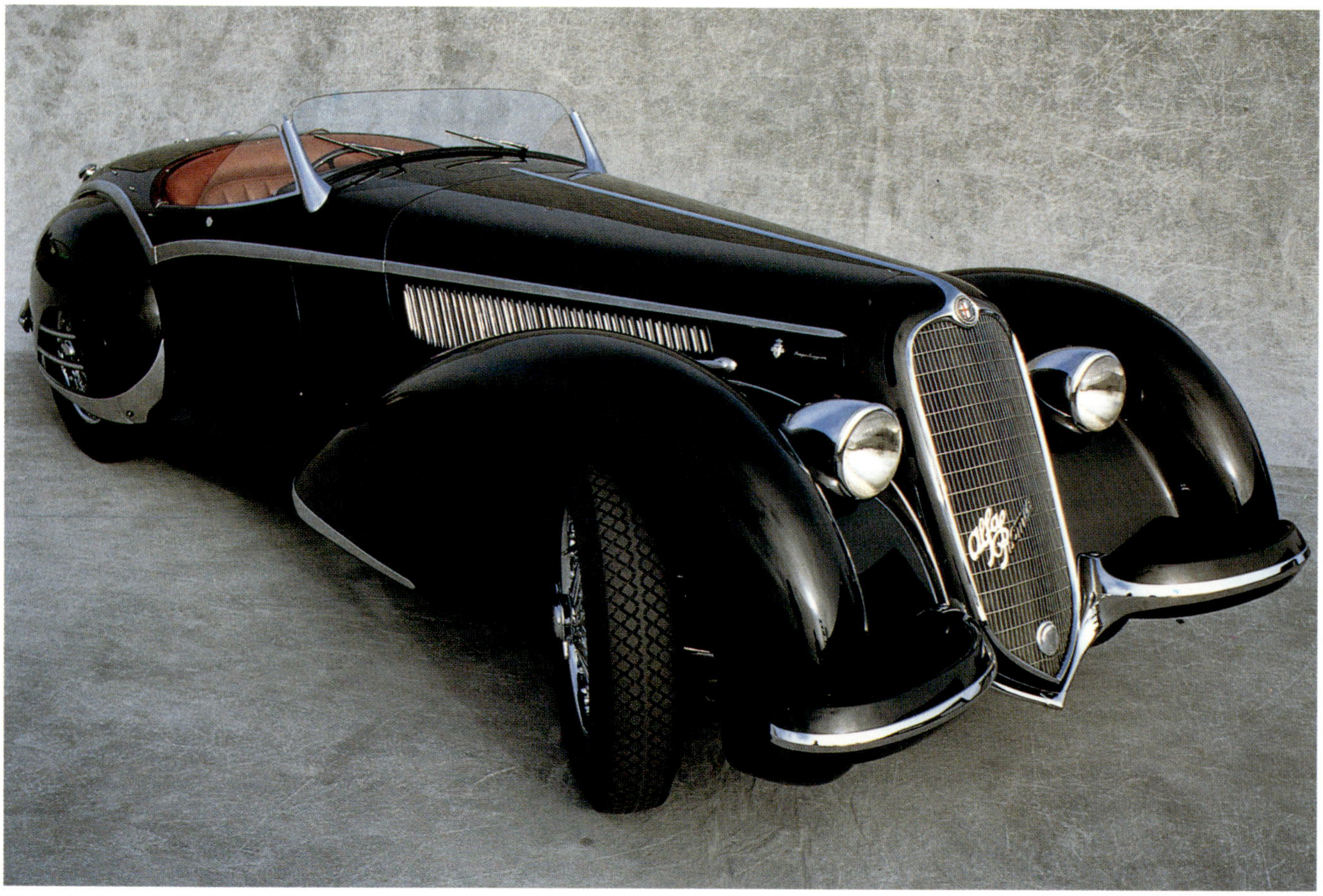

Semi-shiny surfaces

So far we have only dealt with the techniques for lighting highly polished surfaces, but how can you tackle objects which possess only a small element of shine?

Semi-shiny objects are not predominantly matt or glossy, but tend to take on the characteristics of both. Examples of semi-shiny objects include unpolished metals, plastics, human skin and fruits such as oranges and apples.

You can treat these surfaces as you would matt ones, but a more interesting way is to enhance what sheen there is. For example, spraying water on plants gives your light source something to bounce off, creating highlights. Water also livens up people's skin – think of the reflective beads of sweat on a boxer's face.

Suntan oil gives skin a satiny look – go along to a body building competition or capture your friends on the beach. Or try polishing up a bowl of apples so that the reflective quality of their smooth, tight skin is enhanced.

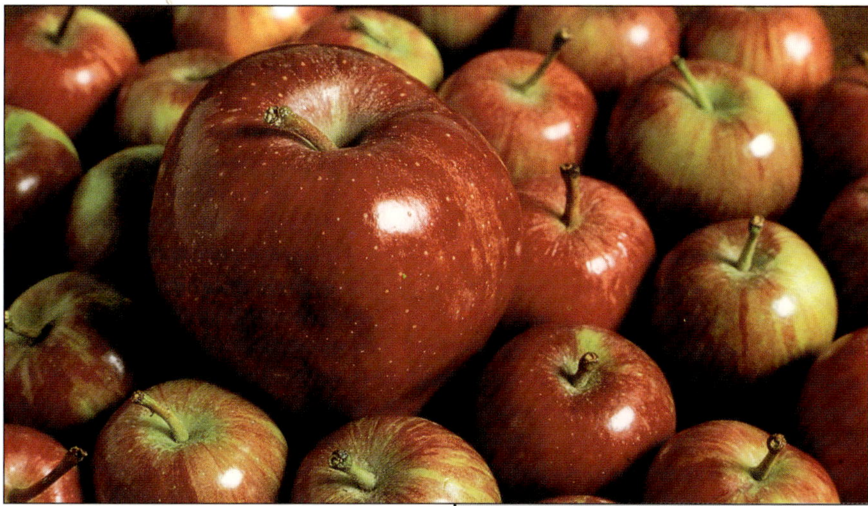

▲ AN APPLE A DAY
Window light produces highlights on the polished surfaces of these apples. The photographer added a focal point by placing one much larger apple off-centre, in the scene.

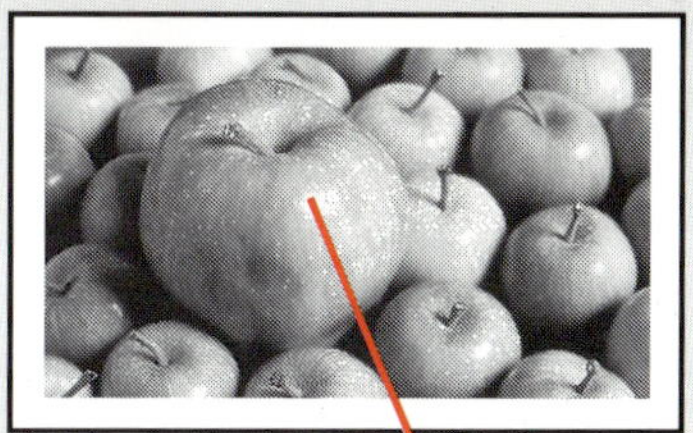

▼ WELL OILED
A mixture of oil and sweat have produced a sheen on these rippling biceps. Sunlight creates reflections on this shiny surface, revealing the contours of the men's muscles.

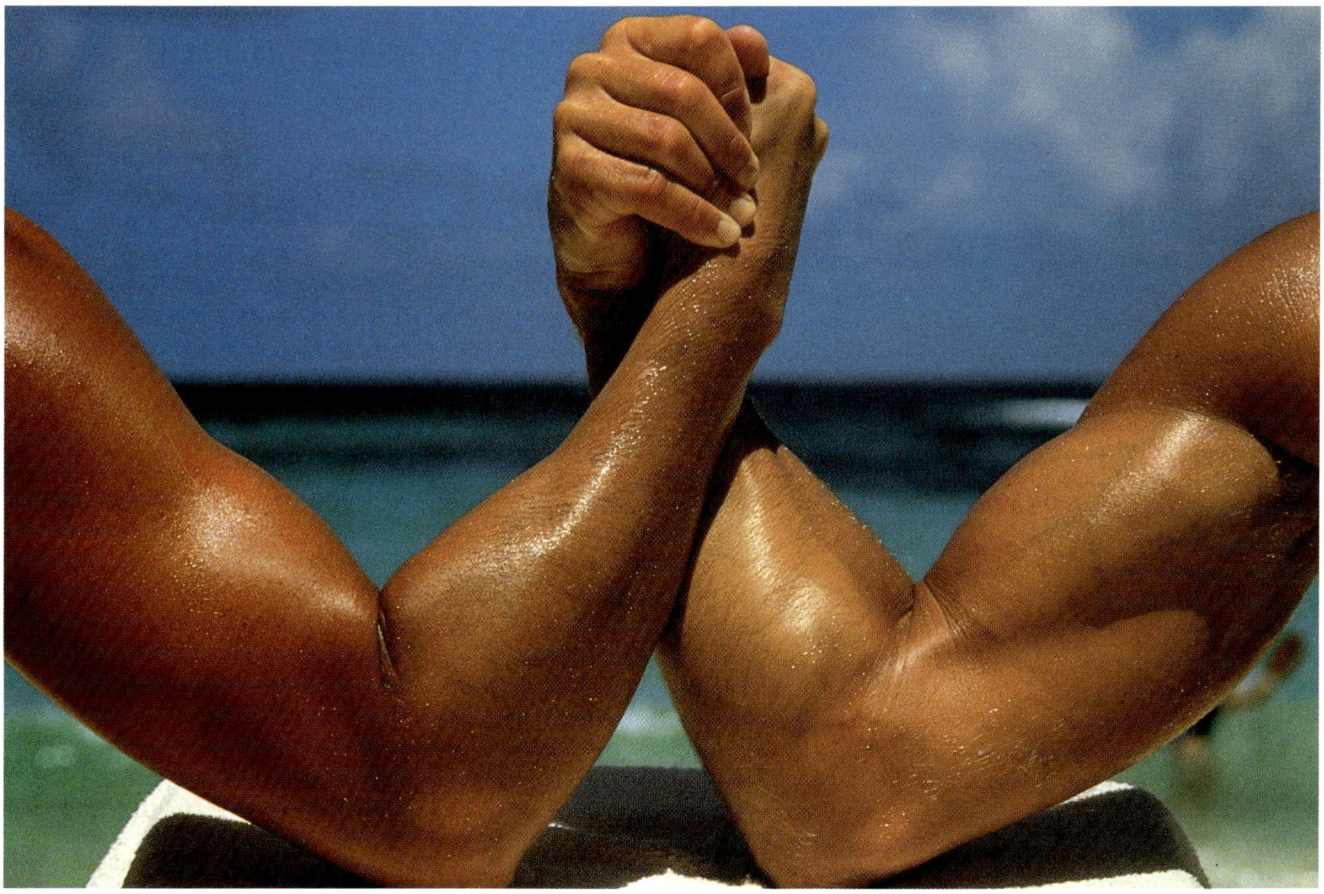

Adding a touch of sparkle

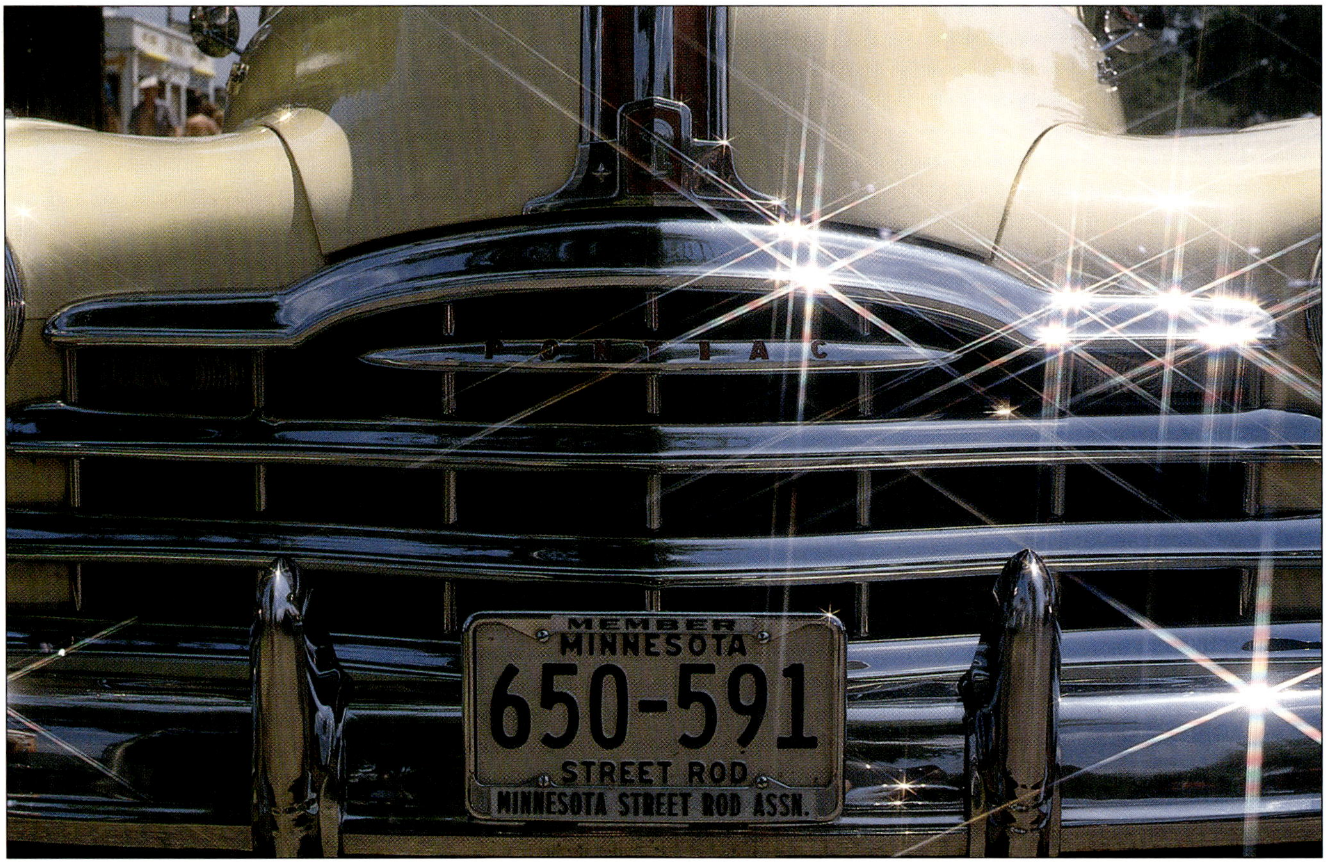

▲ **CRAZY CHROME**
The photographer attached a starburst filter over his lens to turn the highlights on this car, produced by bright sunlight, into spectacular bursts of light.

There are several filters, from cross-screens to diffractors, which, used occasionally, are great for transforming the highlights on shiny subjects into bright bursts of light.

A starburst filter is the most commonly used and comprises a series of parallel lines etched on to a plain glass or plastic filter. These lines produce brilliant stars out of highlights, further enhancing an object's sheen.

Ideal subjects include street lights at night, sunlight on water or in eyes, sparkling jewels worn by a portrait subject, or chrome or bronze statues.

For the most dramatic results make sure your subject is against a dark background so that the highlights show up clearly. (A black velvet backdrop is ideal for studio shots.)

CHECK IT!

Here are a few, quick reminders:

❑ small, hard lighting produces tiny highlights which emphasize the glossiness of an object

❑ large, diffused lighting produces broad highlights which reveal the form of shiny objects

❑ polish up or add water to semi-shiny objects to make them gleam

❑ use a starburst filter to give highlights that extra sparkle

Cut it out

If texture is not a priority, you can use a polarizing filter to cut unwanted reflections from most shiny surfaces, while improving detail and colour saturation.

Position your camera lens at an angle of about 55° to the reflective surface, and rotate the filter so that the reflections disappear. However, polarizers cannot cut out glare from unpainted metal surfaces, such as silver or chrome.

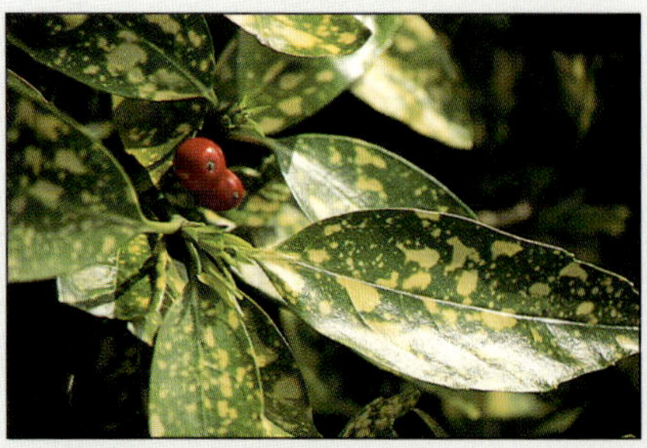

▲ ***Without a polarizer***

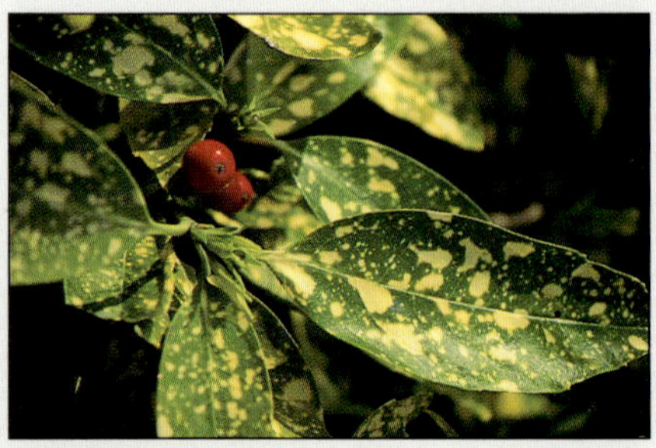

▲ ***With a polarizer***

Using shadows

Shadows are an important, though often neglected, element of composition. In their simplest form they can provide information in a picture; used imaginatively they make powerful subjects in their own right.

Being aware of light and shade – the way light strikes an object and the shadows it forms – is not a natural function of the eye, and often it takes a photograph to make us aware that shadows exist.

This is because our eyes can register a far greater range of light intensity than film, so that when you look at an unevenly lit subject you see detail in both the light and shaded parts. When recorded on film, however, shadows appear much darker than they do in real life.

Shadows are particularly useful for giving your photos the sense of a third dimension. As the sun sinks lower in the sky, the influence of shadow on a landscape's form, for example, increases.

At midday the landscape looks flat and featureless, but in the late afternoon, when the sun is low in the sky, the pattern of shadows formed by the trees and hills add form and interest to the scene.

Clouds, too, cast shadows on the land, helping to reveal its form. Similarly, the contours of the human body can be enhanced with carefully placed shadows.

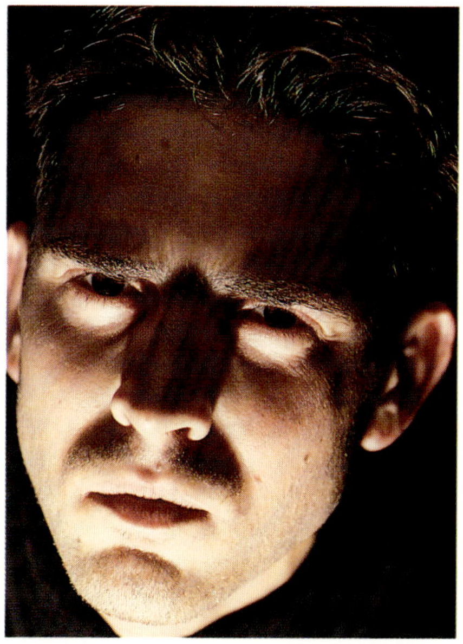

▲ SINISTER FACE
By controlling the direction and quality of a single light source you can create some macabre lighting effects. For this menacing effect the photographer spotlit the man's face from below so that eerie shadows are formed under the eyes and nose.

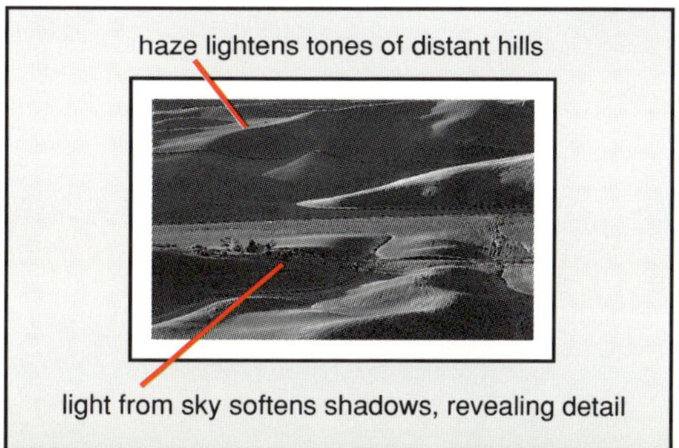

▼ ROLLING GREEN HILLS
Late afternoon sun bathes one side of the hills in a yellow glow, while leaving the other side in shade. Apart from creating a colourful scene, this interaction of light and shade makes the hills look three dimensional.

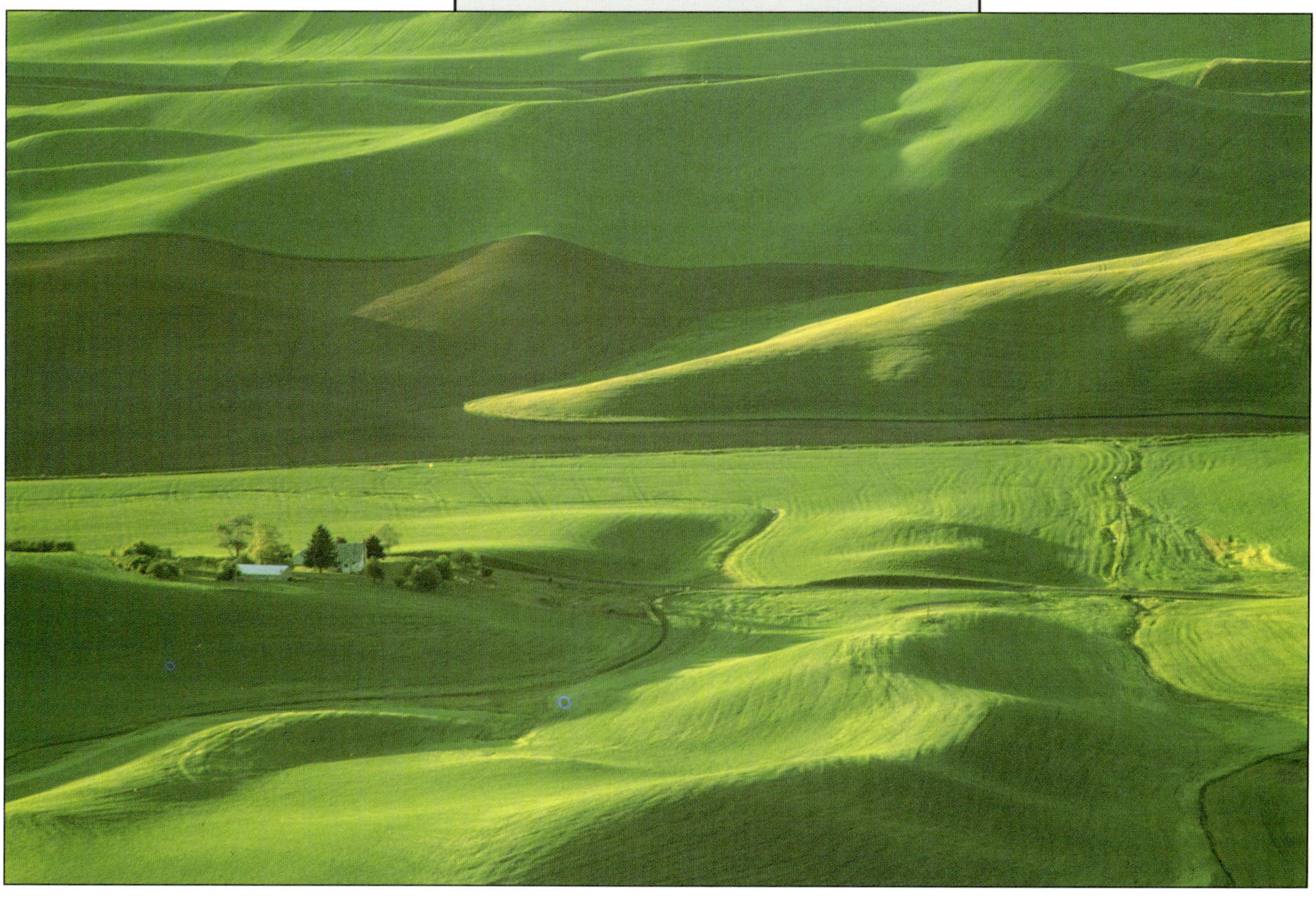

Making the most of shadows

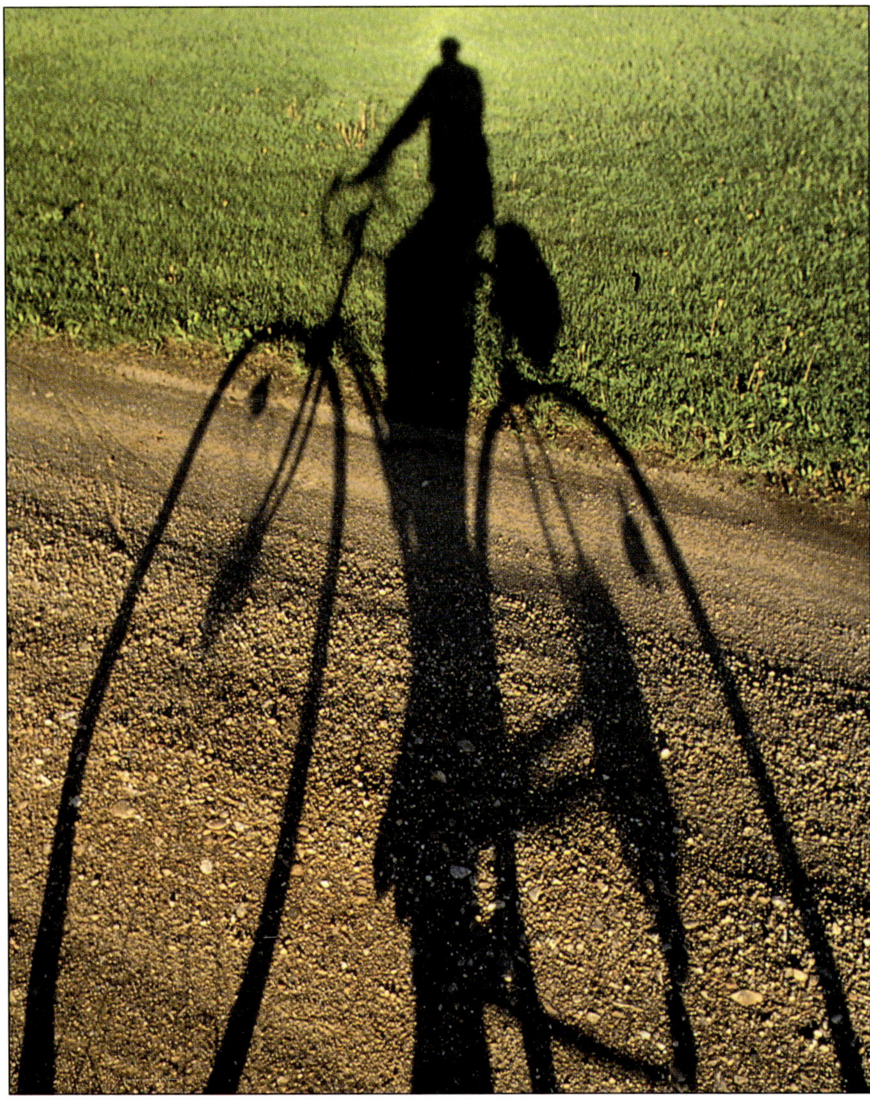

◀ **ME AND MY SHADOW**
Rules were made to be broken occasionally, so why not have a go at shooting your own shadow? Here, the photographer kept the camera close to his chest so that it is hidden from view, and chose late afternoon light so that the shadows are elongated.

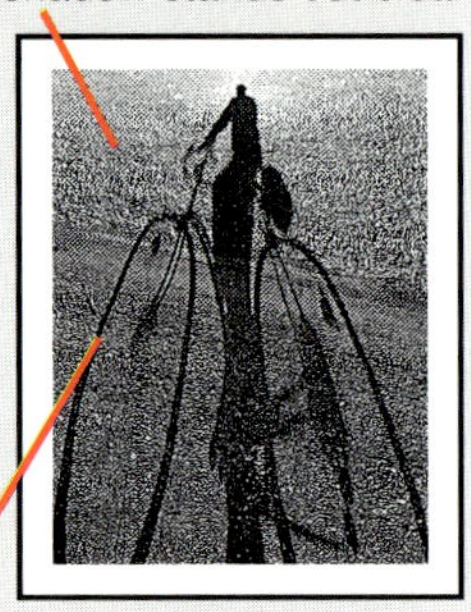

Tip

Calculating exposure

For shadows, you need to meter carefully to get the effect you want. For dark shadows, take your meter reading from the lit area of your scene. For pale shadows, in which some detail can be seen, increase the exposure about one stop.

As well as providing information about an image, shadows give you enormous scope to be creative, whether you make them the subject of your composition or use them to pep up a rather ordinary scene.

Hard lighting produces dark shadows, while soft light results in paler ones. Usually the darker the shadow the more powerful the effect; but occasionally a soft shadow is useful for bringing out a range of subtle hues not found in brighter light.

Self-portraits One old rule of photography says that you should never include your own shadow in a picture. However, you can create some amusing or dramatic effects using your own shadow – as long as the results look deliberate.

For instance, you could position your own shadow so that it looms threateningly over your subject, or use it to add interest to an otherwise plain scene.

Time of day You can use other people's shadows to great effect, too. Photograph your subject early or late in the day to reveal shadows not at their strongest but at their longest, for a distorted effect.

Objects with simple shapes cast the most effective shadows, since the viewer can identify them by their shadows alone. Try to find a high viewpoint so that the elongated shadows are seen in their entirety.

A sense of drama Shadows are also good for creating certain moods. They can produce a menacing, sinister effect – think of the strong, long shadow following a lone figure, for instance.

A portrait sidelit with a single light source, for example, places half the face in deep shadow, and creates a much more dramatic image than a face which is frontlit.

Unwanted detail You can make the most of shadows by using them to get rid of unwanted fore or background clutter. For example, if you want to photograph a building but its surroundings are ugly or distracting, wait until the building is in strong sunshine and the foreground falls into deep shadow, hiding unwanted details.

Patterns Of course shadows create interesting patterns, too. Think of the parallel lines cast by iron railings, or alternate shafts of light and shade formed by the sun streaming through window blinds.

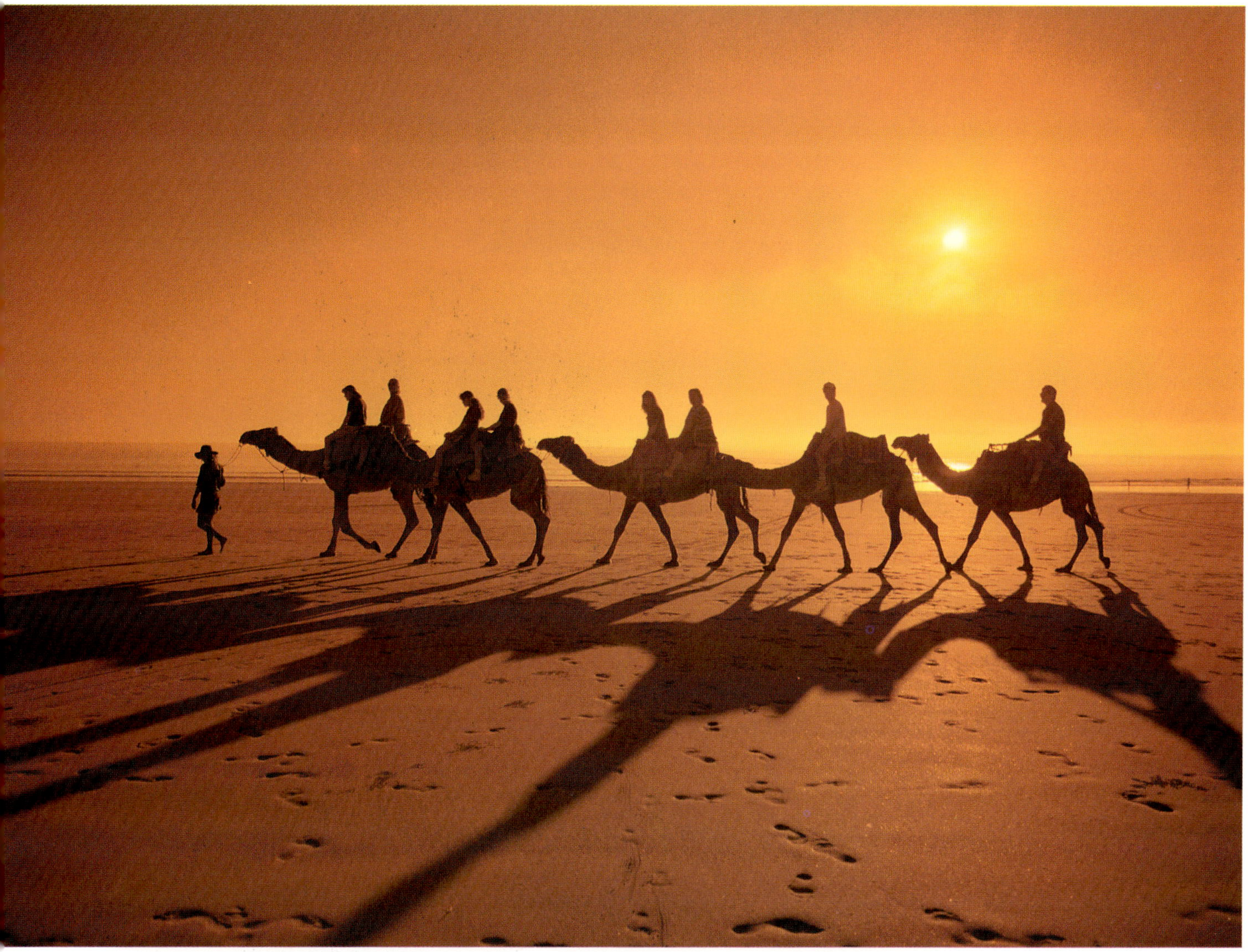

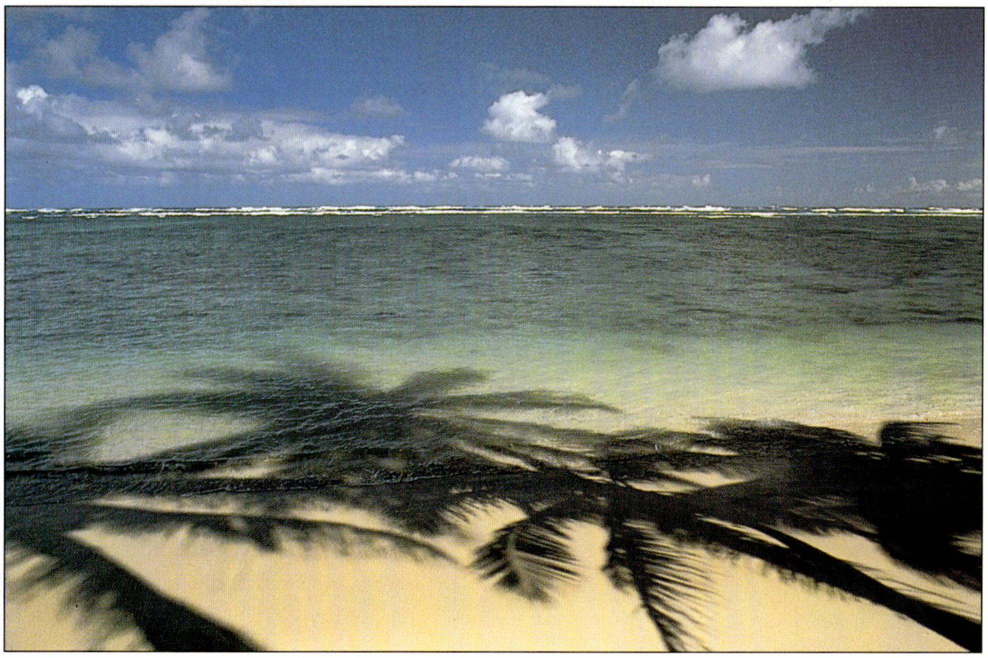

▲ SUNSET TIMES
Early evening is one of the best times of day for using shadows in an image, because this is when they are at their longest. The raking sunlight elongates the shadows of the animals' necks, making them look more like giraffes than camels.

◀ PALM BEACH
Shadows make interesting subjects in their own right. Here, the photographer achieved a more unconventional shot by concentrating on just the shadows rather than including the palm trees themselves.

Shadows indoors

Shadows aren't confined to the outdoors, there are plenty of opportunities indoors, too. If you use a naked bulb, for instance, you get the same effect as that produced by sunlight – well defined, dark shadows.

With a little thought about your viewpoint and the angle of your lighting, background shadows can be used to echo or add interest to your main subject. For instance, a window frame projected behind a portrait can look effective.

Alternatively, you can cast your subject's shadow on to a plain wall behind them. The closer you place your light to the subject, the bigger and more dramatic the shadow will be. You can even fake a shadow by cutting out a piece of card shaped, for example, like a horned devil, and arranging its shadow to fall behind an angelic little child.

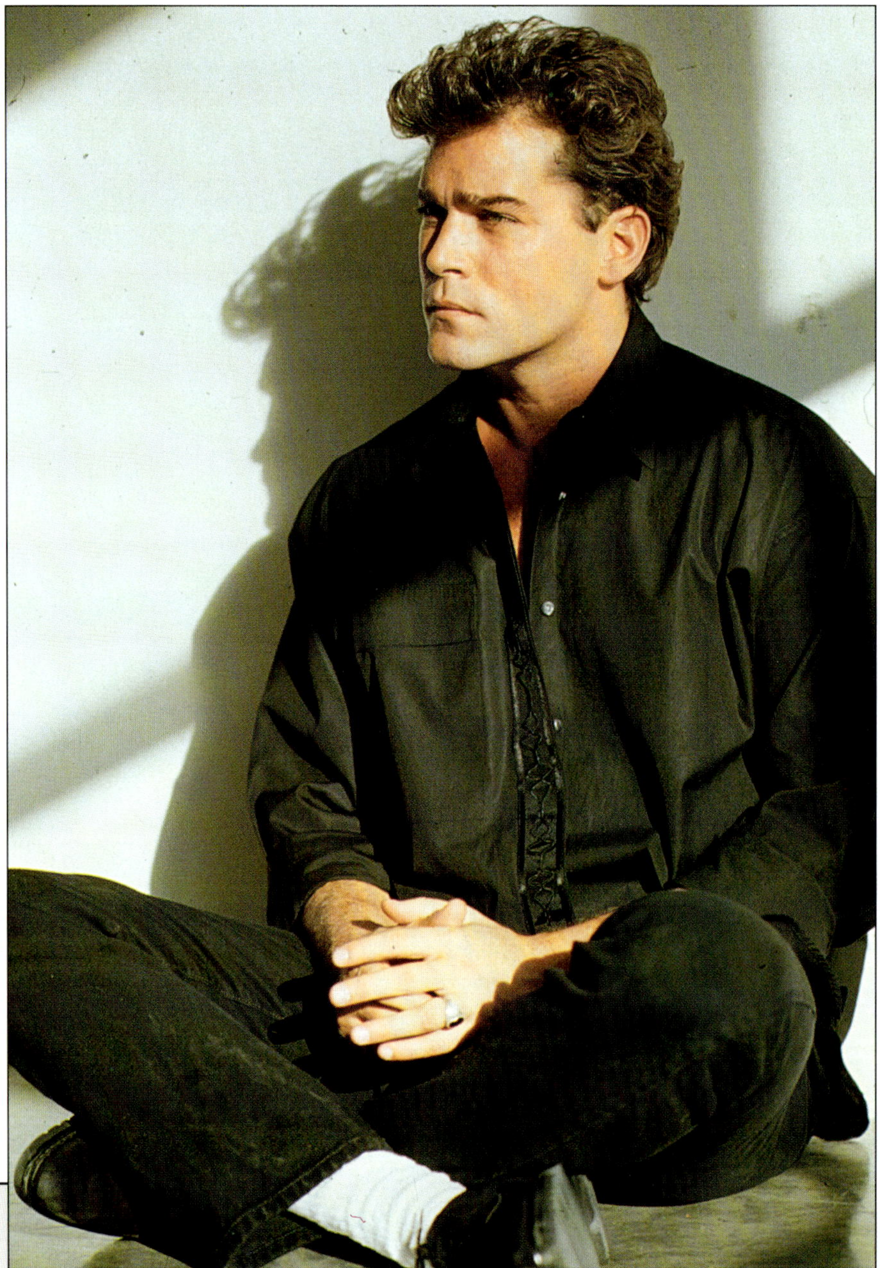

▶ **OFF THE WALL**
The photographer simulated this window scene in his studio by placing a crossbar in front of the light source. He slightly overexposed the shot in order to retain detail in the shadows rather than in the highlights.

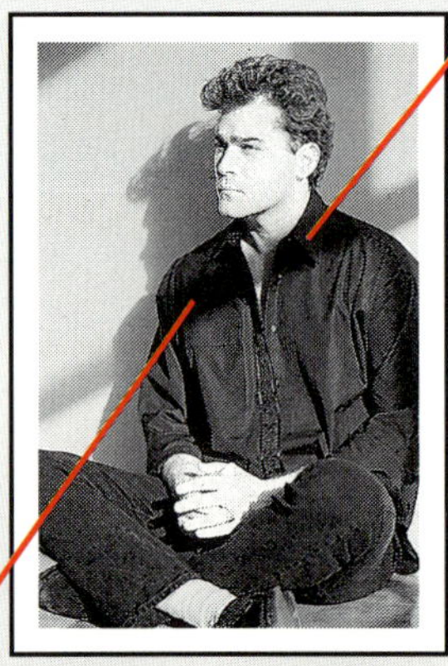

Tip **Don't forget**

If you have deliberately over or underexposed an image for a certain effect, and your final pictures are prints rather than transparencies, you must remember to notify the processors so that they do not try to correct your exposure.

CHECK IT!

Make the most of shadows by:

❏ using them to reveal form

❏ making them the subject of your composition

❏ photographing them early or late in the day to get a distorted effect

❏ positioning them to hide unwanted details

❏ using them to add a sense of drama or mystery to a scene

Creating silhouettes

With their stark, definite outlines, silhouettes make eye-catching images, whether you choose to create a solid black mass or decide to reveal just a hint of detail in your subject.

The attraction of silhouettes lies in their simplicity and power of suggestion – they use very little to convey a great deal. If you look at the profile of a person's face you can usually tell their sex and age, and possibly even something about their character.

Silhouettes are also appealing because they conceal unwanted details. Use this to your advantage to turn fussy subjects into simple, striking ones. If there are several objects in the frame, try to isolate each silhouette so that their outlines aren't confused.

True silhouettes, where every object in the scene appears black, are used occasionally in photography, but usually some amount of detail is included in the image – a little colour or tone or a feature in the background.

Whichever effect you opt for the purpose remains the same – to concentrate the viewer's attention on the subject's shape.

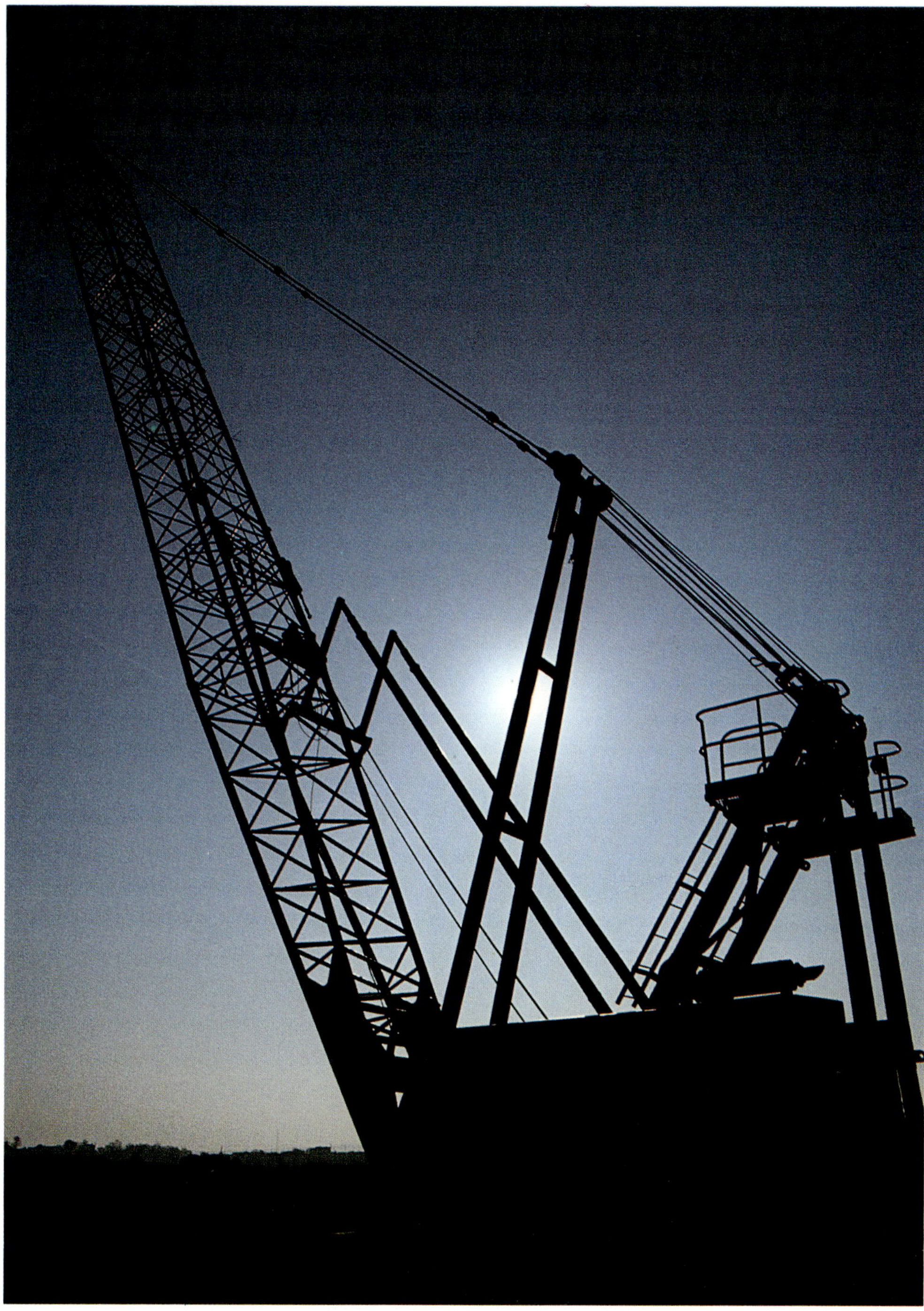

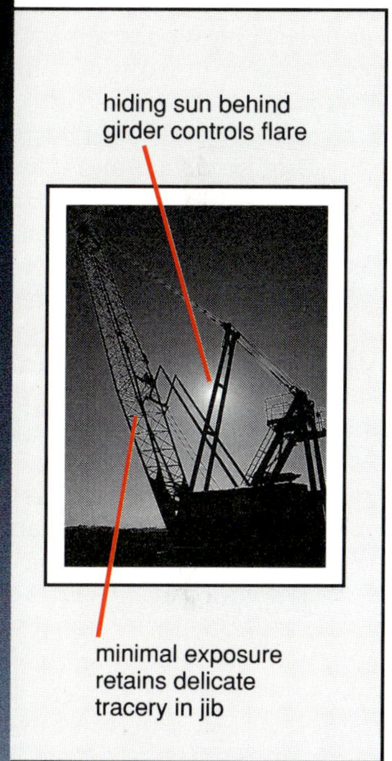

◀ HIDDEN SUN
With the sun directly behind the subject – in this case a crane – there are no stray highlights to confuse the outline, and the body of the crane is kept solid black. The brightness around the sun is localized, so the sky at the edges of the frame appears darker.

Silhouettes in daylight

Silhouettes can be formed in a number of ways: you can use natural or artificial light, shoot into the sun, or make use of foggy or misty conditions. These effects can be created artificially, too.

Contrast is the first requirement for a strong silhouette – namely a dark subject against a light background. The simplest way to provide such contrast is to backlight your subject against a pale background, so that your subject is placed in dark shadow.

If you are shooting indoors you can create high contrast by placing your subject in front of a doorway or window which has light behind it, even if diffused by a curtain.

Shooting into the sun is the easiest way to produce a silhouette, especially if the background has a light tone such as water or sand. However, sun can cause flare, lowering the contrast in an image – so use a lens hood or shield the lens with your hand to keep out any stray light.

If the silhouette is small in the frame try using either a telephoto or macro lens to outline an object against the sun's disc itself.

When shooting towards the sun the time of day influences the result you get. For example, mid afternoon sunlight is strong, creating high contrast. But if you want a more ethereal effect use the soft light of dawn when the contrast is greatly lessened.

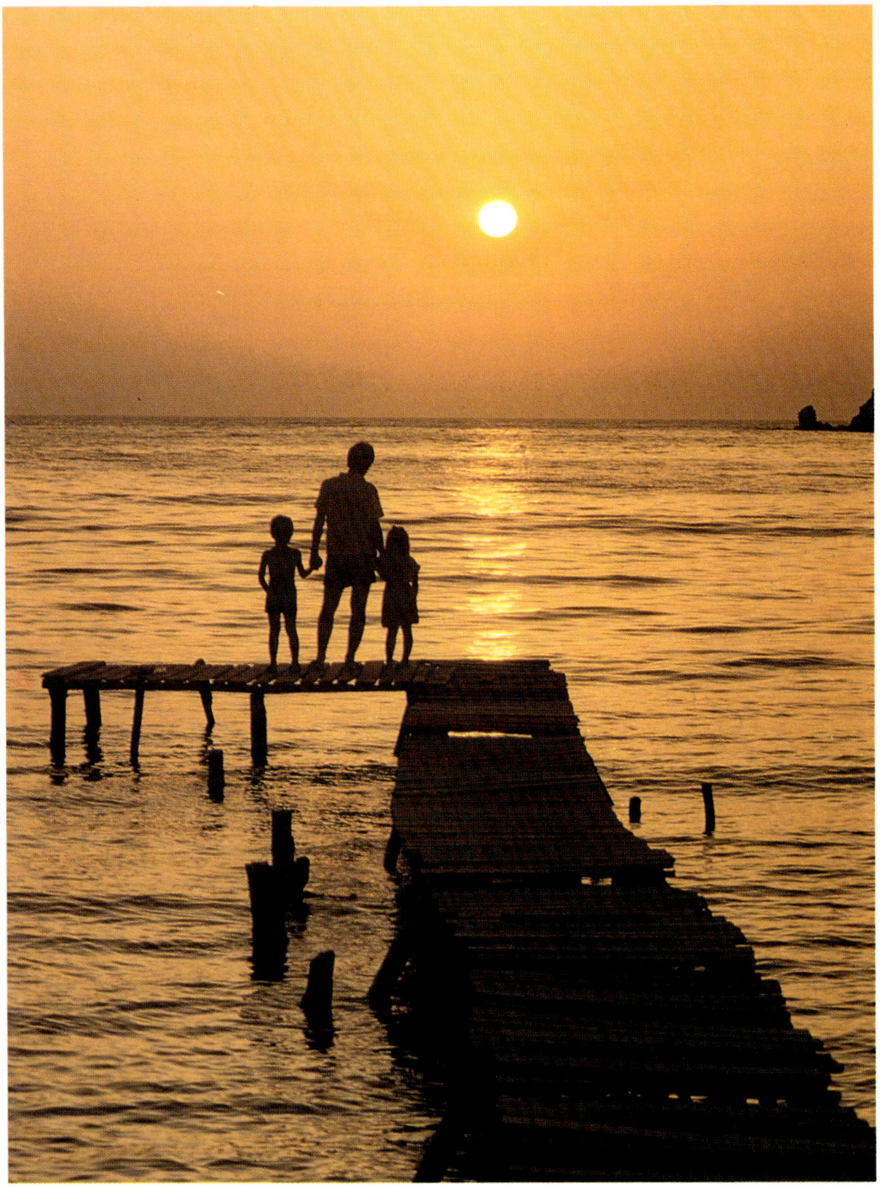

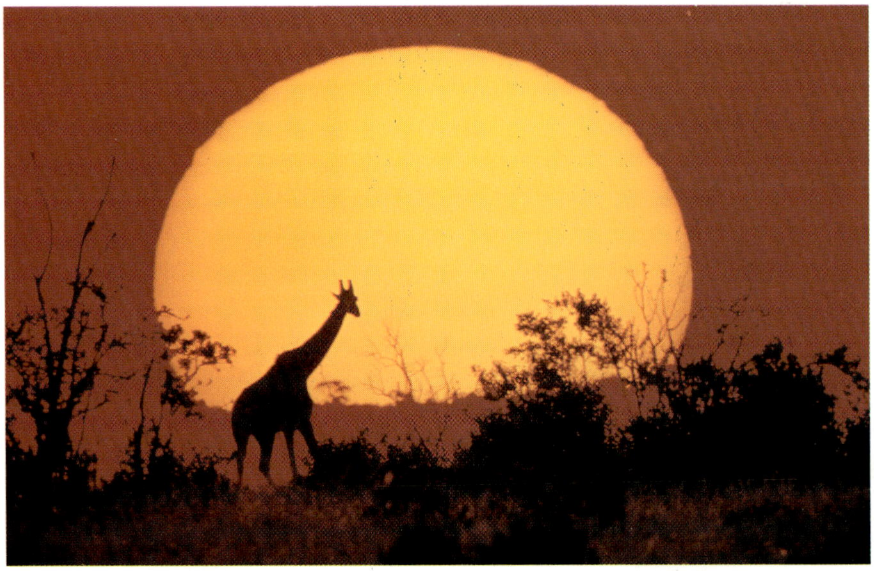

▲ **SUNSET BOULEVARD**
Silhouettes taken against the sun's reflection in water are very popular. Here, the movement in the water has diffused the sunlight to give a broader area of bright background. By adjusting the exposure carefully the photographer has managed to retain detail, and interest, in the foreground.

◀ **ANIMAL MAGIC**
The photographer waited until the last possible moment as the sun was sinking in the sky to capture this shot. A long telephoto lens magnified the sun's disc sufficiently to frame the silhouetted profile of the giraffe.

Tip

A bit of a boost

Silhouettes are created when there is high contrast in a picture. If you develop your own pictures you can boost contrast by printing black and white film on high contrast (hard) paper or by pushing slide film.

Mist and fog Eerie, monochrome images can also be produced in fog or mist because background details are obscured by a white veil, emphasizing the outlines of objects in the foreground. Think of the lone figure of an angler by a river on a misty morning, or a skein of geese in flight.

Exposure is critical in these conditions – underexposure produces muddy tones, whereas overexposure weakens the silhouette. For the best results take an average meter reading from the dark and light areas.

Viewpoint is always an important consideration for any photo, but never more so than when you are shooting silhouettes. It is vital that you separate your subject clearly from the background. Make sure the subject is on high ground, or get down on the ground and shoot upwards so your subject is outlined against the sky.

Even with easily recognizable subjects it's worth moving around to make sure that the subject is angled to create the most striking impact that its shape allows. For example, a profile of a person or pet is usually better than a head-on view. However, some subjects, such as trees and skyscrapers, look good from any angle.

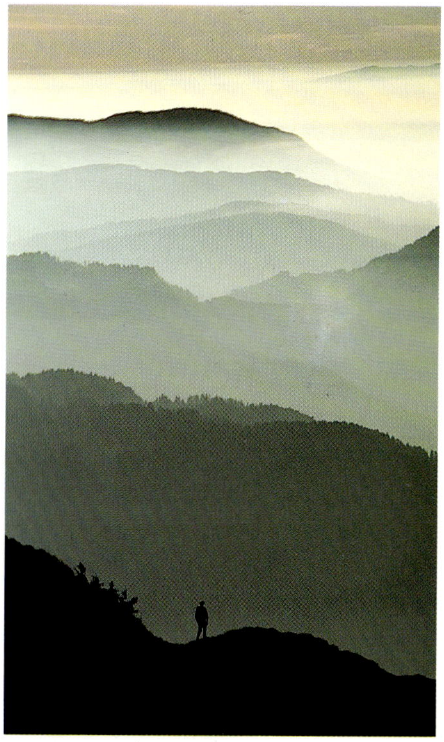

▲ MISTY MORNING
Shooting against the light in the early morning mist throws the mountains and figure into silhouette, producing a moody, monochromatic image.

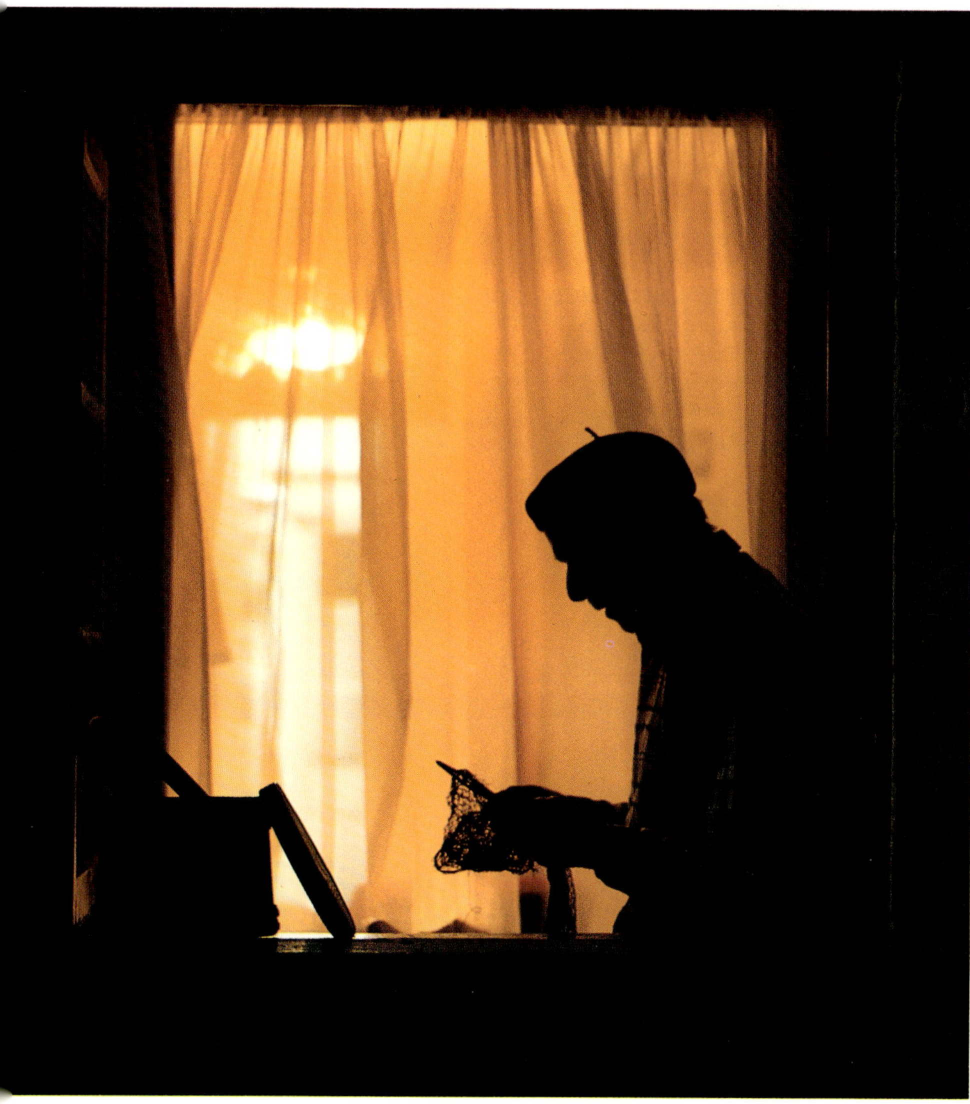

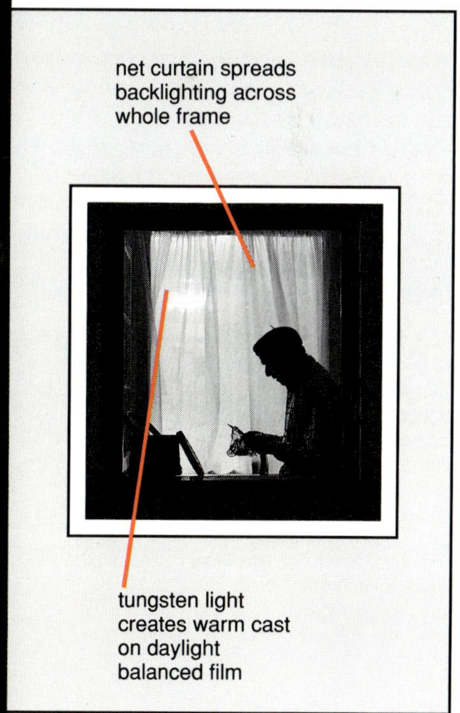

◀ INTERIOR MOTIVES
Window light, especially when diffused by a curtain, is much softer than direct light, so a fair amount of detail is revealed about the man's activities and clothing. Even in complete silhouette the tag on the hat identifies it as a beret.

Artificial lighting

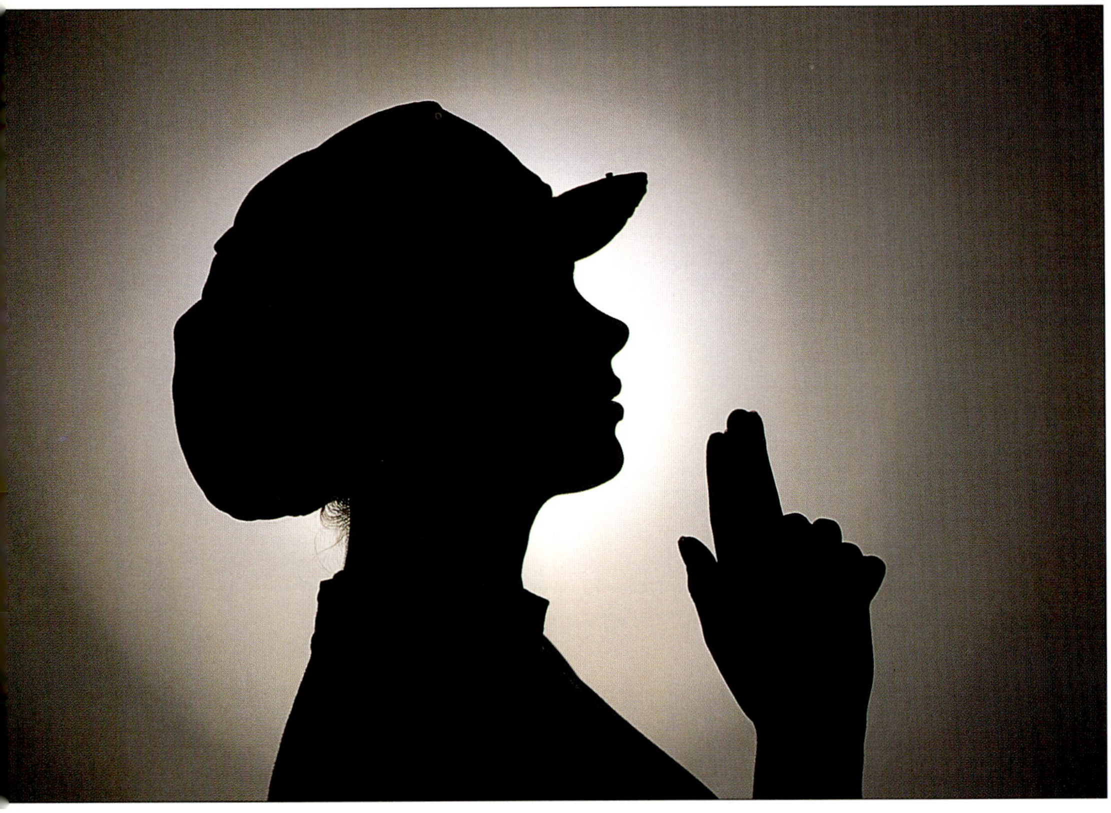

◀ **IN PROFILE**
The photographer created a halo of light around his subject by placing a snoot over the spotlight to project a compact circle of light on the white backdrop.

CHECK IT!

You can create a silhouette by:

❑ shooting into the sun

❑ placing your subject in front of a backlit window or doorway

❑ photographing in mist or fog

❑ directing studio light at the background only

❑ printing black and white film on high contrast paper

Why not have a go at creating silhouettes in the studio, where you have much more control over the strength of your lighting? Place your subject against a plain, white wall and direct a spotlight on to the background. By taping a piece of card around the light so that only the wall is lit and metering for the background, your subject will end up looking totally black on film.

Silhouettes also have a useful place in special effects photography. A backlit horizon line cut out from card, for example, can make a simple and convincing backdrop to a scene constructed in your home or a studio. You could also try using a deep red filter outdoors to darken your subject and produce a vivid backdrop at the same time.

However, a string of silhouettes can become as tired and uninteresting as any photographic device, and it is important to achieve plenty of variety in such images. Look not only at the different technical ways of producing them, but explore all the possible creative effects, too.

▶ **VIVID BACKDROP**
A deep red filter was used for this picture to add colour to the sky and to heighten the contrast between the sky and the wind pumps. Although the silhouettes were created by shooting into the sun, the filter darkens them even more.

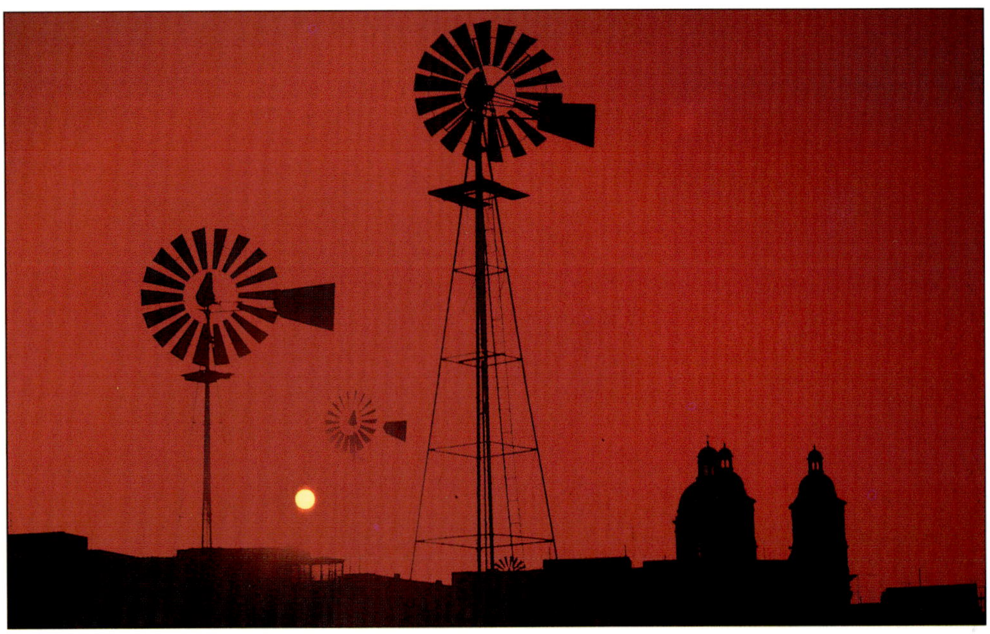

Pre-dawn to mid-morning

The changing colour and direction of light throughout the day transforms everything you see. From spectacular sunrises to mysterious night shots, there are many ways to take advantage of these changes.

So far, we have looked at the 'secrets of light' in isolation. Now it is time to put it all together and to see how different light can totally transform a subject, depending on the time of day.

This is fundamental to many types of photography, especially travel and landscape shots. Be warned, though: it can be very tiring to try to exploit all the different moods of light in a single day. This is especially true in the summer when daybreak may be at four in the morning, and there's still some colour in the sky late in the evening. You have to allow yourself some time to rest, and if you pre-visualize the best times to shoot particular subjects, you should be able to plan your days accordingly.

Check the weather forecast, too: early morning mist can be beautiful, but early-morning rain seldom provides much incentive to get up before dawn. Use dull days to scout out good locations, and to work out the best time to photograph them.

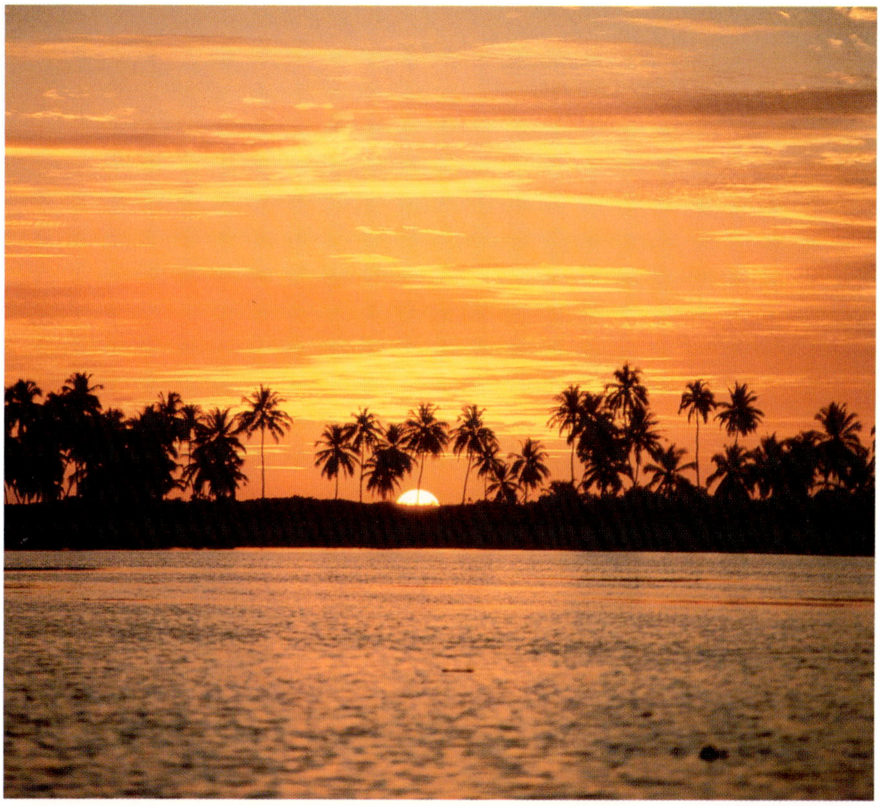

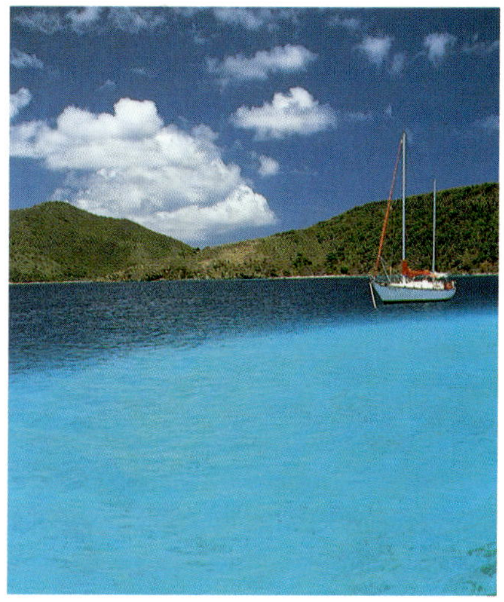

▲ **NOON**
When you want to record a bright and definite image with crisp detail and little modelling, midday is the best time to shoot.

◀ **SUNRISE**
At sunrise the gorgeous colours of the sky are reflected in the water. With the sun at this angle the camera can be safely pointed towards the glowing disc.

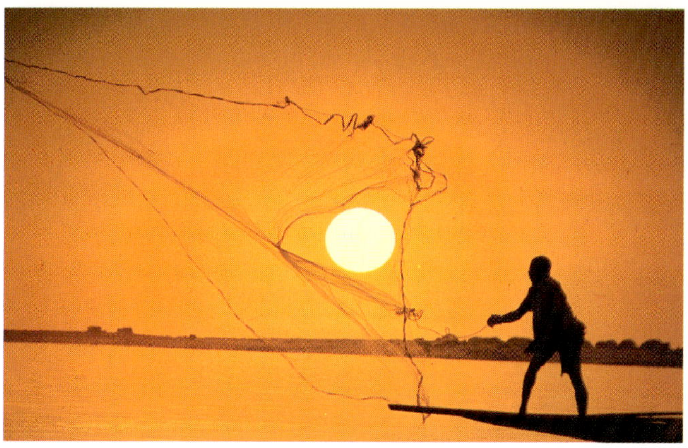

▲ **SUNSET**
Sunsets can often provide wonderful opportunities for silhouettes, such as this stunning shot of a fisherman casting his net.

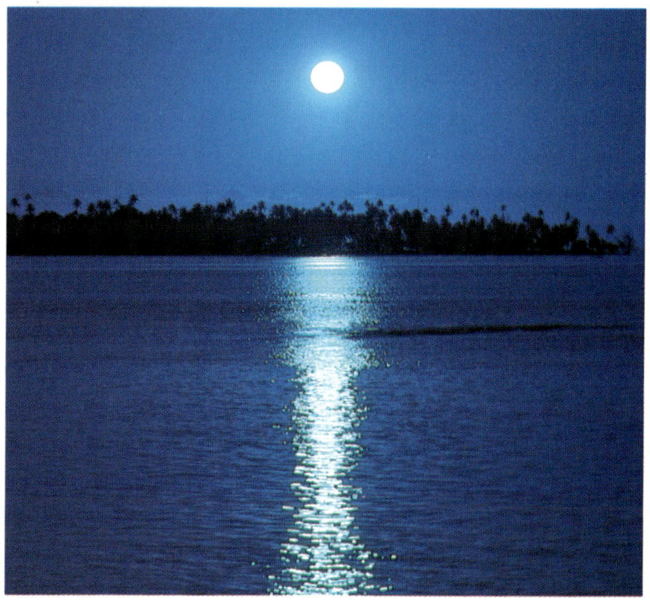

▶ **NIGHT**
Pictures by moonlight are easiest to shoot when they include the moon – the moon is lit by the sun, so it needs relatively little exposure.

Before sunrise

At this early hour there will be little apparent colour anywhere. A subject may appear in silhouette against a dark grey sky as the sun begins to shine over the horizon. Objects will appear in shades of black and grey with, perhaps, a tinge of blue.

When the sun is just below the horizon on a clear day, the sky is filled with the full spectrum of colours from red to a deep blue-violet. Colours change in a matter of minutes and this is the time to shoot the wonderful pink glow caused by haze.

Capturing this light does require quite a lot of effort. Be prepared to get up very early if the location is far away. Remember that low light means slow shutter speeds – so unless you use a high speed film you will need to use a tripod and a cable release to prevent camera shake.

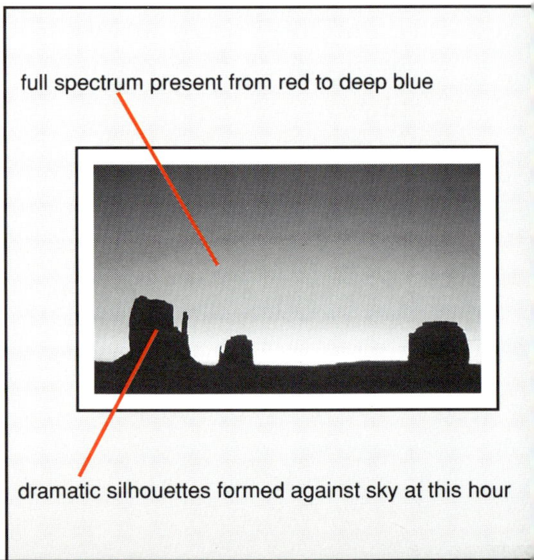

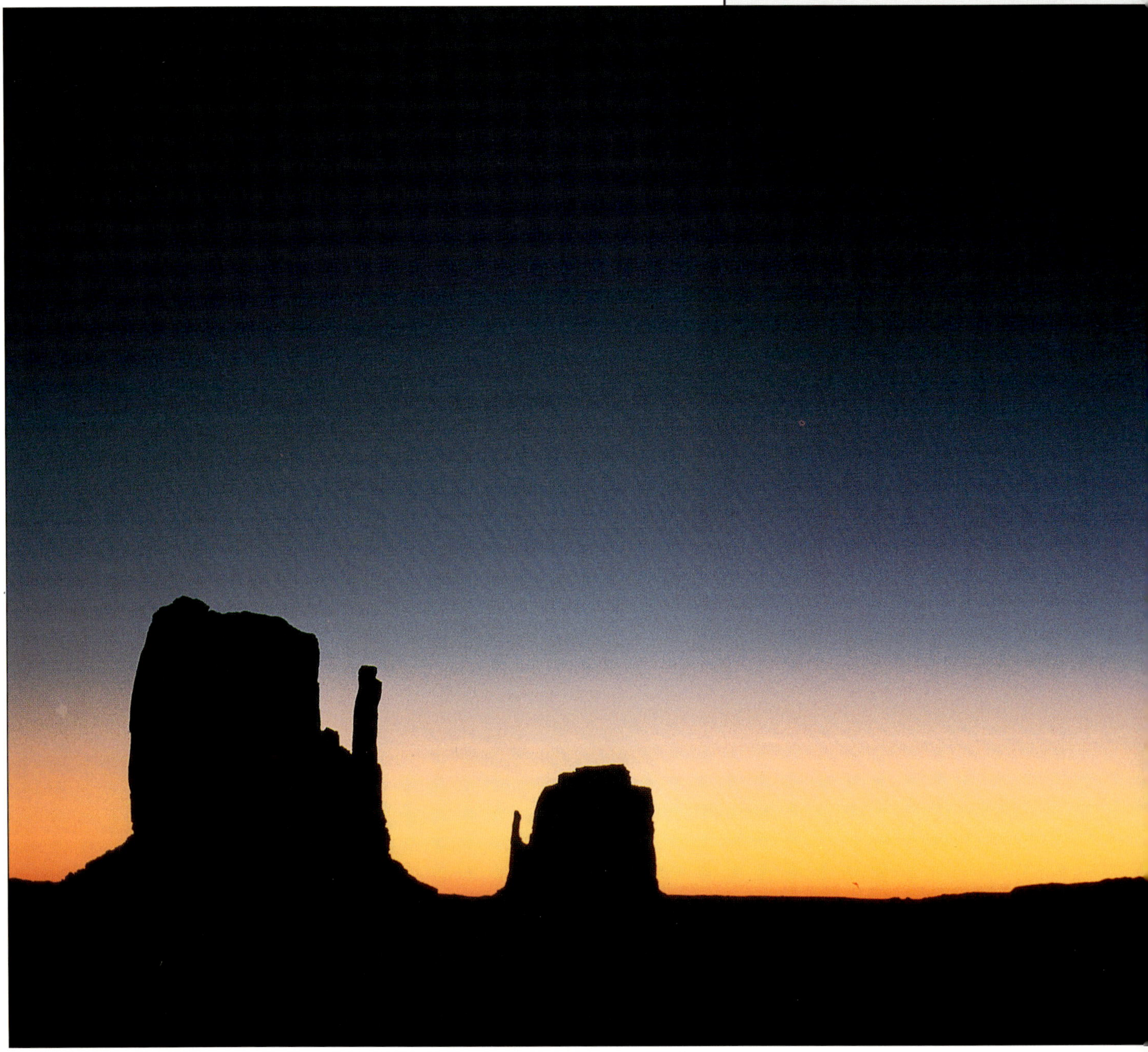

▼ COOL DAWN
First light over the Arizona desert creates a whole range of colours from orange to deep blue. The silhouetted rock formations add even more impact.

Sunrise

As the sun appears over the horizon the light becomes a deep orangey red. This is because all the other wavelengths are scattered at this time of day.

Sunny mornings can provide spectacular opportunities to take photos and you'll often find that there's a mist, too, which will soften the scene's colours and can make landscapes, gardens and cityscapes even more interesting. Be prepared to shoot quickly, though, because around dawn and dusk the light changes very fast.

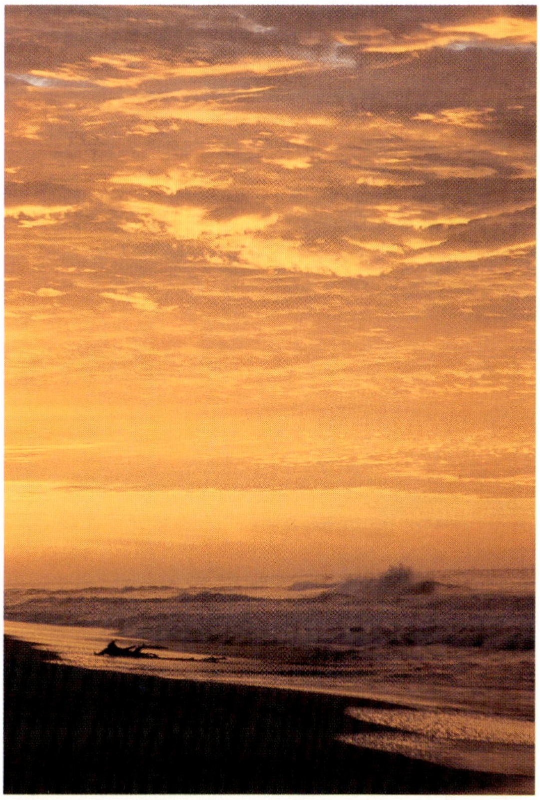

◀ FIRST SUN
Sunrise lights up the sky with a rich orangey red glow. The photographer has chosen to fill three quarters of the frame with the cloudy sky, which makes for a more dramatic picture.

▼ MISTY MORNING
Early morning mist over this meadow creates a gentle, pastel coloured scene. Notice how aerial perspective makes background objects fade away into the misty haze. The cows provide foreground interest.

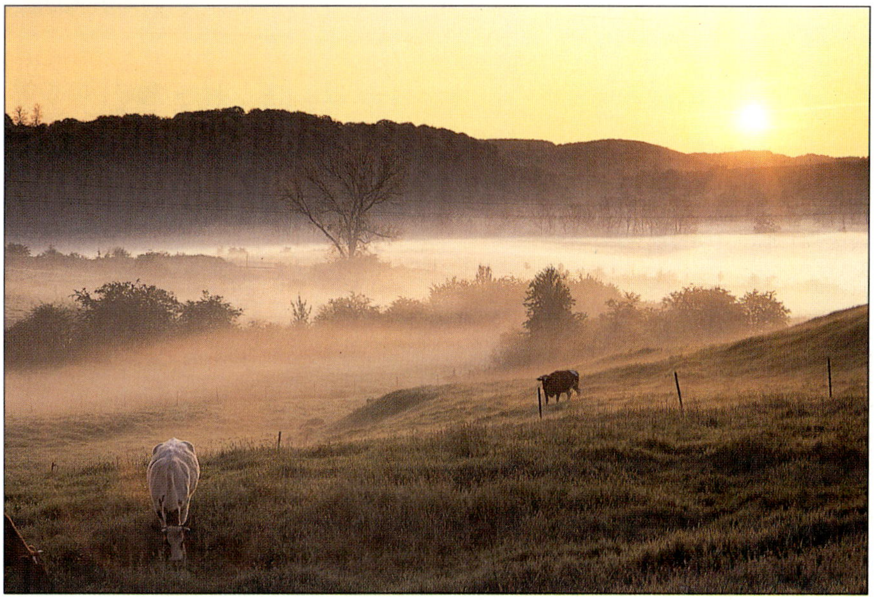

After sunrise

A low sun provides you with many more photographic opportunities than when the sun is high in the sky. The low angle of light gives you the choice between front, back and sidelighting.

After sunrise, shadows are often deep blue and cold although subjects lit by the sun can sometimes have a yellow or golden tint. The low sun casts strange deep blue shadows which make for some striking pictures.

It's worth bracketing exposures at this time of day. With slide film, even half a stop can alter the atmosphere of a picture quite dramatically. Slight overexposure will add to the lightness of the scene. Underexpose, on the other hand, and you will end up with much richer colours.

Mid-morning

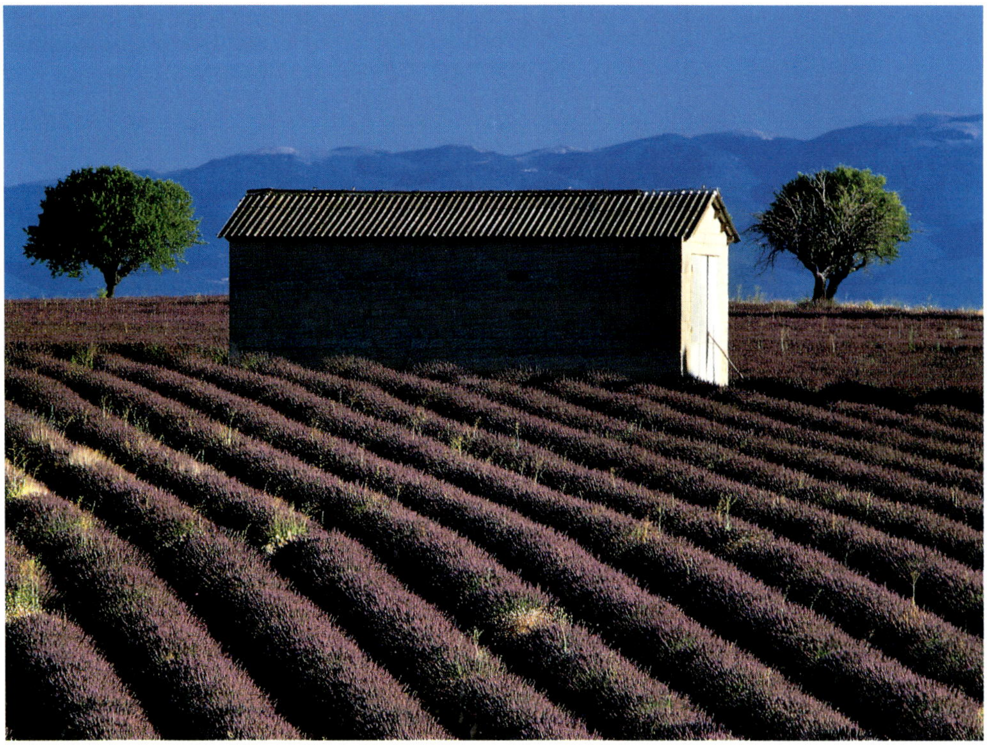

◀ **HARD BLUE**
Photographing in mid-morning enhances an already striking picture. The hard blue light makes an interesting contrast with the softer colours of the lavender rows in the field.

As morning progresses, the light shifts towards a more neutral colour. Now is a good time for those more detailed shots which are impossible to get at dawn, with its low raking light.

The hard-edged shadows thrown by the relatively low-angled sun are long enough to make an interesting picture. Relief and texture show up well, which makes mid-morning a good time to shoot architecture.

If the sun is directly behind you, don't forget to make sure your own shadow isn't in the picture.

CHECK IT!

Points to remember:

- ❑ At dawn use a tripod, if possible, to avoid camera shake
- ❑ Early to mid-morning light is ideal for buildings as it enhances textures and reliefs
- ❑ A low angle sun lets you choose between frontlighting, backlighting and sidelighting
- ❑ Because of the unpredictable light early in the morning, make sure you bracket your exposures

Tip **Check your light**

Because light levels change rapidly early in the morning, it is often difficult to get an accurate reading from your meter. There are two ways of overcoming this.

Either try to find a view which has an equal balance of light and darkness. Or, if you can control the exposure on your camera, take a reading of the brighter part of the sky and then increase the exposure by 1½-2 stops. This should ensure a more accurate reading.

▼ **MODELLING LIGHT**
The mid-morning sun produces strong shadows which can create fascinating patterns as in this desert scene. Notice, too, how the low sun brings out the textures of the sand.

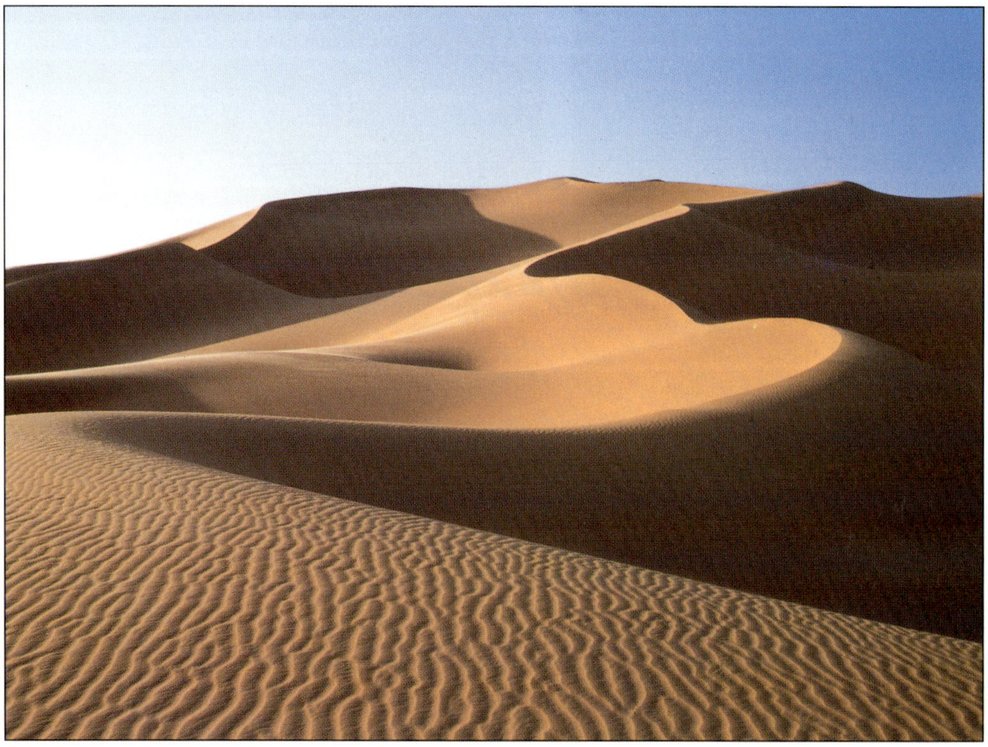

A small port at dawn

A view including a harbour, rows of pretty houses and moored boats is a combination full of possibilities. Mike Busselle and David Jones photograph a French port at the start of the day.

Honfleur is an extremely pretty little village. Situated on the Normandy coast just to the west of Le Havre, it originally relied on fishing for its livelihood but has now become a popular tourist attraction, and is especially busy during the summer months.

Avoiding the crowds is one good reason for photographing the village early in the morning, but lighting is an even better one. Mike has taken pictures of Honfleur several times before, and told me that all the best views along the harbour look stronger when the sun's still low in the sky. So I went to bed early the night we got there and braced myself for an early morning start.

A cloudy start

We left our hotel at 5am on a dark and ominously cloudy June morning and walked down to the harbour. Mike wanted to set up as early as possible so he'd be ready to shoot when the sun rose. The weather had been overcast for the past few days, and we were both afraid of not getting the early sunlight we needed. But just as the dawn was breaking, the clouds parted to give us an even chance of good light.

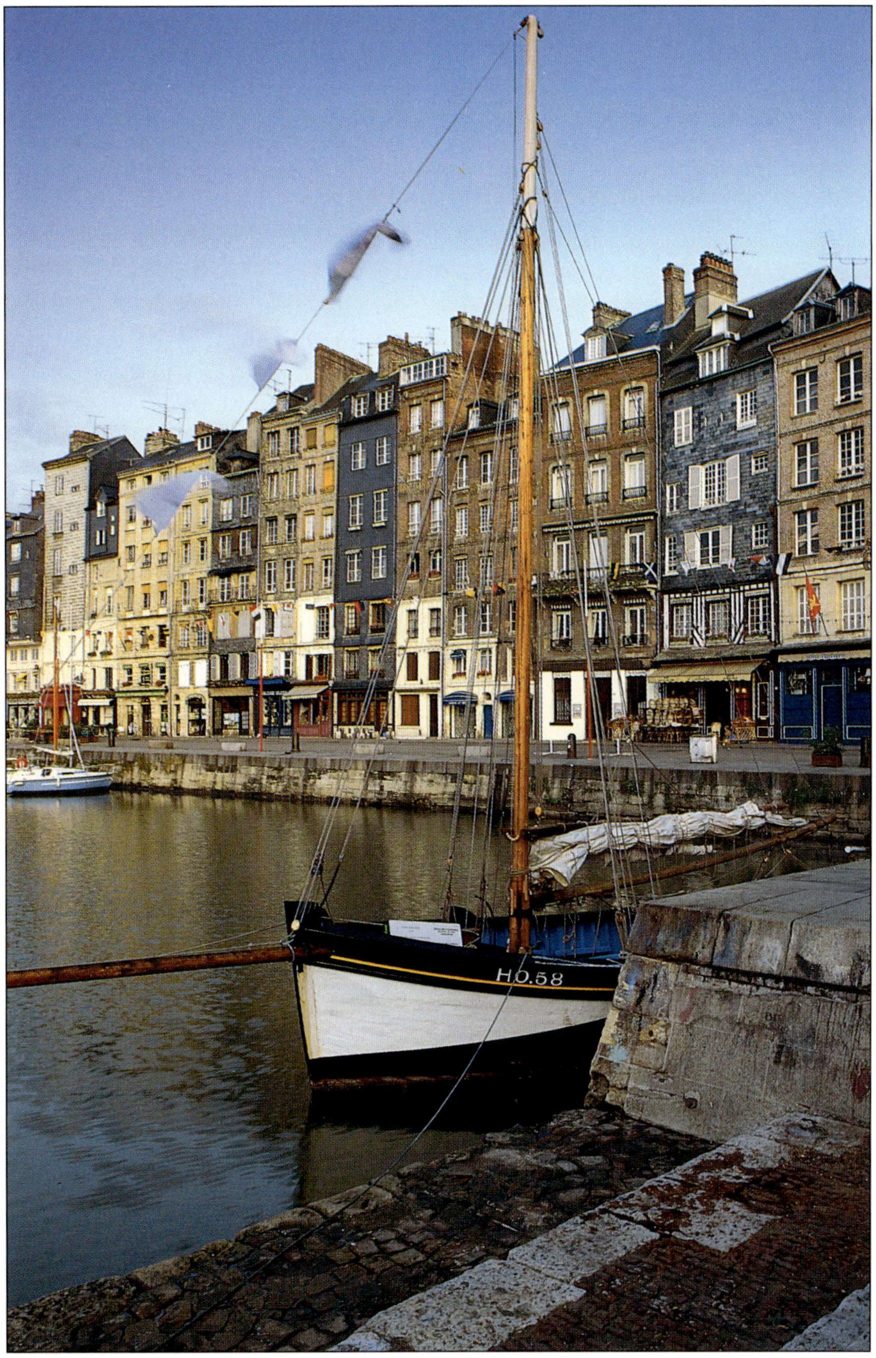

1 ▲ BLUE LIGHT Mike began at the southern end of the harbour, where he found an old moored fishing boat. He took a tightly framed shot with the boat in the foreground and some seafront houses behind, and included a lot of sky to capitalize on the clear, blue early morning light.

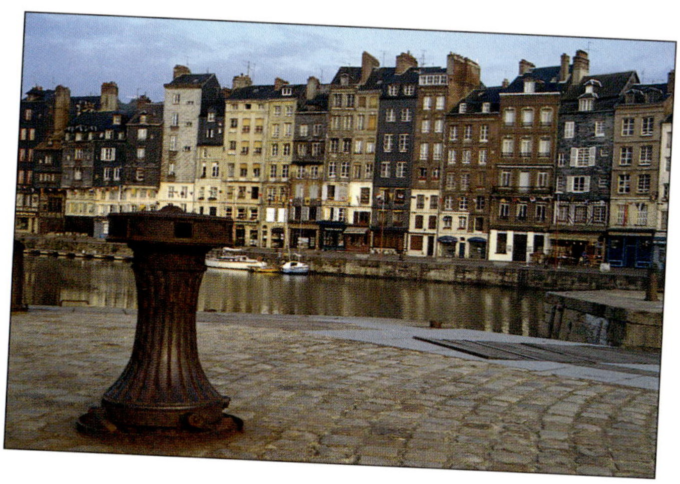

▶ David took this shot at first light. He used a 35mm lens to frame a view across the harbour towards the tall houses, and included a rusty old capstan in the foreground. But the capstan only looks intrusive in the picture.

The set up

Mike and David were photographing the village of Honfleur in Normandy, northern France. The village was at its best in the morning because the prettiest rows of seafront houses are east facing and therefore only lit by the sun early in the day. They began shooting at 5am and watched the light change dramatically as the sun slowly rose. At about 6am a patch of rain clouds appeared in the north, and by 7am they had blotted out the sun entirely.

As soon as it was bright enough I started shooting, using a Nikon F4 on a tripod with a 35mm lens and Fuji ISO 50D slide film. My first shot was a view across the harbour towards the rows of tall, thin shops and houses with an old metal capstan in the foreground. It was a good idea, but the capstan isn't interesting enough.

Cold light

The first thing Mike did was have a good look around. Only when he'd picked out three or four prime viewpoints for future reference did he start shooting. He used a Nikon F801s on a tripod with a 28-70mm zoom lens and Fuji Velvia ISO 50 colour slide film, and took full advantage of the cold, blue light that preceded sunrise. A traditional fishing boat was moored at the southern end of the harbour, and Mike decided it would make an excellent foreground.

He set up behind it and took an upright shot looking towards the houses. Then he moved back to where I'd taken my first shot, but moved a little closer to the water so he caught the houses' reflections on film. The light in the resulting shot

▶ When the sun came up David tried again. He moved to the southern end of the pier and shot back towards the sunlit houses. It's a better shot, but the foreground lacks interest – a moored boat or even some reflections in the water would have helped.

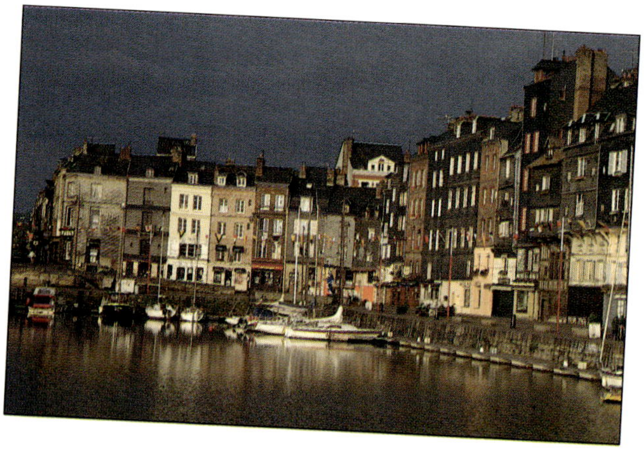

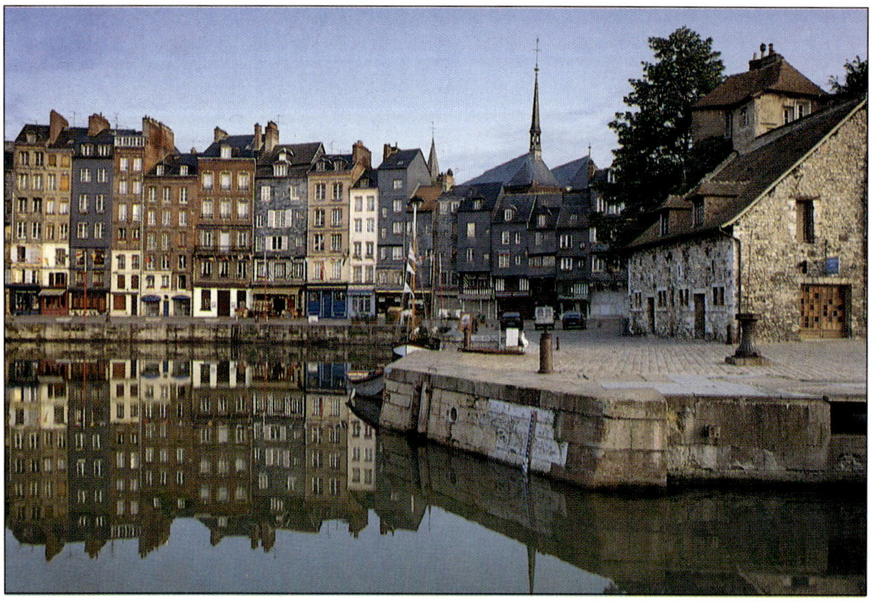

2 ▲ REFLECTIONS
Mike then moved around to the western side of the harbour so that he was shooting directly across the water towards the houses. He included a lot of water in the foreground so he could capture the houses' reflections on film. As you can see, the light was improving all the time.

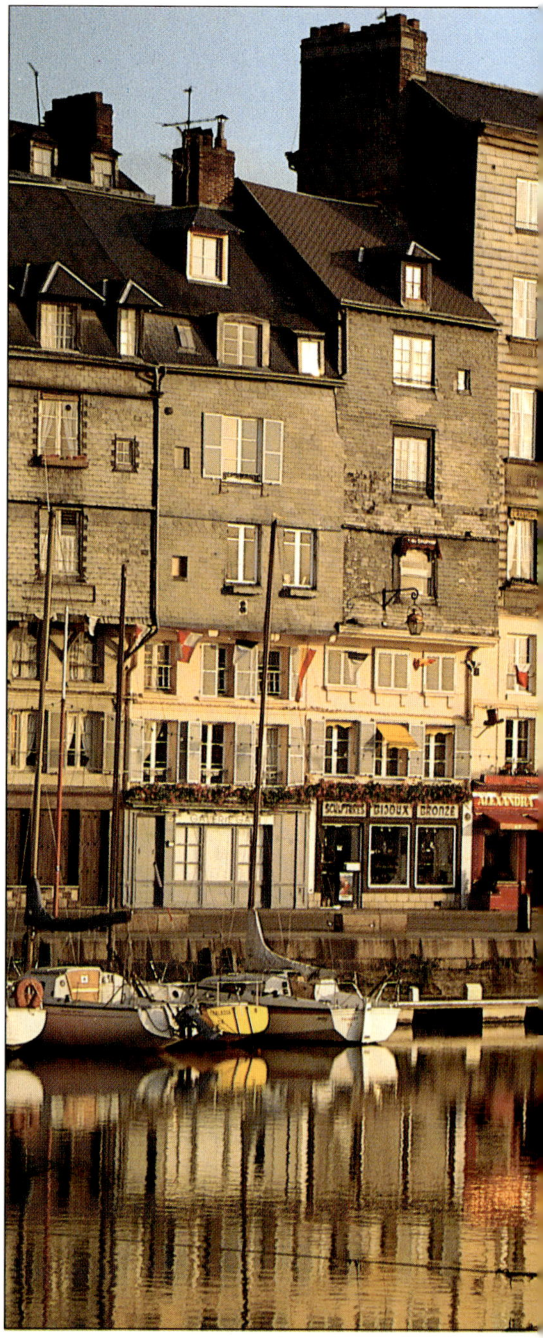

3 ▶ A BURST OF COLOUR
When the sun came up it brought out all the rich colours in the scene. Mike moved up to the north end and took another shot across the water towards the houses. In the warm sunlight the scene looked completely different, and there was no need to resort to filters.

was cool and clear, but the sun was beginning to emerge.

The sun bursts forth

When the sun came up properly I realized why Mike had insisted on getting up so early. The first rays lit up the east facing house fronts and made them really stand out against the dark, cloudy sky to the north. It was a spectacular scene, and one we were both determined to take advantage of.

I stood at the southern end of the pier and framed a shot of sunlit yachts and houses backed by the dark sky. It was better than my first effort, but given the conditions, I was disappointed. By underexposing I lost some of the colour in the view, and a stronger foreground or some clearer reflections would have helped the picture.

Working fast

Mike wanted to make the most of the sunlight, but he could see that the dark clouds were spreading so he had to work fast. Because he'd had a good look around to begin with, he knew exactly where the best viewpoints were.

He started by taking a view of the brightly lit houses reflected in the water from the northern end of the harbour. Then he took another shot from that end with a yacht in the foreground. To finish off, he went back to the old fishing boat he'd started with and took an excellent landscape shot along the seafront.

It was now around 7am and people were beginning to appear, but as they did the sun was blotted out by the advancing clouds. It started to rain, and remained overcast for the rest of the day. Mike and I didn't mind too much though. It felt very satisfying to have achieved something so early in the morning.

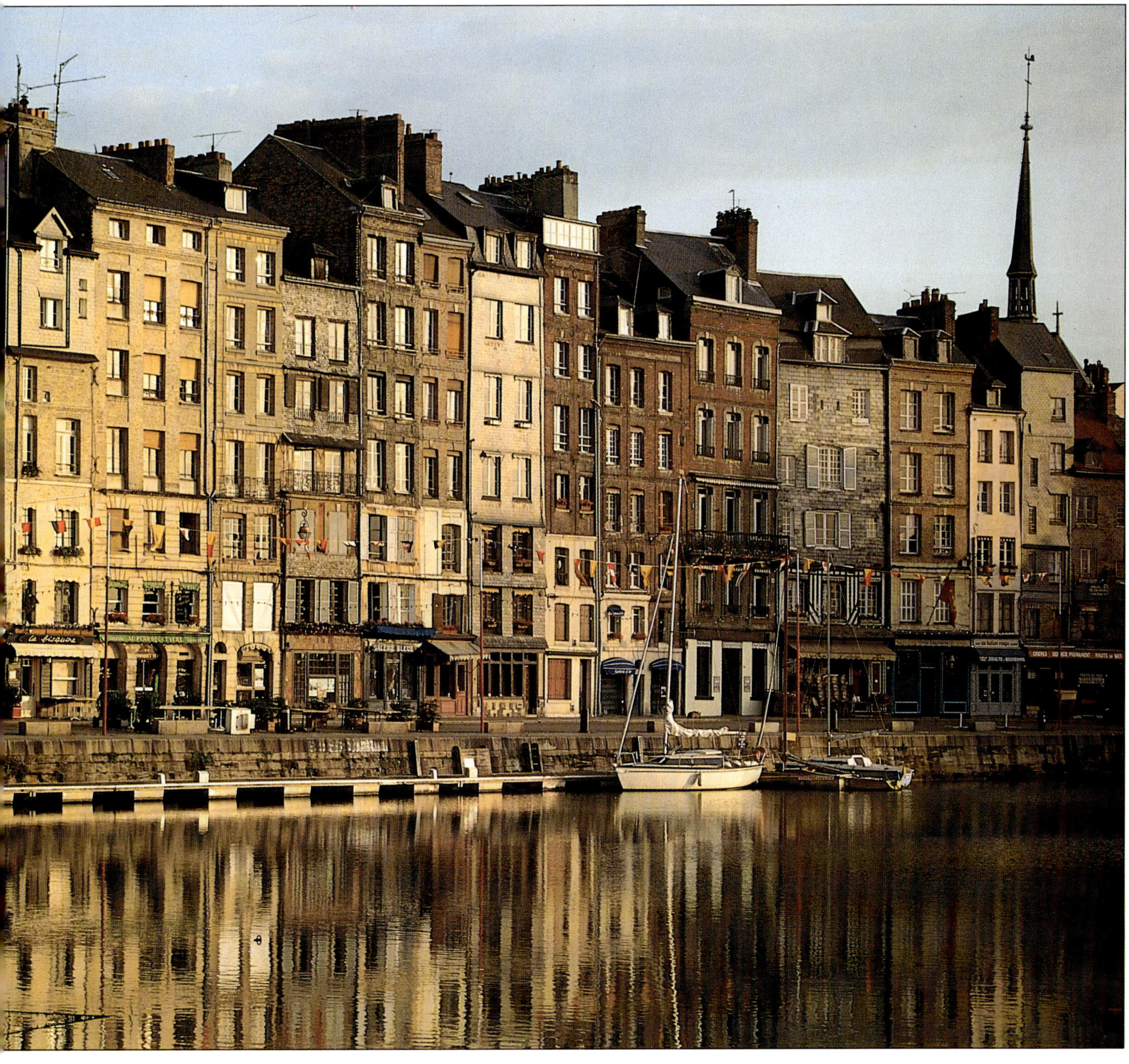

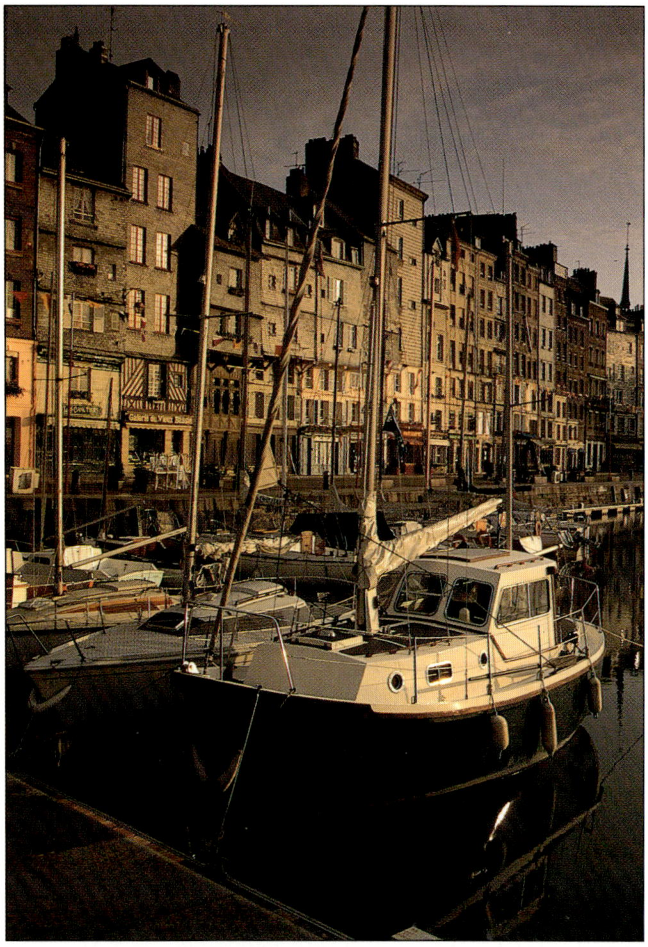

Compact tip

❑ Most compact cameras will switch on the flash in dim early morning light, despite the fact that subjects like this village are too distant for the flash to have any effect on them. To take atmospheric available light pictures, switch the flash off. If you're getting a slow shutter speed, avoid camera shake by using a tripod or by resting your compact on a handy surface.

SLR tip

❑ When strong vertical lines dominate your pictures, it's sensible to keep them parallel by levelling the camera carefully. However, this leaves the horizon at the centre of the frame, allowing the foreground to dominate the shot. Professionals often use a shift lens to pull the horizon down, but if you can't afford one, look for reflecting surfaces that will actually add to a shot.

4 ◀ STRONG FOREGROUND
Mike knew the sun wasn't going to last long so he had to work fast. He wanted to take a shot of the houses that included a strong foreground, so he set up behind a group of yachts and shot through the rigging. It was a lovely shot, but the boats looked too modern.

5 ▼ THE PERFECT BALANCE
Mike moved back around to the southern end of the harbour to take this concluding photograph. He included the moored fishing boat again, but this time took a landscape shot of the view. The contrast between the dark foreground and the brilliantly lit buildings behind is striking.

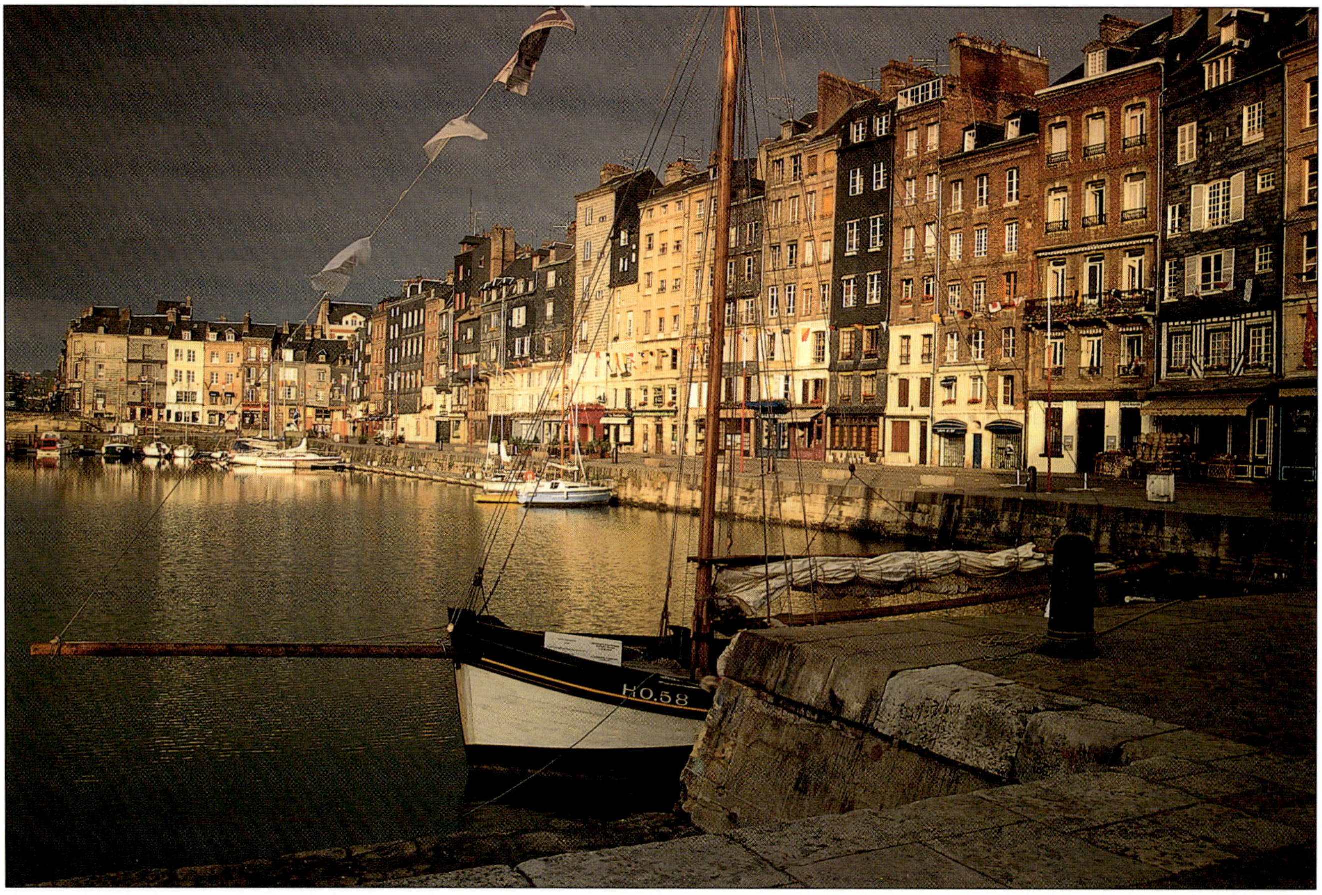

Midday to twilight

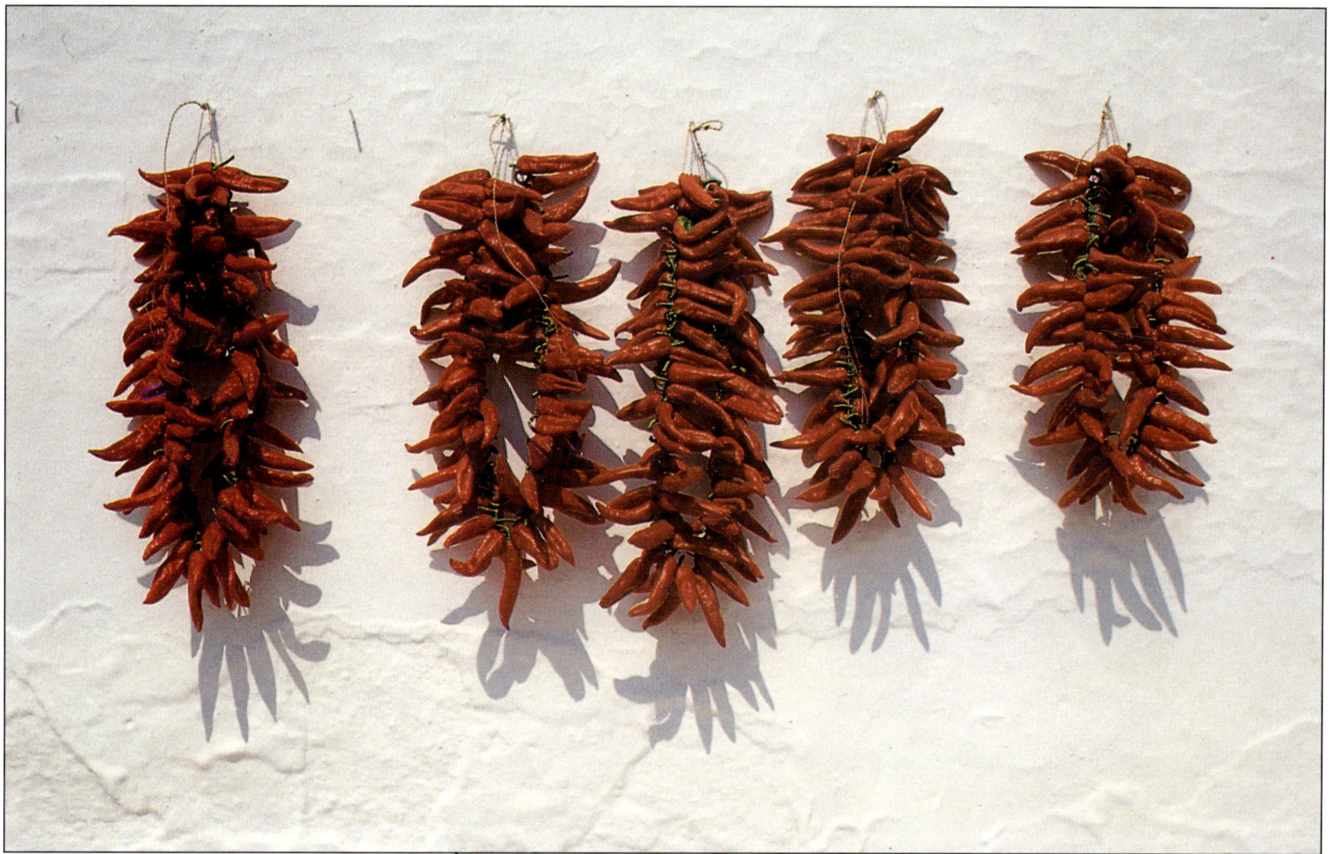

▲ **HOT PEPPERS**
This simple but striking composition was taken at midday. The noonday sun projects sharp shadows which fall underneath the subject, simplifying rather than complicating the picture. To obtain the right exposure, a meter reading was taken from the white wall and two stops were added.

Between noon and dusk, daylight offers a rich variety of natural lighting conditions. The challenge for you is to match the subject to the time of day.

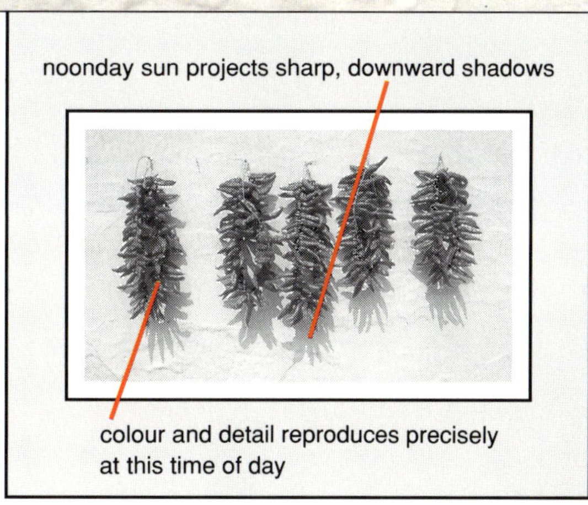

During the middle hours of the day, when the sun is high up in the sky, the light is more consistent in quality and colour than at any other time. Light is neutral, which means that the colour balance of daylight film matches it correctly. But this doesn't mean that it's also the best time for all types of photography.

You need to think carefully about taking photos when the sun is overhead. Some subjects are far more suitable than others. On the plus side, a high sun makes for crisp, sharply detailed pictures. Subjects which are strong in shape and colour, and where shadow is unimportant, can make good subjects in this type of light. For example, think of brightly painted beach huts at the seaside.

Colour reproduces very accurately during this part of the day, but there are a number of disadvantages. Light during these hours gives little form or modelling, which makes it unsuitable for subjects with interesting texture. The higher the sun the more the shadows will fall underneath. This can be very unflattering for some subjects such as portraits, where the eyes will look concealed and sunken. It's unlikely that your subject will be over-impressed with the results!

Flat, horizontal subjects, like landscapes, don't work either, as the lack of shadow hides texture. At best you'll be left with a sharp, but uninteresting shot.

Tip

Sunny f16 rule

On a bright sunny day even an advanced exposure system can sometimes be fooled by a shiny subject. But there's a quick and easy way to overcome this – the 'sunny f16 rule'.

This simply means that when the camera is set at f16 the correct shutter speed is the one with the number closest to the film's ISO rating. For example, if you are using ISO 64 film, the correct exposure for bright sunlight at f16 is 1/60th sec, the shutter speed closest to 64.

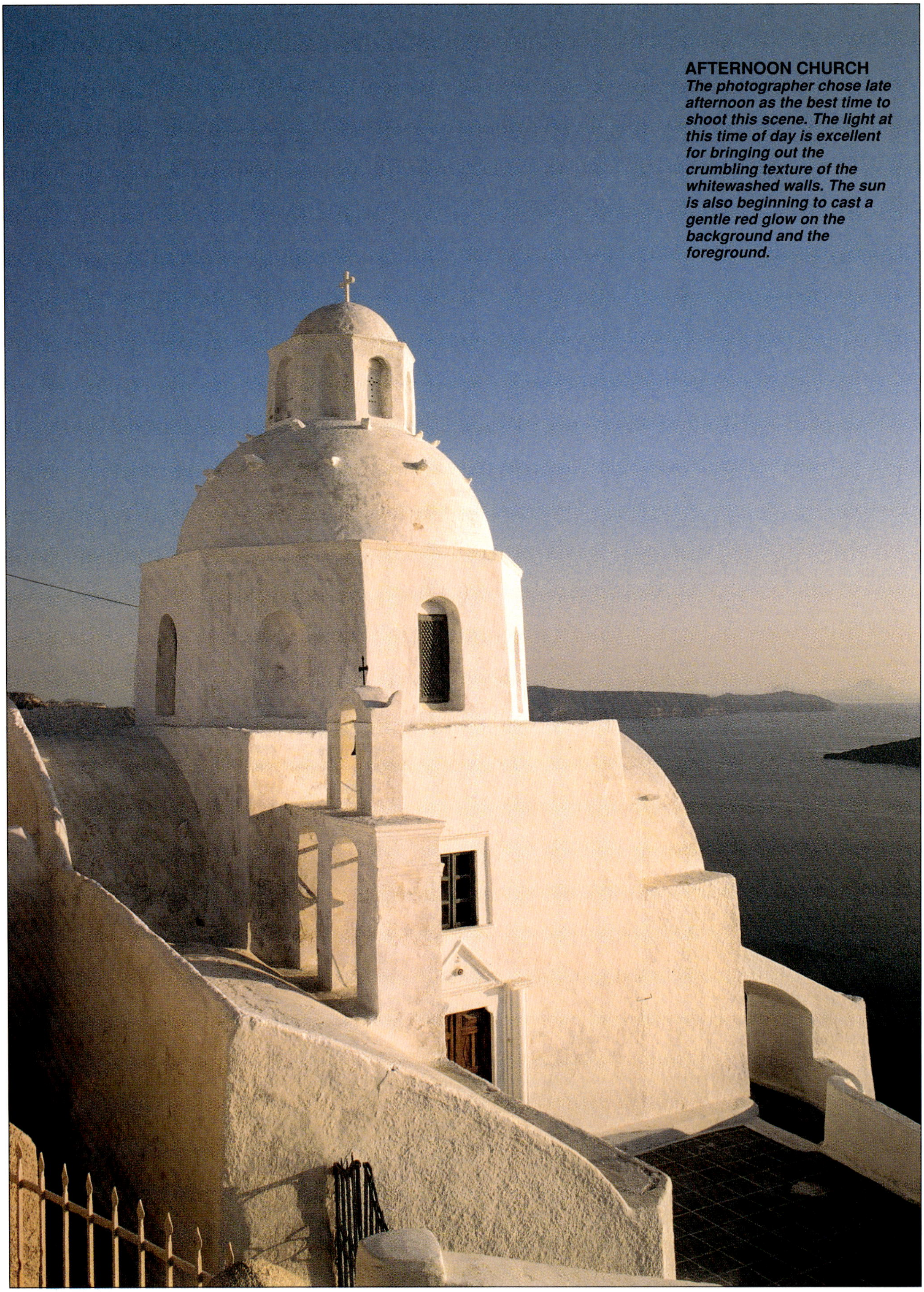

AFTERNOON CHURCH
The photographer chose late afternoon as the best time to shoot this scene. The light at this time of day is excellent for bringing out the crumbling texture of the whitewashed walls. The sun is also beginning to cast a gentle red glow on the background and the foreground.

Afternoon light

In the early afternoon, changes in the light are hardly perceptible from midday. If there is dust and moisture in the air, the light may appear slightly warmer, but photographic opportunities are still limited.

By mid afternoon, daylight takes a definite shift towards the red end of the spectrum, and this becomes more and more pronounced over the next few hours. By late afternoon, shadows are lengthening and the lower light creates modelling. Now is an excellent time for photographing subjects such as buildings where the texture is important.

▼ SUN AND SAND
Afternoon light is good for shooting beach scenes and people. The angle of the sun projects interesting shadows on sand, and faces aren't spoilt by the distorting downward shadows of midday.

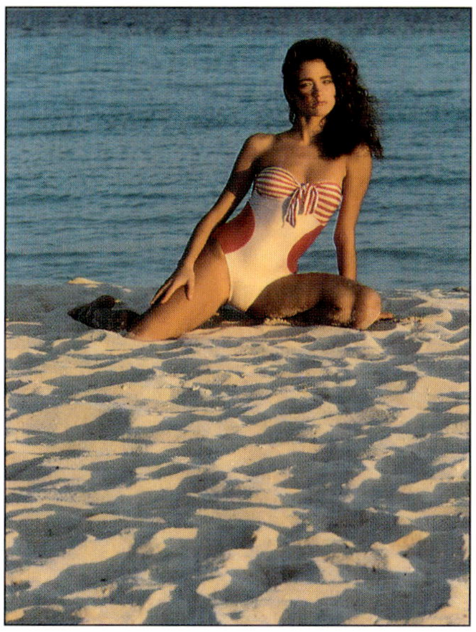

Tip

Special effects

Use a yellow or orange filter to intensify the natural sunset colours. A starburst filter will create a star-shaped explosion of light from the sun.

Flare, which should usually be avoided, can be used creatively at this time of day. A small aperture will give star shapes, with light bursting out along points of the star. A larger aperture gives a more circular spread of light.

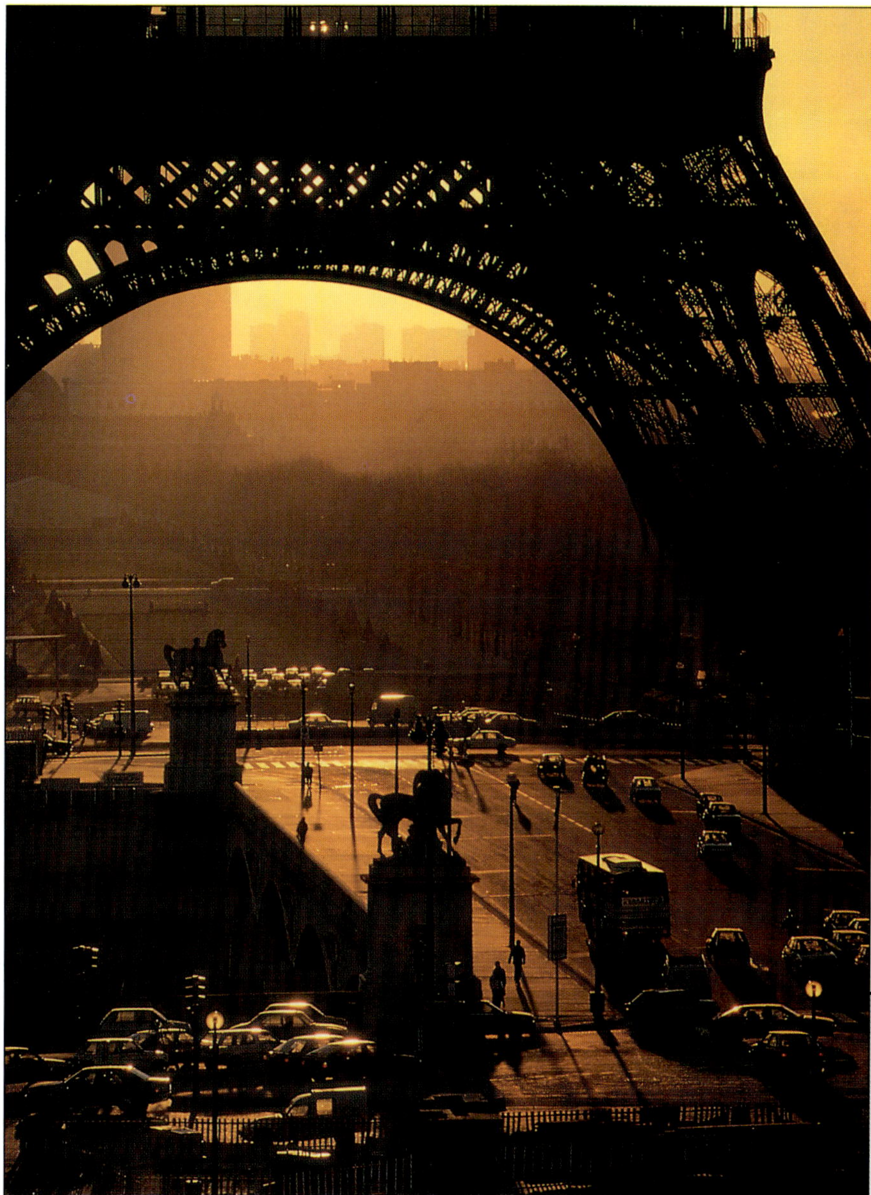

Sunset

Spectacular sunsets are one of the most popular photographic subjects, but all too often the results turn out rather ordinary.

Not all great sunset shots have the sun in the frame. Attention to the clouds or concentrating on a foreground silhouette against a glowing sky can often be more interesting.

If the sun is going to be the centre of attention, it's best to use a long telephoto lens and focus on infinity. A lens longer then 300mm ensures that the sun features significantly in the frame.

Light changes rapidly at this time of day so it can be difficult to get an accurate exposure reading. If you take a reading from the sun, the rest of the sky appears underexposed, while if the exposure is taken from the foreground, the sun is overexposed, so meter for the sky with the sun just outside the frame.

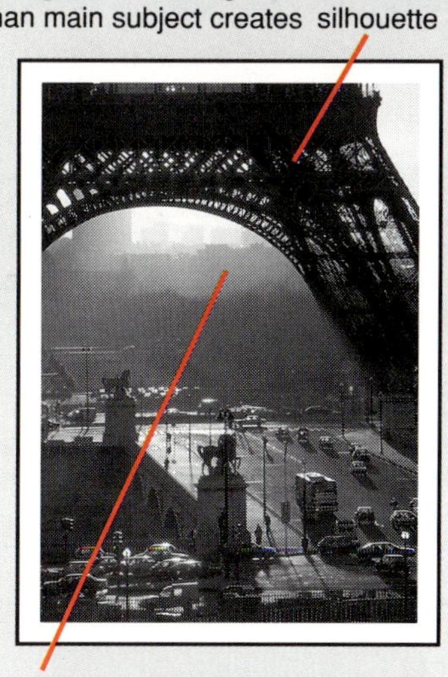

▲ SUNSET TOWER
Here a familiar subject – the Eiffel Tower – is treated in an unusual way to frame this view of Paris. Shooting into the sunset creates a silhouette of the tower, and the background haze adds atmosphere.

Twilight

When the sun is just below the horizon, the lighting conditions can produce some highly unusual opportunities. Light fades very quickly – at the equator, sunset is almost like turning off a light – so ideally you need a tripod and a long exposure.

The purest twilight colours can be seen when there are no clouds in the sky and no dust in the atmosphere. In these conditions the full range of colours in the spectrum is usually present. Dust makes the sky look yellow or even grey. An overcast day, on the other hand, will make your pictures rather too blue.

Colour film isn't very good at dealing with a relatively bright sky and an unlit ground. Some of the most successful twilight pictures are therefore silhouettes. Try to isolate a distinctive foreground subject – a tree or high building for example – and expose for the sky to create a silhouette.

CHECK IT! ✔

To make the most of daylight in the second half of the day:

- ❑ at midday avoid portraits or subjects where it's important to show texture
- ❑ use late afternoon to bring out texture and form
- ❑ to cope with rapidly changing light at sunset, bracket your exposures
- ❑ try including a silhouette at twilight to add impact to a shot

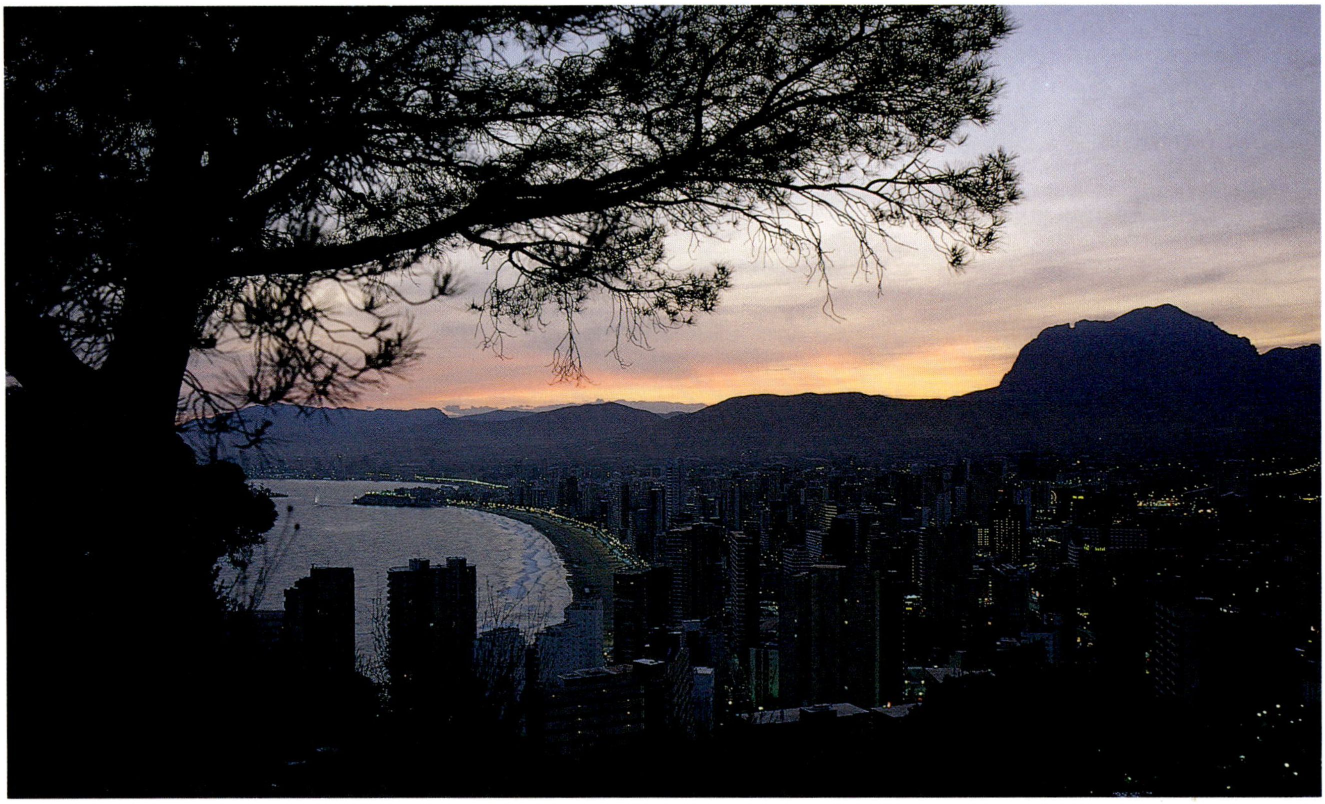

▲ DUSKY TOWN
When the sun has fallen below the horizon, the sun's afterglow splashes rich colours across the sky. With the great contrast between ground and sky it's best, as in this photograph, to provide an equal balance of light and dark in the frame.

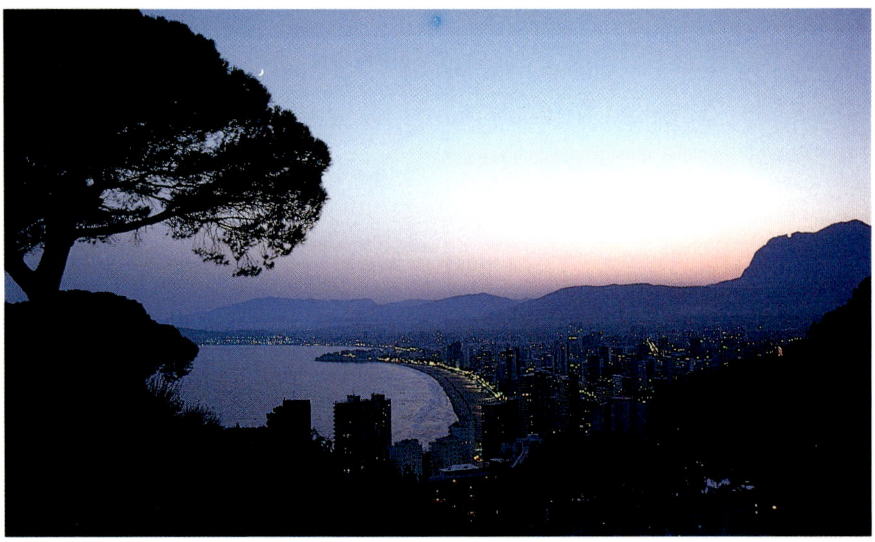

▶ TWILIGHT HOUR
Light changes rapidly at this time of day, as this photo of the same scene taken ten minutes later shows. Using a wide angle lens allows the photographer to get more of the sky in the frame and include a tiny moon just above the silhouette of the tree.

Night photography

Night photography can be far more challenging and exciting than photographing by daylight. By employing a little trickery the camera can see a host of images and effects that are invisible to the eye.

During the day, our eyes see clearly and we expect the camera to reproduce what we see. At night, most people's eyes not only take in a bare minimum, but often see less brilliant colours, fewer details and with less clarity. Given enough time, however, the camera can see colours which we can't and look into shadows where our eyes can't penetrate.

At night, moonlight makes landscapes appear unreal and mysterious, and cityscapes are totally transformed. There is a surprising variety of different coloured light sources, including street lamps, car headlights, neon signs, candlelight and fires. All create interesting and diverse effects for photography.

These light sources are often eyecatching enough to be the subject of the picture, rather than simply illuminating a scene. For instance, think of a street light seen through mist or the colour and movement of flames from a glowing bonfire.

Tip

Night exposure

If you want to record clear detail at night, measure the brightest part of the scene and open up the aperture by three f stops or choose a shutter speed three settings slower. This method is equally effective with a hand held meter or with the camera's own TTL meter when it is used close to the subject of the shot.

As most artificial lighting is weaker than daylight, you will need both a slow shutter speed and high speed film. Even in a brightly lit city scene shot on ISO 400 film, the exposure will typically be 1/60th sec at f4.

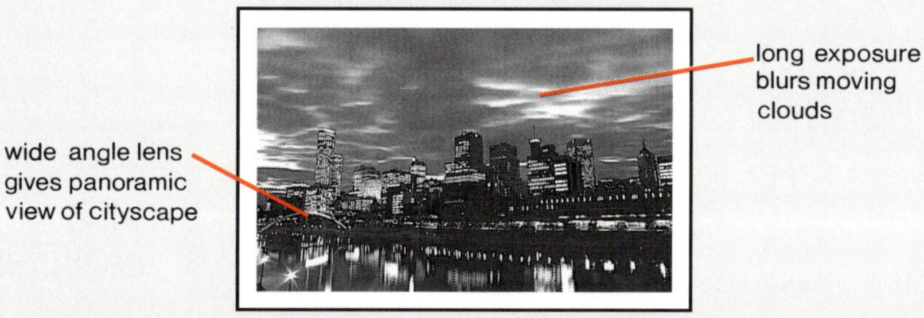

▼ **SKYLINE ALIGHT**
Photographing at late dusk when there is a little light still left in the sky has the advantage of turning the buildings into silhouettes. Deliberate use of daylight film results in an attractive green cast from the fluorescent office lights, which is then reflected in the water.

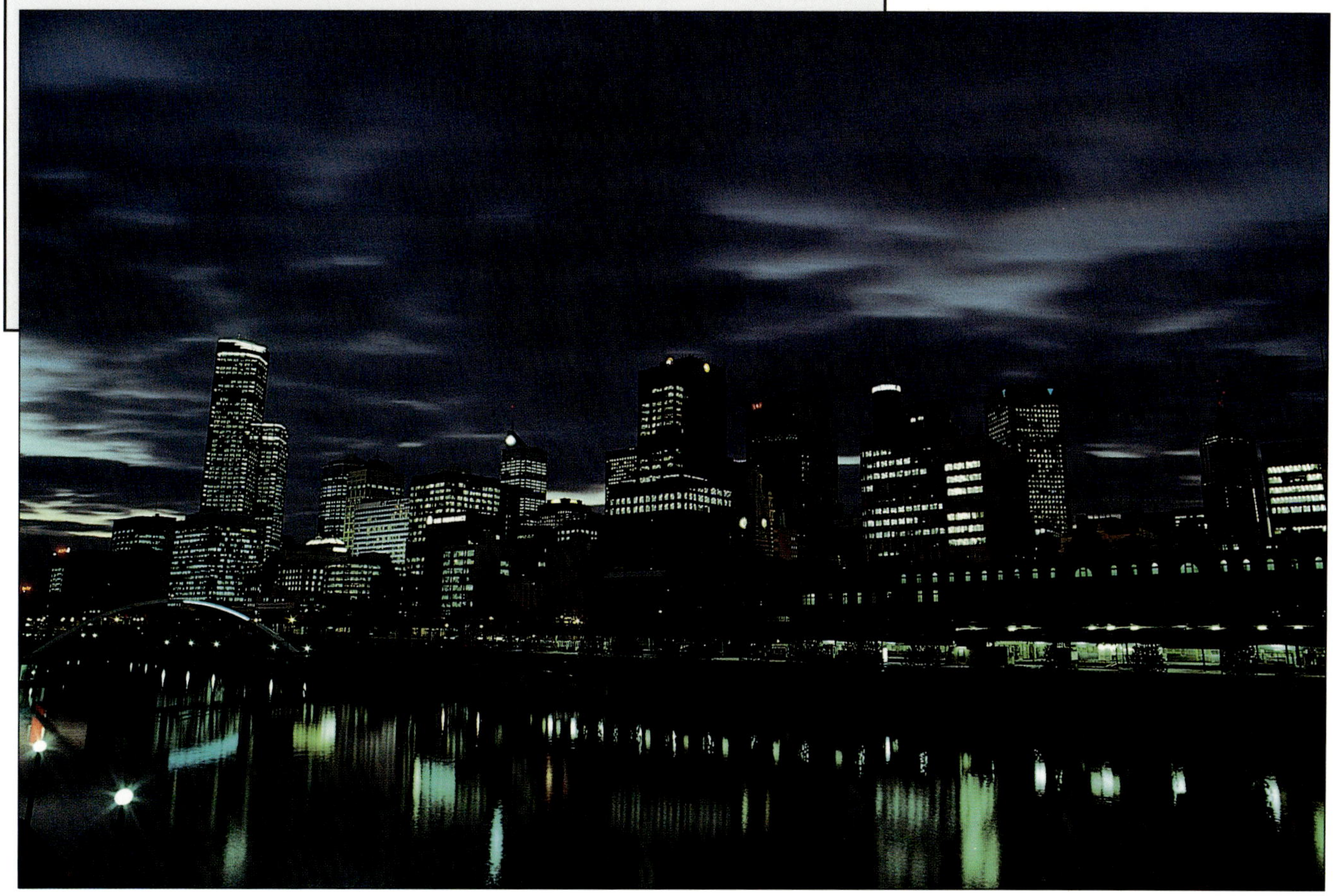

Light and subject

Sometimes you will want to include both the light source and the subject which it illuminates as features in the shot. Think of a child holding a sparkler, for example, or an urban street lit by streetlamps or shop displays. The closer the subject is to the light, the better the result.

There will be an extreme contrast between a bright light and a dark subject. One way of overcoming this is to include a reflective surface in the picture – such as a window or a wet street. Anything which reflects the light source will produce a more effective photo.

Backlight

The human face has a slightly shiny surface and reflects better if you photograph it with the light behind it and slightly to one side rather than with the light coming over your shoulder. This technique lets you obtain some effective shots, particularly if you are using candlelight. Instead of a dim full-face portrait, the result is a brighter, rim-lit profile, leaving the rest of the face in semi-silhouette.

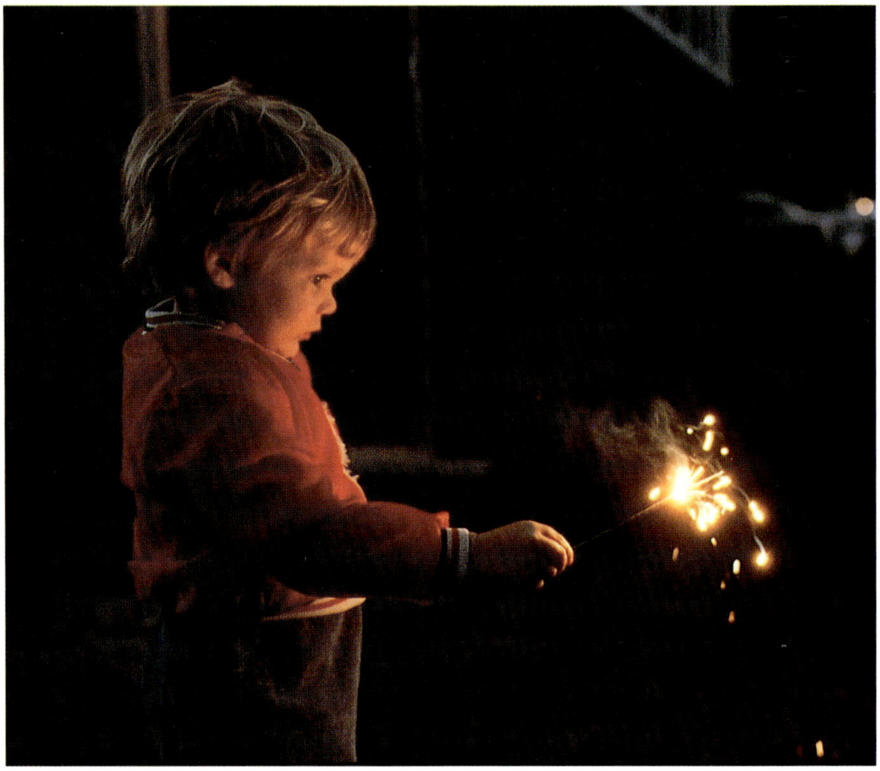

▲ **NIGHT SPARKLE**
Because the child's face reflects the light from the sparkler, there is not too great a contrast between light source and subject. To capture the warm glow, the photographer took a reading from the face.

▼ **STREAMS OF LIGHT**
With an exposure of around 15 seconds, the photographer has caught the streams of white and red light from the cars' head and tail lights. They rival the sky and office lighting for brightness.

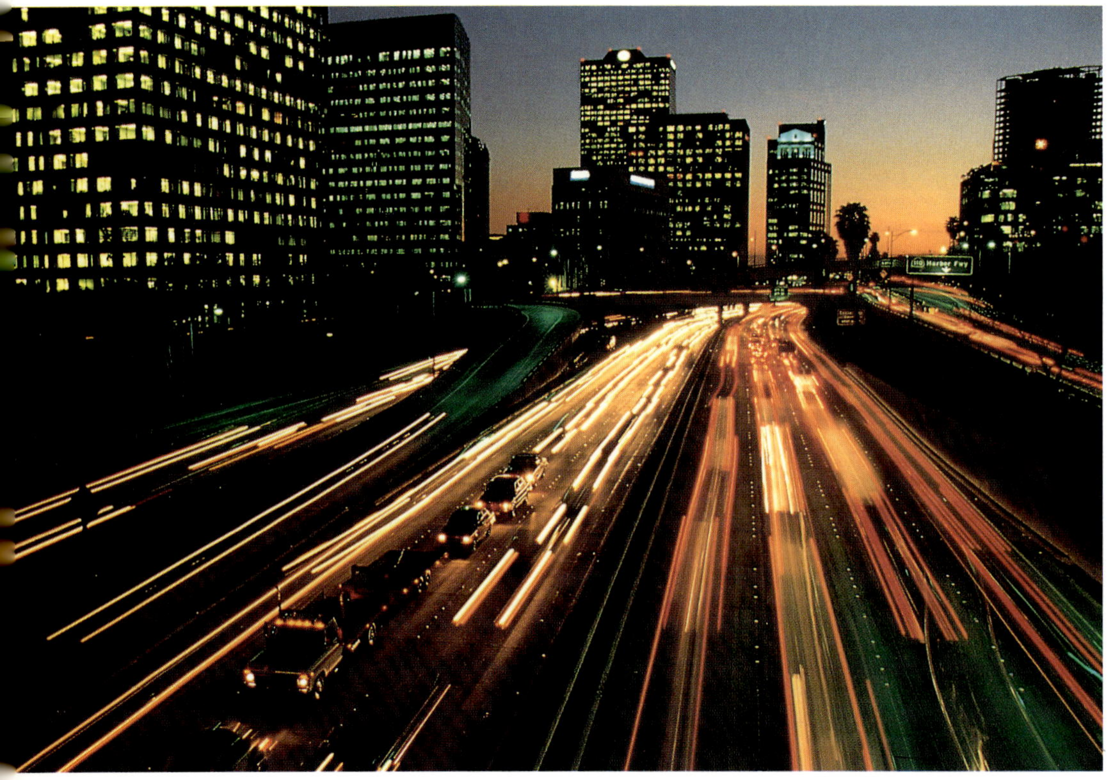

Tip **Night measures**

You'll find that shooting at night requires a little more preparation than daytime photography.

As visibility is much more limited, make sure you can put your hands easily on everything you'll need.

You may wish to remove film from its outer wrappings to save fumbling, and take along only one kind to avoid confusion.

Because you are likely to need long exposures, a tripod or other fixed support is almost always essential when it's dark. Ideally, try to choose a model with a quick-release fitting. This removes the risk of jamming the screw when you remove the camera.

A small torch can also prove useful and a watch with a luminous secondhand is invaluable for those very long exposures.

Moving light

With your camera mounted on a tripod and the shutter held open with a locking cable release, any moving light is recorded on film as a continuous streak. If the light source slows, the brilliance increases; if it speeds up, the effect is dimmed. The lights from cars streaming under a bridge, for example, create long streaks of red and white on film and will enhance any photograph of a city sight.

Fireworks

Fireworks provide you with wonderful photographic material. You can capture on film both their spectacular colours and their movement. To the eye, a roman candle projects a coloured ball, but to the camera, it draws a coloured line across the sky. If you use ISO 400 film with a shutter speed of around 1/30th sec, you should be able to take most of your shots without a tripod.

You can capture several air bursts on one picture by keeping the shutter open and covering the lens with its cap when there's a lull in the proceedings. Set a small aperture, such as f11 or f16, to prevent the sky appearing pale blue.

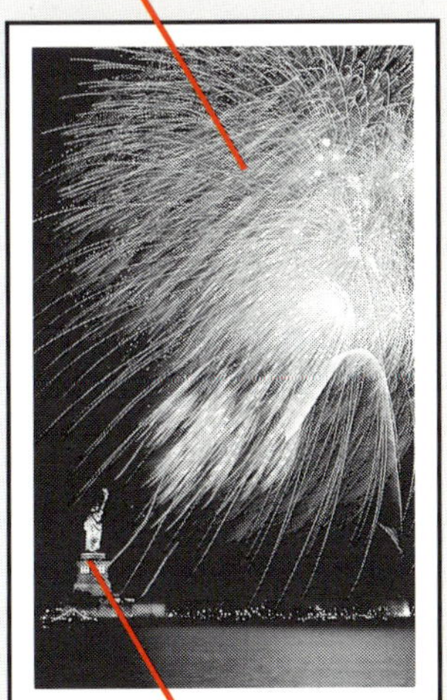

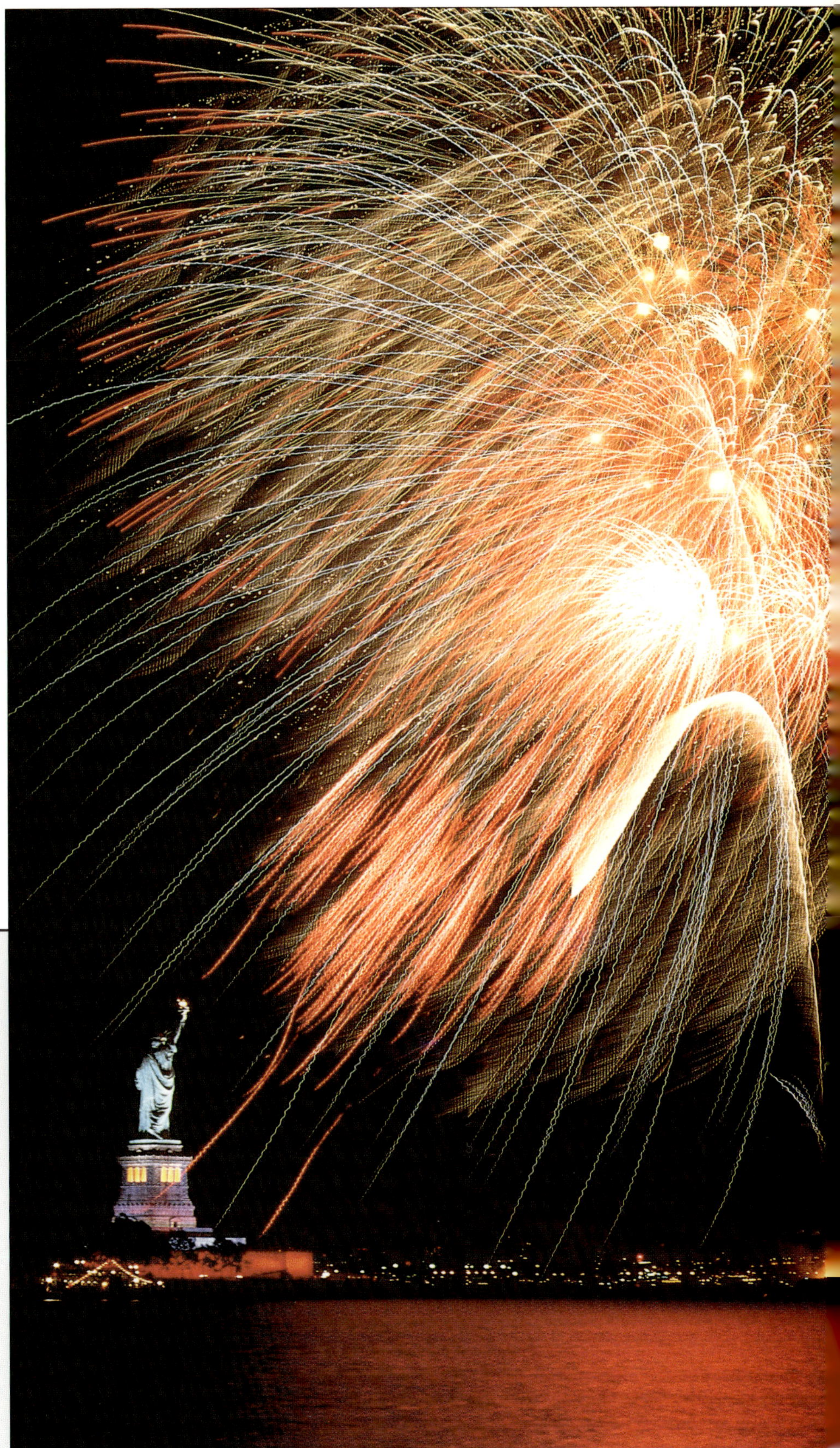

▲ **GRAND DISPLAY**
In reality, this scene never existed. The photographer used a long exposure to record consecutive bursts of fireworks and used the lens cap to cover up the lens between each burst.

Shooting by moonlight

Photographing by the light of the moon can create magical pictures but it does pose some problems. Very long exposures are needed even with fast film as the light intensity is around 15 stops less than daylight. Scenes with water, snow and sand often work best as they reflect a lot of light. Bracket your exposures as widely as possible and don't be deterred by a few disappointing results.

Photographing the moon itself is less difficult. Dates of the full moon are published in diaries. Keep exposure times reasonably short. Anything over a few seconds will cause the moon to be recorded as an oval, because of its path across the sky.

Double exposure

Some of the best moon shots are faked using the technique of double exposure. The moon can be photographed before or after the background. A powerful telephoto lens (anything over 400mm) will make the moon appear a respectable size in the frame.

It's important to compose the shot carefully so that you leave enough space in the frame for your second image. Then, using the double exposure button on your camera, take the second shot, again composing carefully to avoid an overlap between the two images. Make a sketch of the scene and mark on your subjects to be on the safe side.

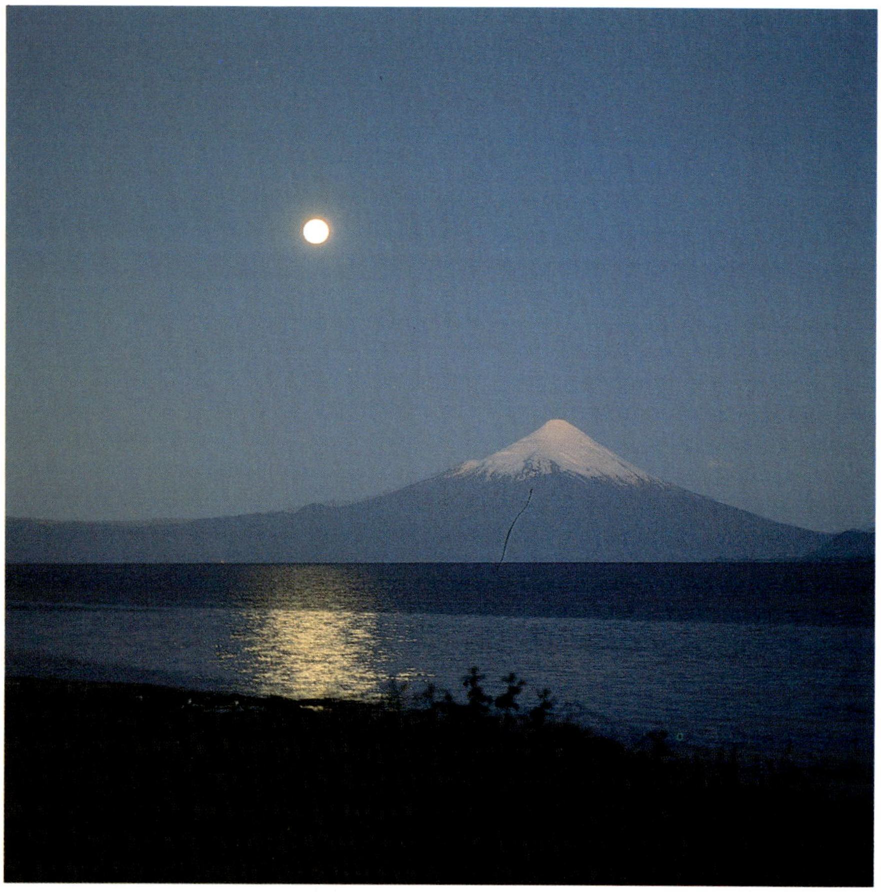

▲ MOON AND MOUNTAIN
Photographing by moonlight is often most effective when there is a reflective surface such as water in the scene. Here the photographer used a relatively short shutter speed to prevent the moon from blurring as it moved across the sky.

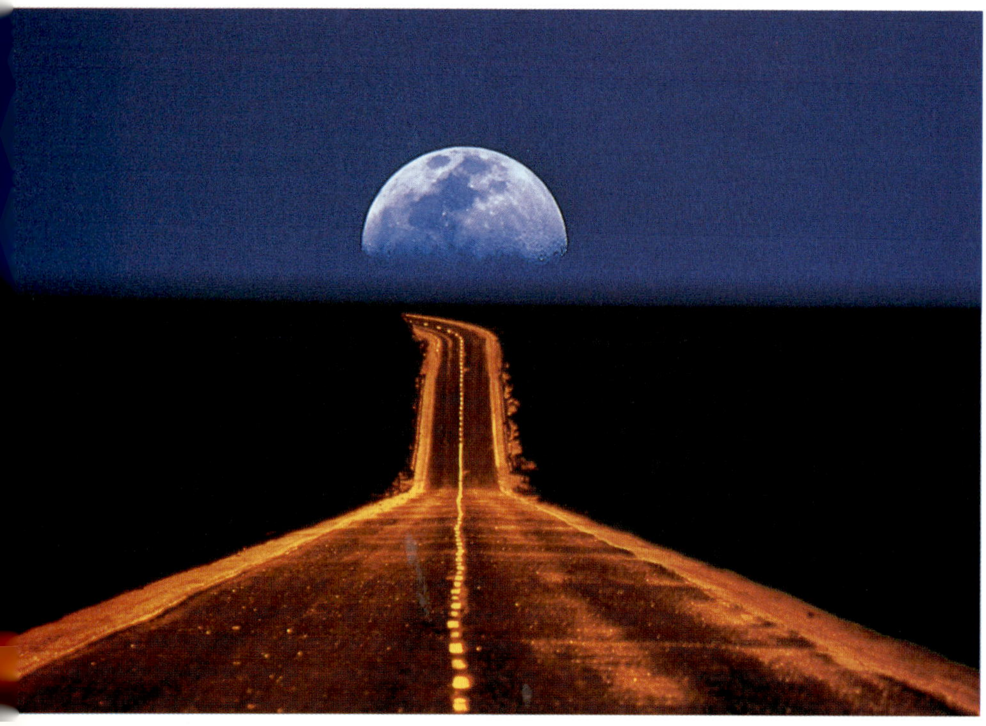

CHECK IT!

When shooting at night:

❑ bracket your exposures to ensure good results

❑ look for reflective surfaces

❑ use a time exposure to capture light trails of traffic or fireworks

❑ use a telephoto lens and double exposure to create spectacular moon shots

◀ ROAD TO THE MOON
To create this stunning shot, the photographer made use of double exposure – shooting the road and the moon separately. The glowing, orange appearance of the road was produced by heavily underexposing for the scene.

Shooting a building by night

Night time offers you wonderful possibilities for photographing architecture. Graeme Harris shows Martin Elliot how to exploit darkness to the full.

A building that looks quite ordinary during the day can be completely transformed at night if it is lit up, and becomes a great subject for photographs.

We decided to shoot Admiralty Arch, in the heart of London – a building that looks attractive by day but more imposing at night. It's photographed by hundreds of tourists every year, but Graeme decided he was after something different from the usual postcard view.

We arrived at the scene while it was still daylight, so that we had an opportunity to look around, find some good viewpoints and decide which lenses we might need.

Martin's shot

I used a Pentax LX SLR, loaded with Kodak Ektachrome ISO 64 slide film, and borrowed Graeme's 80-200mm zoom. I knew a tripod is essential when you're using such a slow film at night. I could have used a much faster film, but the final photograph would show obvious grain and paler colours.

In daylight I had picked out the traffic island nearest the arch as a good – and safe – vantage point for photography. It gave the clearest view of the arch and allowed me to cut out the annoying traffic cones at the side of the road.

I waited until some cars were coming towards me before pressing the shutter, so that I could capture the glow of their headlamps. The result, however, could do with lots of improvement. Graeme was sure the scene had the potential for a more dramatic shot.

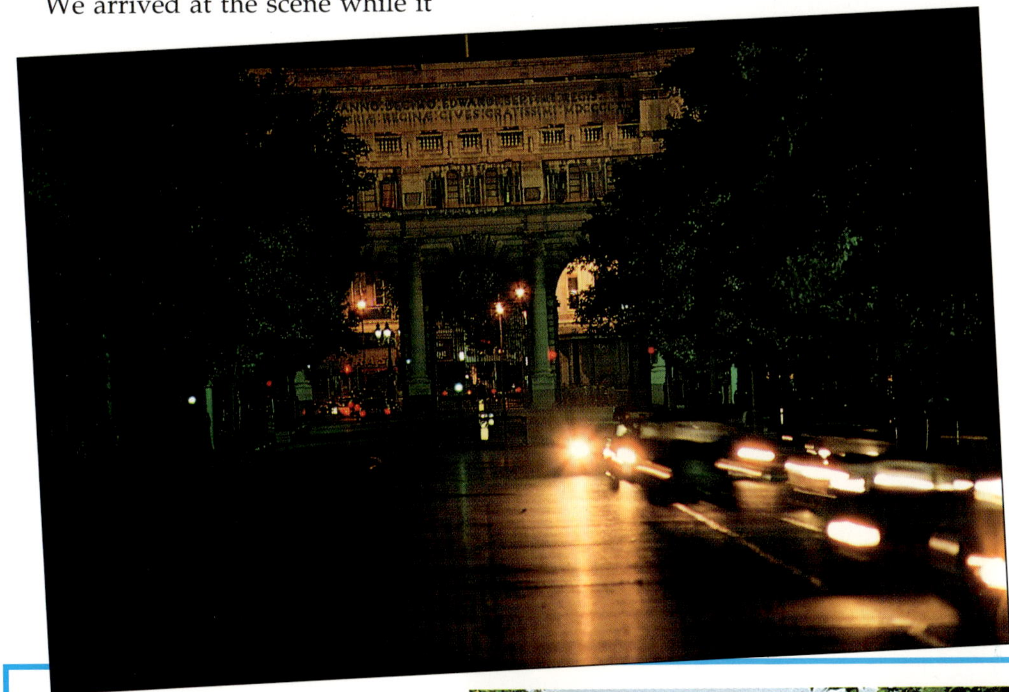

◀ ***Martin borrowed Graeme's 80-200mm zoom lens and stood on a traffic island in the middle of the road, using a tripod. Although he's captured the car headlamps, they appear as blurs instead of streaks of coloured light because the chosen shutter speed was too fast.***

The rest of the frame is far too dark, even though the camera was set on manual instead of aperture priority mode. The arch is underexposed and the left hand side of the photo is uninteresting.

The set up

Graeme and Martin were shooting Admiralty Arch, in central London. Before it got dark Martin photographed the arch from the side of the road with a standard 50mm lens.

Both Martin's and Graeme's shots were taken while they were standing on a traffic island in the middle of the road, well protected from the moving cars. Graeme's final photos were taken from a second traffic island, further out of shot.

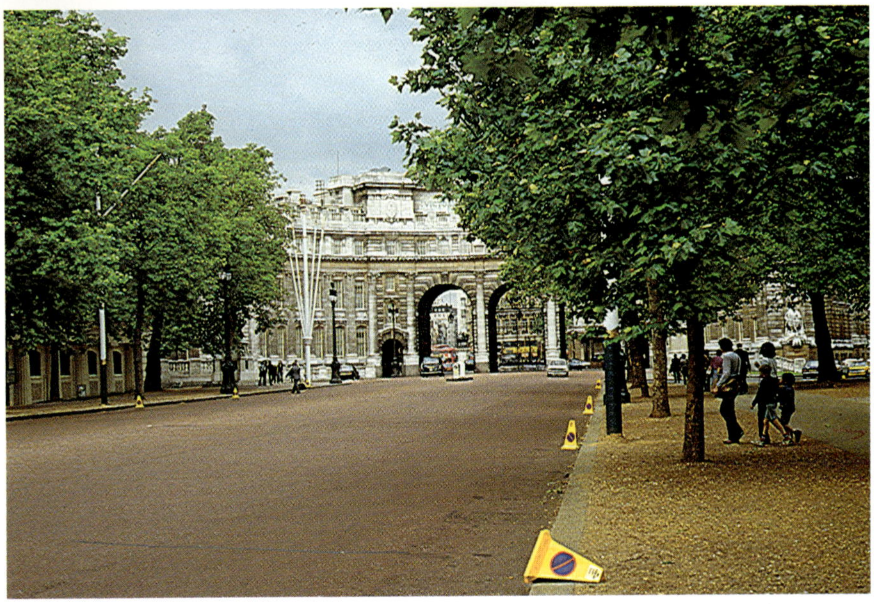

GRAEME'S SHOTS

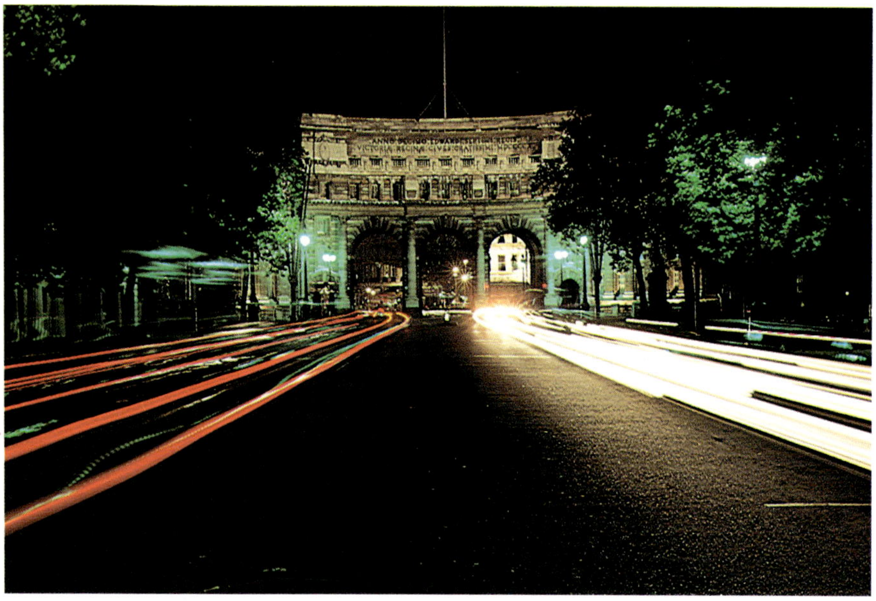

1 ▲ INCREASING THE EXPOSURE Graeme stood in the same place as Martin but with a 50mm lens, also using a tripod. He waited until cars were moving in both directions and then opened the shutter for 4 seconds so he could capture light streaks in two colours. But the arch still looks a little too dark.

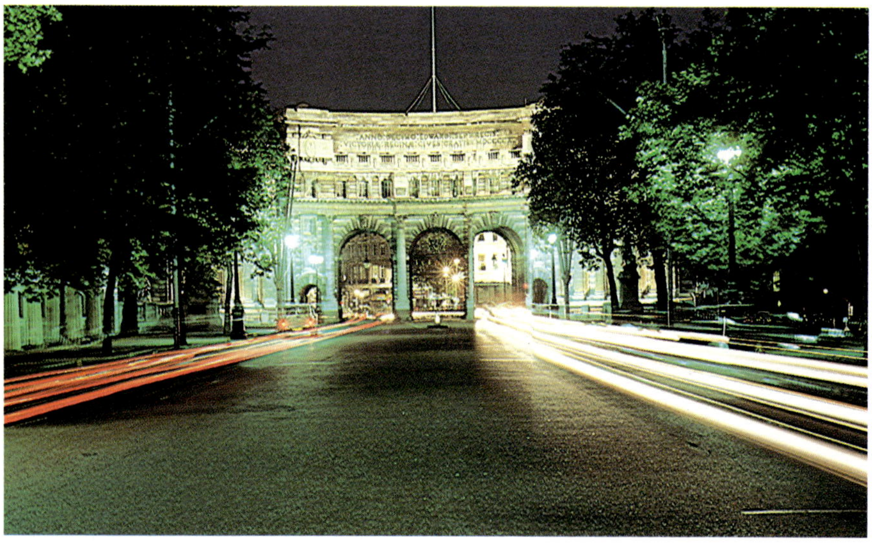

2 ▲ BRACKETING Using the same composition, Graeme took a series of four bracketed shots at 4, 8, 16 and 32 seconds so that one would be correctly exposed. This image was shot at 16 seconds. The longer exposure means the arch looks a little overexposed, but this suits the picture and shows more detail in the trees. The arch, however, looks too small.

3 ▶ CHANGING THE LENS Now Graeme decided to make the arch seem bigger but he couldn't move closer without risking being run over. So he walked back to the next traffic island and used his 300mm lens. This gave better perspective and allowed the arch to fill the frame more.

4 ▼ THE FINAL SHOT Graeme guessed that the last shot was correctly exposed but didn't contain enough car trails. So he used the same shutter speed – 16 seconds – but exposed the film only when he could see plenty of cars in the viewfinder. For the rest of the time, he covered the lens with a piece of black card. The resulting shot is awash with light trails in the bottom half of the frame.

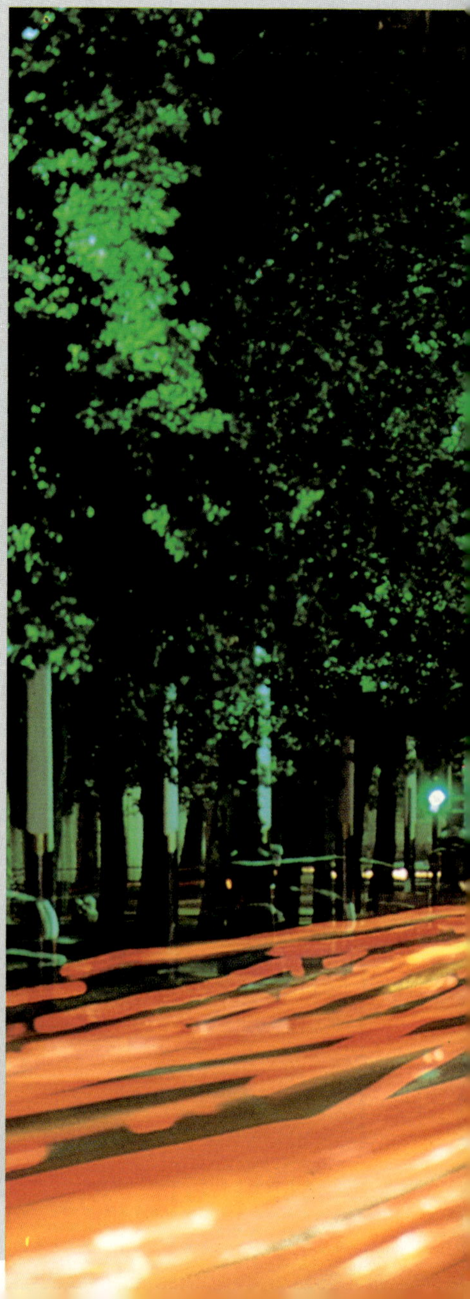

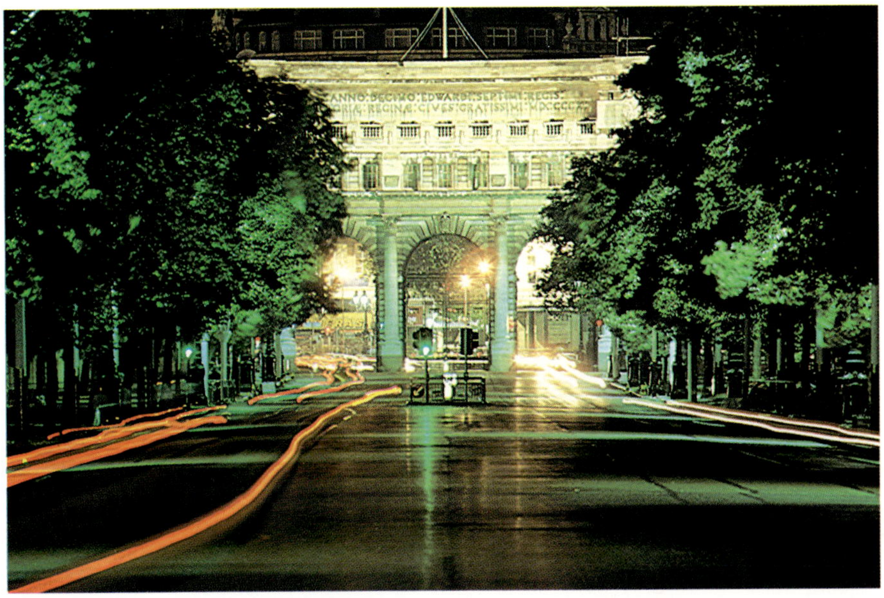

Tip

Reciprocity failure

If you use very long exposures (over 1 second) the colours you remember from a night time scene can look very different on film. This is known as 'reciprocity failure'.

Manufacturers recommend using colour correction filters to counteract this effect, but leaving it uncorrected can result in attractive colours which go well with a night time scene. For instance, when using long exposures, some films turn the blue of the sky into a purple tint.

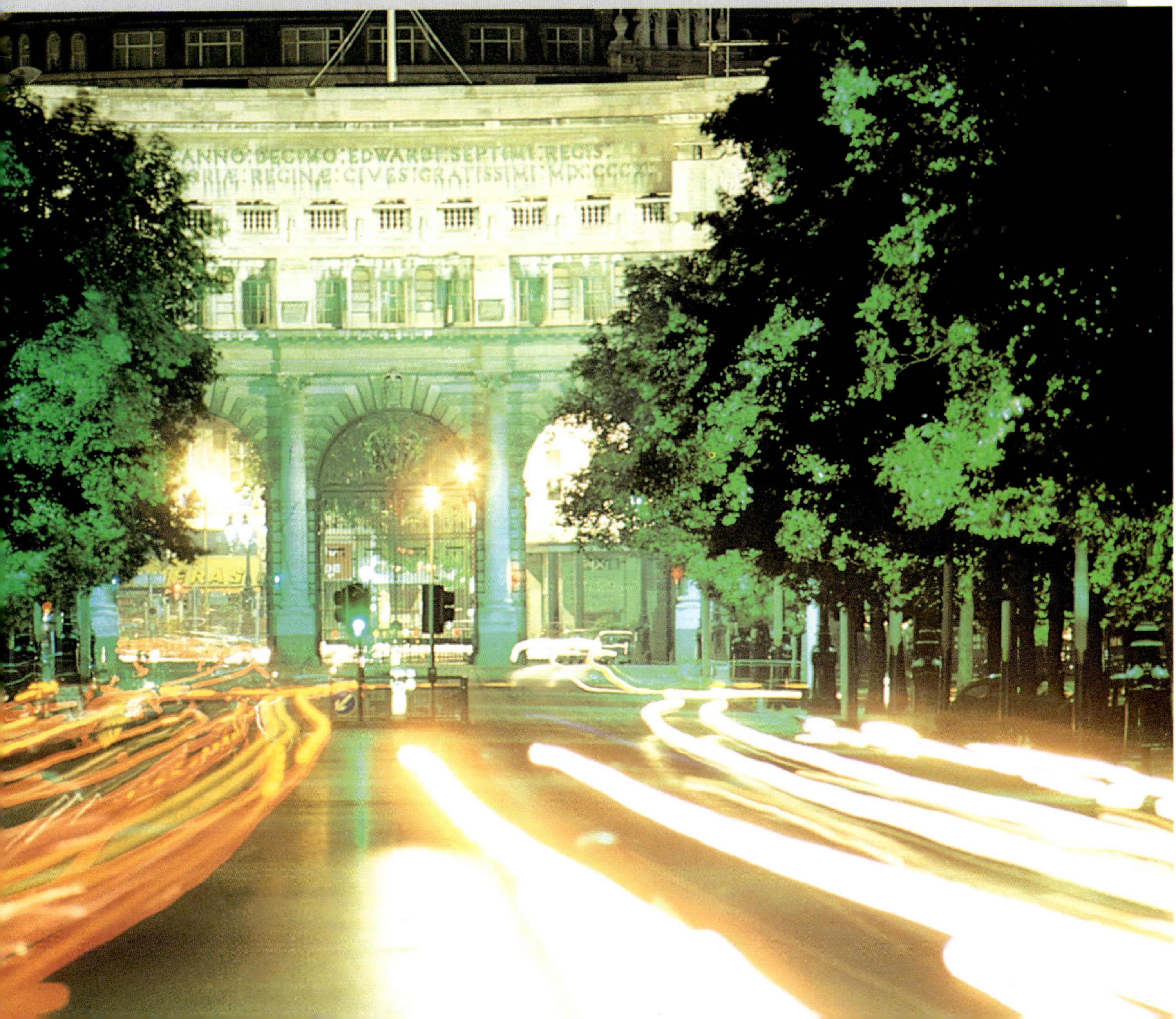

Graeme's turn

Graeme used the same film and camera as Martin. As well as a standard lens he brought along an 80-200mm zoom and a 300mm fixed lens, together with a very sturdy tripod. 'It's because of the traffic', he explained. 'With it roaring past on both sides of us, an ordinary tripod is going to shake. That will ruin the picture, especially with the 300mm lens and the long exposures. So the heavier the tripod, the sharper the picture will be.'

Graeme used the same viewpoint I'd taken and started off with a 50mm lens. He chose a longer shutter speed and, to make the scene paler in colour, increased the exposure slightly.

He felt the composition needed attention. There was too much road in the foreground and the arch was a little small. Instead of staying where he was and fitting the 80-200mm zoom, Graeme decided to move further back to the next traffic island and use the 300mm lens. This gave a foreshortened perspective which makes the lights more obvious. But the shot was let down by the lack of car trails.

By the time Graeme took his final shots, it was getting late and there were only a few cars driving along the road. But his last shot was the best one – it's full of trails of light which turn the picture into something special.

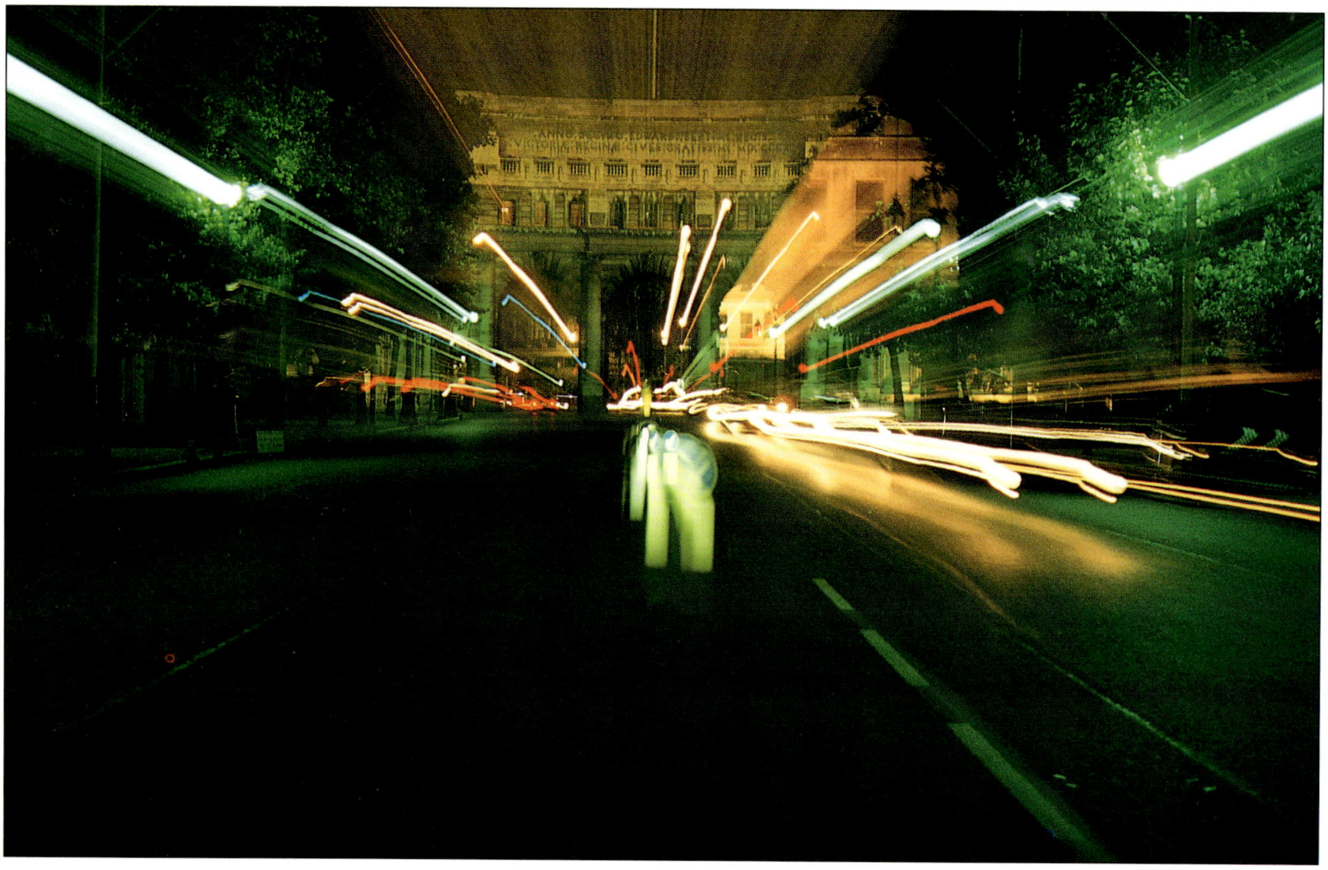

▲ ***Graeme decided to experiment. He fitted the zoom lens to his camera, still mounted on the tripod, and set a very slow shutter speed so he had enough time to zoom during the exposure. The blue-green streaks are caused by the street lights – using a daylight balanced film like Ektachrome to photograph artificial light results in a colour change.***

SLR tip

❑ It's all too easy to underexpose at night, so for a good chance of spot-on exposures, bracket every shot. For example, if your meter indicates that the shutter speed is 4 seconds at a given aperture, take a photo at this setting and then, keeping the same aperture, shoot at 8, 16 and 32 seconds. Repeatedly doubling the length of time the shutter stays open should ensure that one of your photos is correctly exposed.

Compact tips

❑ With compacts it's more tricky to arrive at correct exposures for night time scenes. Use print film because this has a wider exposure latitude than slides.

❑ If you want to blur car headlamps, look in your camera manual to see if your compact is capable of making exposures lasting several seconds or more. If it is, find out the slowest film that your camera accepts and load up with this. The camera will compensate by setting slower shutter speeds.

Pictures by moonlight

Moonlit scenes take on a distinctive quality. Why not venture out after dark with your camera and experiment?

1 Film

ISO 100 film is a good choice for sharp images. Reciprocity failure affects shots where the exposure lasts more than about one second. The actual effects – including any colour cast – depend on the kind of film you use, so experiment.

So that you can combat underexposure caused by reciprocity failure, start by increasing the exposure length by a factor of two, then three and four. Make a note of your exposures for future reference.

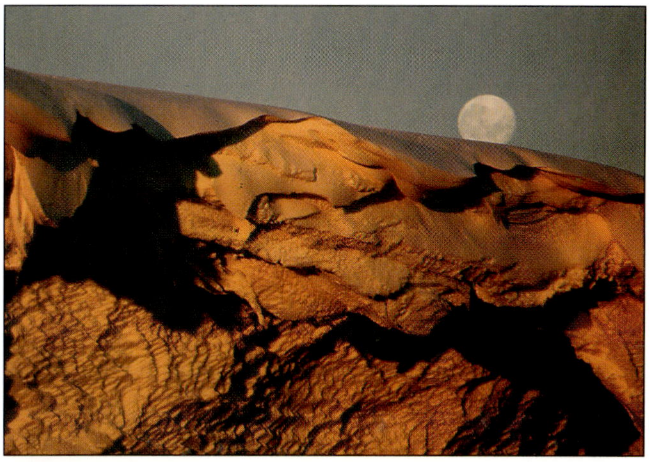

▶ ***Here the moon rose while the sun was still casting light on this ice cliff in the Antarctic.***

2 Composition

A classic image is of a silhouetted subject – say, a plane – in front of a large full moon. However, most of these shots are not 'straight' photographs. Either they involve a double exposure or two slides have been 'sandwiched' together and then copied to form a new picture.

If you want to do the same, make sure that the two shots are taken with roughly the same focal length lens. This looks more realistic.

Images that are just as eyecatching can be created when the moon is only a tiny size in the frame. If the rest of the sky is black, the viewer's eye will automatically rest on the one bright spot, which becomes the focal point.

Another option is to exclude the moon from the shot altogether. Take advantage of the eerie light thrown on the scene. Include the moon's reflection in water to show its presence indirectly.

3 Exposure

Obtaining the right exposure is tricky. Always bracket widely when shooting by moonlight, just as you would if you were shooting at night with the illumination coming from an artificial light source.

If the moon is the only lighting, the contrast between a full moon itself and dimly lit objects is huge. So on one frame of film you won't be able to record both a well exposed moon and all the details of the landscape. The answer is to record trees, mountains and buildings in silhouette so that you don't grossly overexpose the moon. For more detail, make a double exposure.

With a standard lens, an exposure of more than ten seconds records the moon as an oval blur, because you record its movement in the sky. So to capture an image of the moon that's as sharp as possible, set the fastest shutter speed you can in the available lighting conditions.

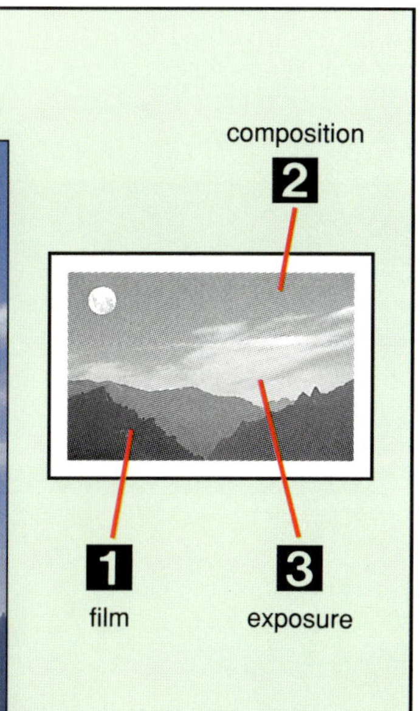

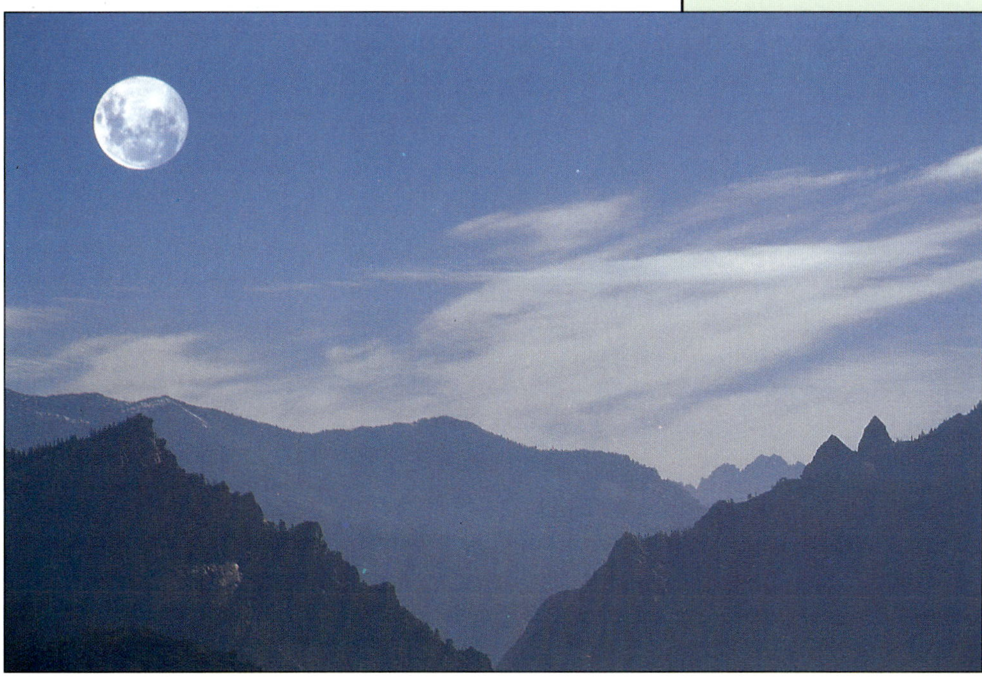

◀ ***A cold, bluish cast is characteristic of shots taken by the light of the moon. Here the shot was taken in late afternoon, when the sun was still lighting the scene.***

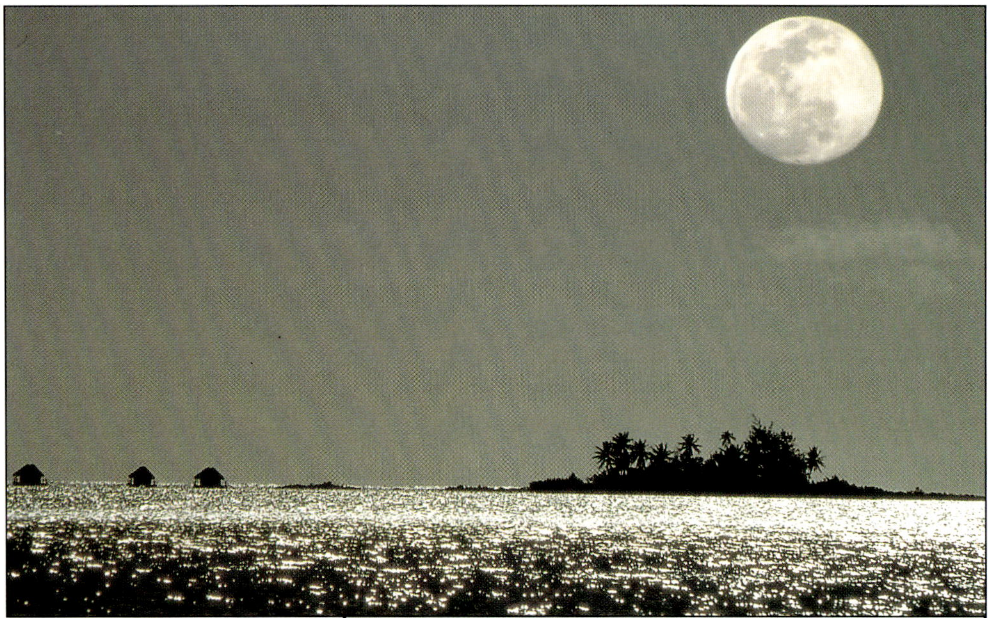

▲ ***This image was created by a double exposure in camera. Careful exposure ensures that the moon does not look burnt out – you can still make out some detail on its surface.***

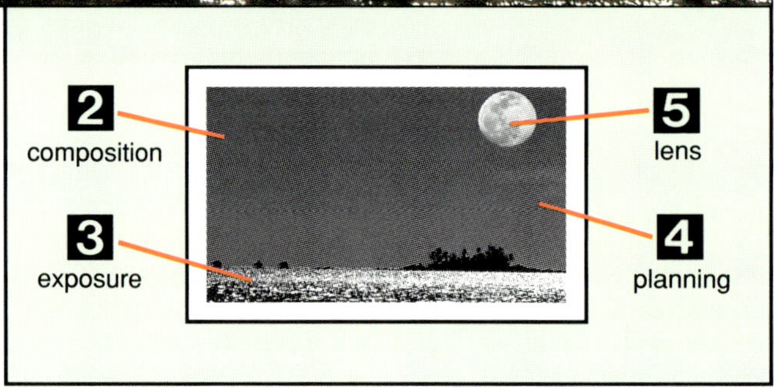

CHECK IT!

Camera: SLR with manual exposure compensation.
Lens: the longer the lens, the bigger the moon appears. Fit a teleconverter to increase the focal length.
Film: ISO 100 slide film. *Don't* load fast film because the results won't be as sharp.
Filters: try fitting a blue filter to enhance the sky's colour, especially at twilight.
Camera support: a tripod is essential, together with a locking cable release.
Time of year/day: check newspapers for dates of the phases of the moon and rising and setting times.
Other equipment: if you want to take double exposures, take a notebook with you to record the position of the moon in the frame. This allows more accurate positioning of the two separate images.

4 Planning

Naturally, a full moon throws more light on the scene than a crescent. Because of the very long exposures involved anyway, it's easiest to shoot only when there's a full or nearly full moon.

Should you want the moon to be in a specific place, bear in mind that its position is less easy to predict than the sun's. If you'd like the moon to be near the horizon, for example, choose a date when sunset and moonrise coincide.

You can find out the phases of the moon from some diaries and newspapers. Rising and setting times can also be found in newspapers.

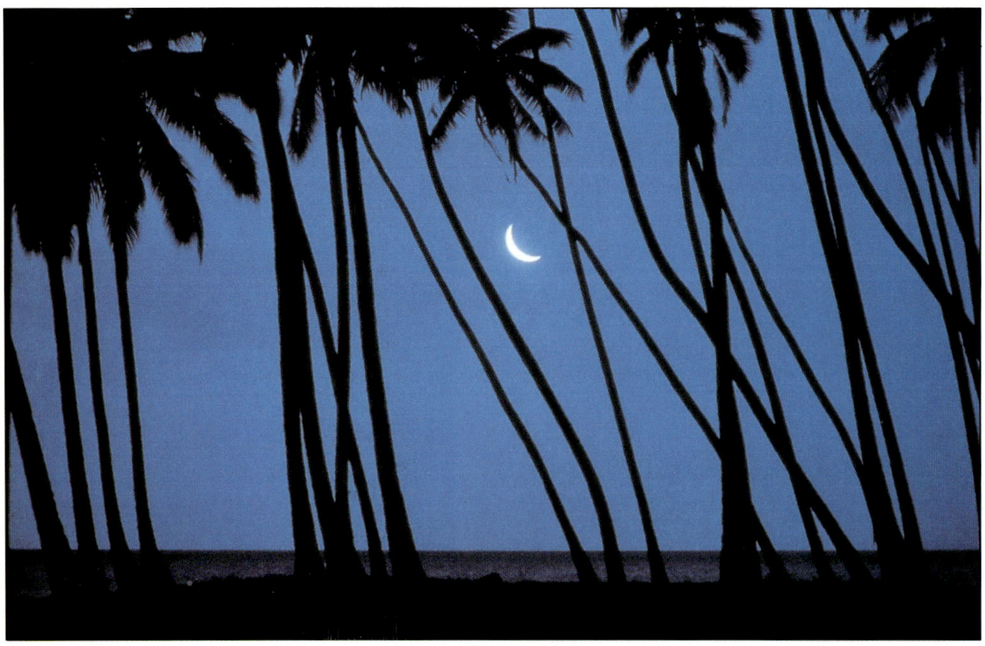

5 Lens

Unless you have access to a very long telephoto, the moon will look small in your shots. With a 300mm lens, for example, the moon measures only about 3mm across on 35mm film.

So to make the moon appear as large as possible, fit your longest telephoto lens. Bear in mind that the longer the lens, the more blurred the moon looks at any given exposure. For example, to minimize blurring with a 400mm lens you'll have to set a proportionately shorter shutter speed than if you were using a 200mm lens.

◀ ***In this graphic shot, a viewpoint was chosen so that the moon was framed by palm trees. The sky was naturally deep blue, but you can fit a filter if it's too pale.***

Jim Henderson – The Northern Lights

With a great deal of patience and perseverance, Jim Henderson has produced a stunningly colourful series of photographs of the Northern Lights.

In recent years, Jim Henderson has spent a lot of time outside his home in Scotland peering up at the night sky. He has been looking for the Aurora Borealis, also known as the Northern Lights, which have provided him with some of his most exciting photographs.

To the naked eye, the Northern Lights often seem little more than pale white marks. However, in Jim's photos they turn into wonderful explosions of colour. He explains: 'Loaded with fast film and using exposures of 40 seconds, the camera is much more sensitive than the human eye. The great thing about my photography of the Lights is that I am often taken by surprise by the colours that come out in the processed film.'

Sunspot activity

The Northern Lights are created by sunspot activity which sends out solar flares into space. Some of these flares enter the earth's atmosphere and create light displays in the night sky of the northern regions of the globe. One of the best areas for viewing them is in the Grampian region of Scotland where Jim lives.

Jim captures the Lights with surprisingly simple equipment. He prefers 35mm to medium format: 'The trouble with 120 film is the lack of good-quality fast films. Also there is the cost of medium format film – generally I prefer to capture every shot I want on 35mm than be more selective with 120 film. After all, every display is unique – it will never be repeated.'

Jim also steers clear of all filters. 'I tried a UV but didn't notice any difference, and all a polarizer seemed to do was to cut down the light. The film manufacturers recommend using a 5G colour compensation filter when doing my standard 40-second exposure because reciprocity failure causes some colour shifts. However, I have noticed very little difference with or without the filter. I defy anyone to say which photo has been used with a 5G and which hasn't.'

Jim has experimented with exposure times as well as filters. 'My lightmeter has never once given me a reading because the night sky is just too dark,' he states. 'I started out by bracketing exposures widely. With anything longer than 40 seconds, I found that the stars looked like lines rather than points of light. This is because the earth rotates, so the camera is actually moving in relation to the stars. In the end, I found that 40 seconds on ISO 1600 film usually gave me an adequate exposure and stars that look like stars.'

"This is one of the shots I tried on medium format with a minute exposure. With the long exposure, you can just see the stars beginning to turn into lines because of the earth's rotation. The silhouete is of a hay baler." Taken on a Bronica ETRS with a 40mm lens on Fuji RHP ISO 400 film (pushed to ISO 1600) at f4 for 1 minute.

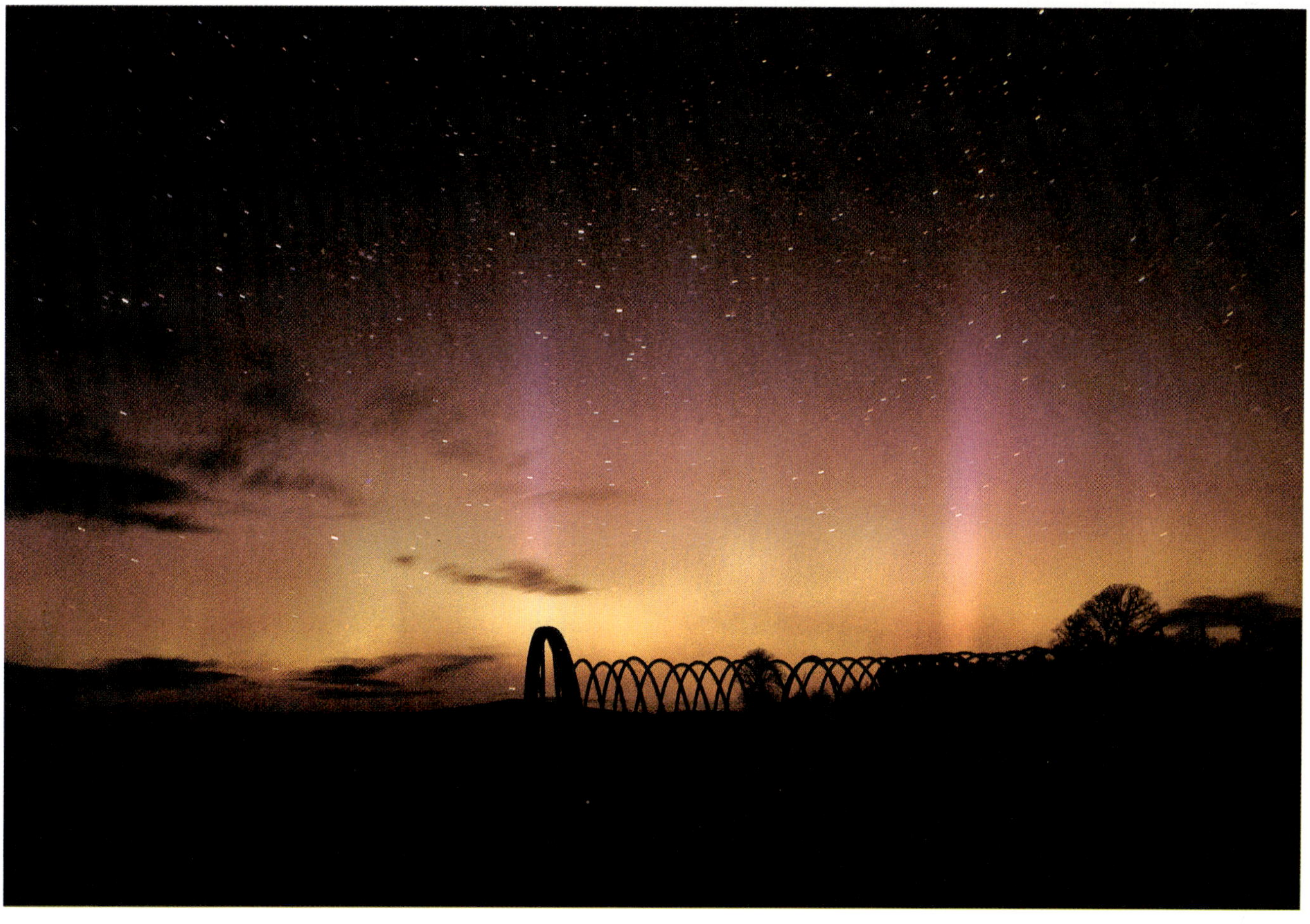

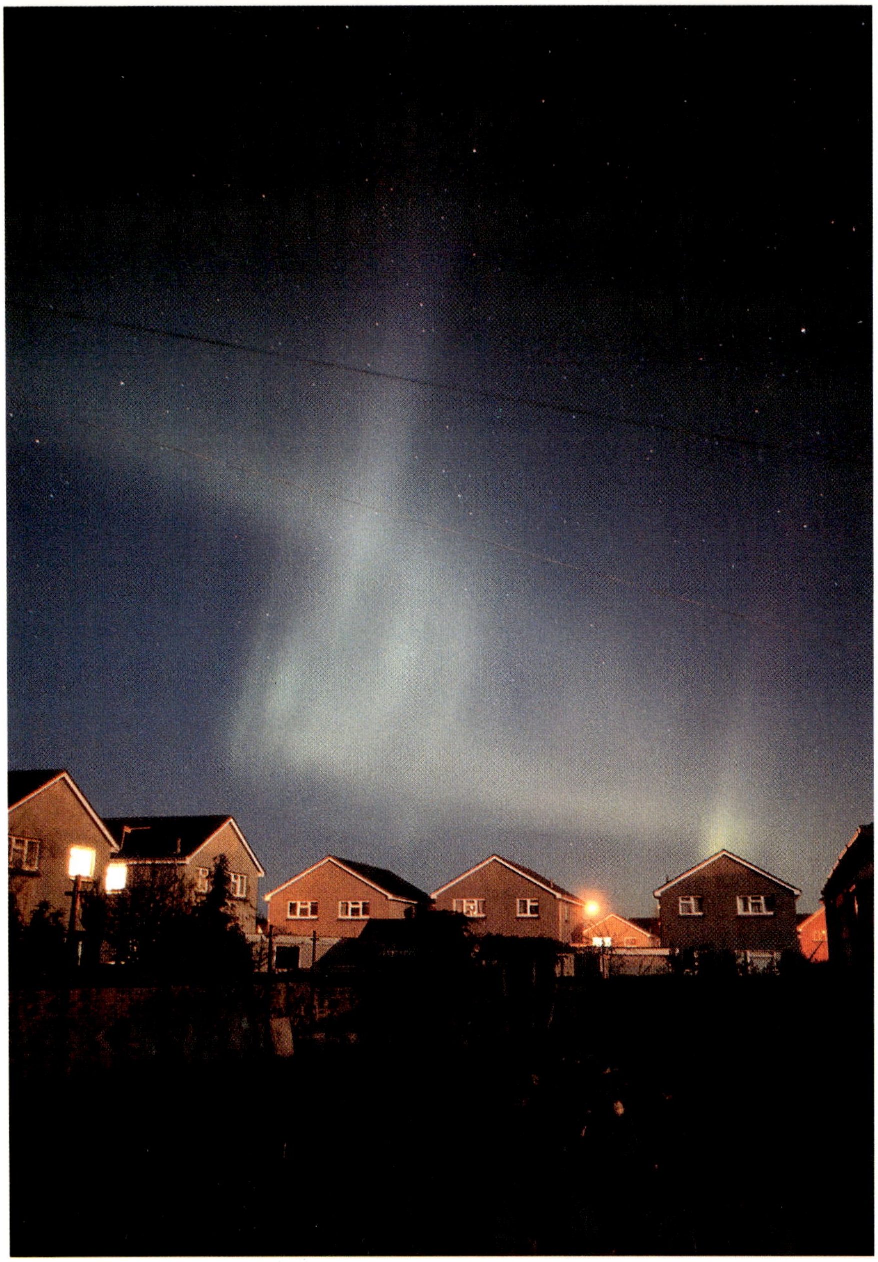

"In this shot, all I saw were some pale white beams in the sky. I had absolutely no idea that these lovely pinks and violets would register on the film."
Taken on a Nikon FG20 with a 28mm lens on Fuji RSP ISO 1600 film at f2.8 for 40 seconds.

"I saw this curtain of light quite unexpectedly before I went to bed one night. The full moon provided quite strong illumination on the houses in the foreground. The down side of a full moon is that the vibrancy of the colours of the Northern Lights is impaired."
Taken on a Nikon FG20 with a 28mm lens on Fuji RSP ISO 1600 film at f2.8 for 40 seconds.

"This was taken on the first day of May – I find that in the spring months you get much more muted colours and pastel shades. I positioned the tree in the composition to show the colours off against a strong silhouette."
Taken on a Nikon FG20 with a 28mm lens on Fuji RSP ISO 1600 film at f2.8 for 40 seconds.

Technical Details

The equipment that Jim uses is pretty straightforward: an old Nikon FG20 body with a Nikon 28mm wide angle lens, a solid Benbo tripod and a locking cable release.
Jim is particularly keen on the Nikon body as it allows him to make B setting exposures without the need for battery power. He notes, 'I will often shoot two rolls of 36 exposure film in a night. With each exposure lasting 40 seconds that can mean a lot of replacement batteries. In any case, you can't always rely on batteries on frosty nights in Scotland.'

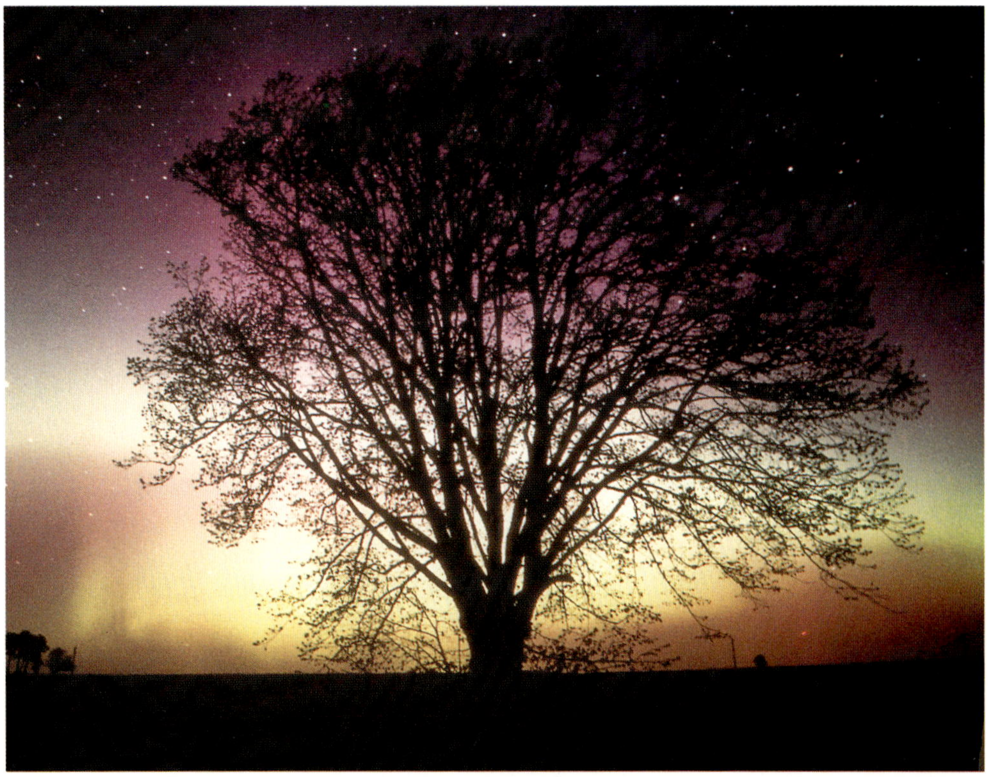

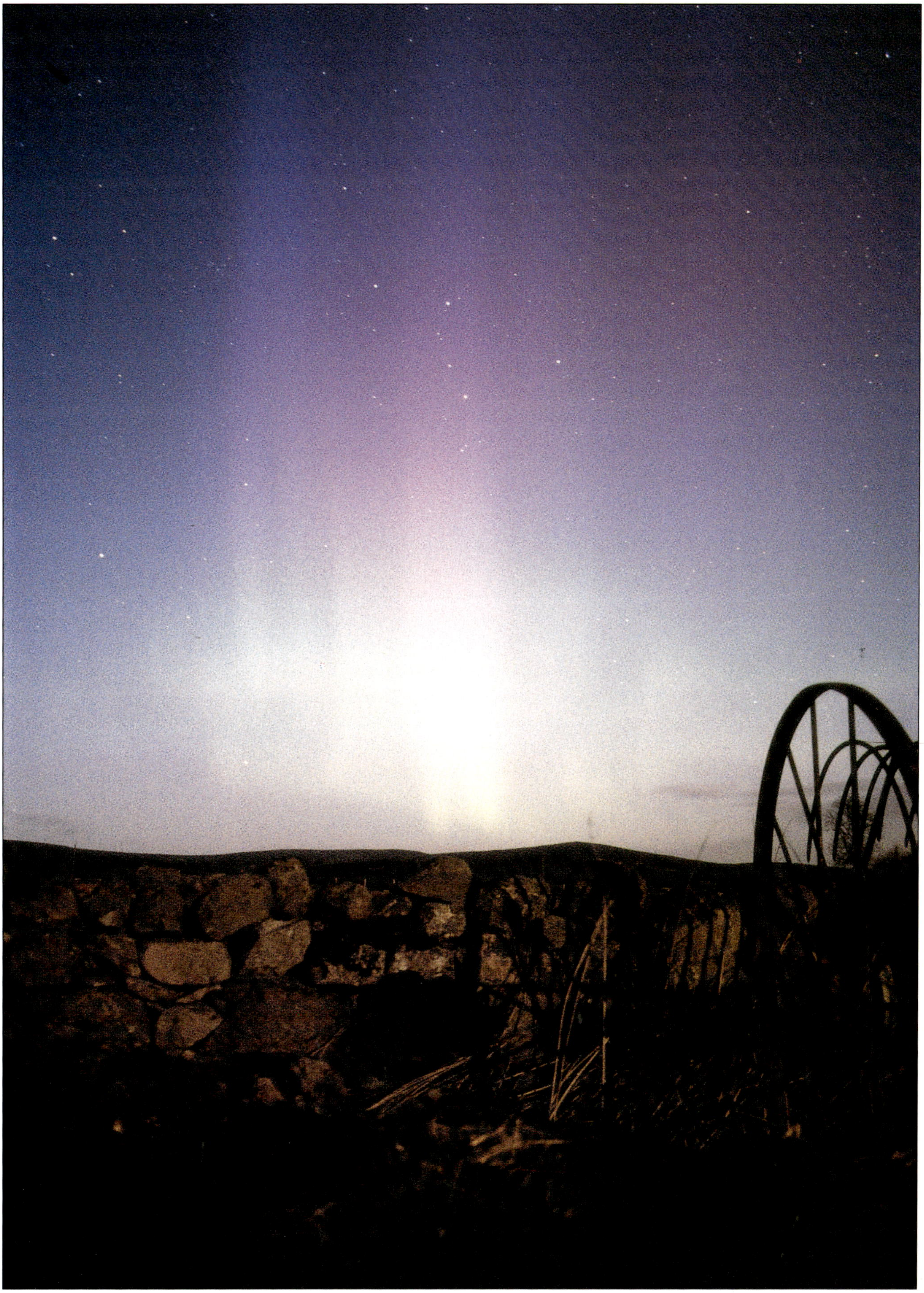

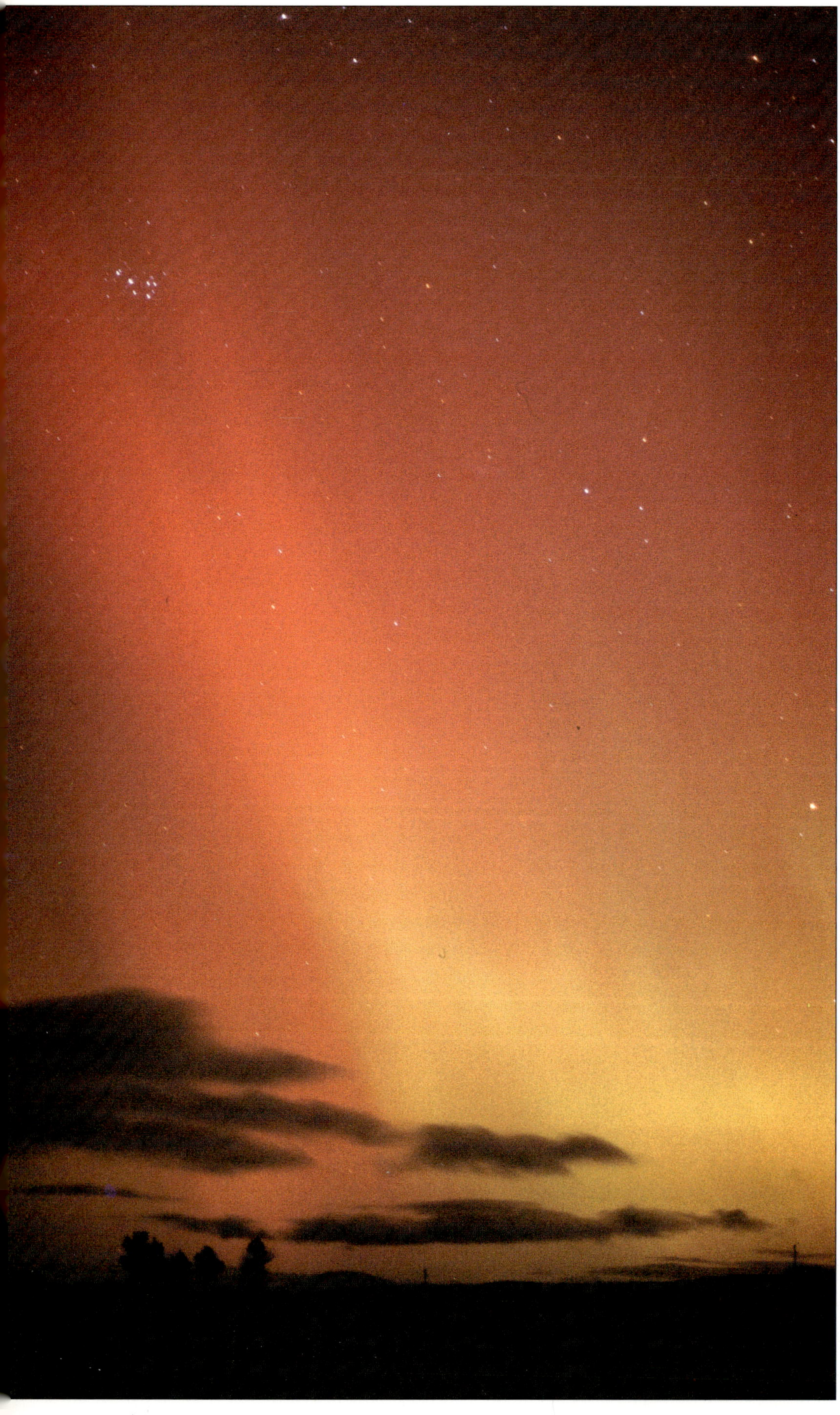

You can do it

One of the biggest difficulties Jim encounters is working in the dark. He states in exasperation, 'I lost one of the biggest and best auroras because the aperture setting was on f16 instead of f2.8. It's also possible to lose shots by not loading the film properly and by not having the focus setting on infinity. Even a slight movement away from infinity can cause an unsharp image.'

To avoid these problems, Jim suggests using a small pen torch to check all the settings. He also uses it to illuminate his watch so that he can time exposures.

Jim warns against using anything stronger than a pen torch, though, as it might affect your night vision. 'Your eyes must be thoroughly attuned to the dark to be able to see some auroras,' he warns.

"This was one of the more spectacular displays. I could see the blood red colour with the naked eye. And you could see the colours in all directions – it was like being in a fishbowl." Taken on a Nikon FG20 with a 28mm lens on Fuji RSP ISO 1600 film at f2.8 for 40 seconds.